The Creative Vision
of Bessie Head

The Creative Vision
of Bessie Head

Coreen Brown

Madison • Teaneck
Fairleigh Dickinson University Press
London: Associated University Presses

Associated University Presses
2010 Eastpark Boulevard
Cranbury, NJ 08512

Associated University Presses
Unit 304
The Chandlery
50 Westminster Bridge Road
London SE1 7QY, England

Associated University Presses
P.O. Box 338, Port Credit
Mississauga, Ontario
Canada L5G 4L8

The paper used in this publication meets the requirements of the American National Standard for Permanence of Paper for Printed Library Materials Z39.48-1984.
Library of Congress Cataloging-in-Publication Data
Brown, Coreen, 1947–
The creative vision of Bessie Head / Coreen Brown.
p.   cm.
Includes bibliographical references (p.) and index.
ISBN 0-8386-3982-8 (alk. paper)
1. Head, Bessie, 1937—Criticism and interpretation.   2. Politics and literature—South Africa—History—20th century.   3. Women and literature—South Africa—History—20th century.   4. South Africa—In literature.   5. Romanticism—South Africa.   6. Racism in literature.   7. Sexism in literature.   I. Title.
PR9369.3.H4 Z58   2003
823′.914—dc21   2002014380

Contents

Acknowledgments

I WOULD LIKE TO THANK THE RESEARCHERS AT THE NATIONAL English Literary Museum in Grahamstown for their regular update on Bessie Head material. I am grateful to the staff at the Khama III Memorial Museum in Serowe for their hospitality and co-operation, and to Howard Head for his introduction to Serowe town. Thanks are also due to the Philip Reckitt Educational Trust for their grant towards the cost of travel to Botswana, to the Brynmor Jones Library at the University of Hull, and to Christine Retz, Managing Editor of the Associated University Presses, USA. However, I owe my greatest debt to Professor James Booth of the University of Hull, UK, for the benefit of his knowledge, his patience and encouragement.

❧

The chapter *A Question of Power* has, in a modified form, appeared in *VOICES: The Wisconsin Review of African Languages and Literatures*.

Abbreviations

THE FOLLOWING ABBREVIATIONS FOR THE WORKS OF BESSIE HEAD
are used for page reference throughout the text:

ABC   *A Bewitched Crossroad*
AWA   *A Woman Alone*
C   *The Cardinals*
CT   *The Collector of Treasures*
M   *Maru*
QP   *A Question of Power*
S   *Serowe: Village of the Rain Wind*
TTP   *Tales of Tenderness and Power*
WDIW "Why Do I Write?"
WRCG *When Rain Clouds Gather*

The Creative Vision
of Bessie Head

Introduction

BESSIE HEAD WAS A COLORED (THAT IS, MIXED-RACE) SOUTH AFRICAN whose books, with the exception of *The Cardinals,* were written during her self-imposed exile in Botswana. It was there that she died in 1986. She lived, for most of her adult life, the solitary existence of a single mother, struggling for financial survival in a country whose language she never mastered. The fact that for many years she was refused citizenship of Botswana also caused her considerable anxiety. Her sense of identity was surely marked by the knowledge that her white mother, from whom she was separated at birth, had died in the mental institution to which she had been committed, because, as Head wrote in a letter, "the ultimate horror had been committed, . . . a white woman had had sex with a black man" (Appendix 22).

Thus, as a victim of racial discrimination in South Africa, Head was ideally placed to present a postcolonial critique of that society. Her personal letters often reflect on the extreme deprivation confronting the black man or woman in white South Africa, the sense "that even the birds and trees belong to the white man" (Appendix 14). Her novels present a powerful exposé of this racism. Also, as a woman struggling to survive alone in a tribal culture, she experienced the hardships of a patriarchal hierarchy. She wrote in a letter: "This particular society is VERY dangerous. It is male dominated. A man has no faults. They move straight towards a woman and would kill her" (Appendix 20). *A Question of Power* and *The Collector of Treasures* examine this issue. However, the overwhelming impetus of Head's writing is to transcend these problems. The protagonists in her novels, both male and female, struggle to survive the vicissitudes of their lives, and in so doing create their own individualistic, egalitarian utopias.

Early critics of Head's work saw this artistic realization as evidence of Head's experience of exile in Botswana, arguing that she "exults at having been given the opportunity to dig her roots into the sands of the semi-arid land" (Ogungbesan 1979, 103).

However, Randolph Vigne's publication, in 1991, of the letters that Head had written to him during her early years in Botswana portrays a vastly different experience of exile. Reading these descriptions of loneliness, isolation, and even ostracism, it becomes clear that the utopian, romantic resolution that closes *When Rain Clouds Gather* was a reaction against, rather than a response to, Head's early experience of Botswanan exile. Indeed, it is Head's letters to Vigne that help to explain the evolution of *A Question of Power.*

This novel, although autobiographical and deeply personal in its portrayal of mental illness, is elliptical and enigmatic in its depiction of the actual origin of, or reasons for, Elizabeth's breakdown. For although Head describes in detail both Elizabeth's ability to relate appropriately to reality and her awful experience of her delusions, this clear separation between Elizabeth as subject of her consciousness and Elizabeth as object of her unconscious is not in process at a crucial juncture of the novel—that part which explains Elizabeth's conscious feelings for the *real* Sello in Motabeng village. It is Head's letters to Vigne that provide a clue to the strange drama that she was conducting in Serowe, one that concerns her relationship with a VIP and the hostility that she felt this attracted from the local people. This hostility seems to have little effect on Elizabeth in *A Question of Power,* and yet her aggressive, unprovoked attack against the black assistant in the post office suggests the presence of feelings of dislike and resentment, hitherto suppressed. It is Head's letters to Vigne, rather than the narrative of *A Question of Power,* that shed light on the author's relationship with the local people.

The desire to make sense out of madness is strong. It seemed possible to me that access to Head's unpublished personal papers might provide further clues to issues that are veiled or simply omitted from her literary output. It also seemed that they might provide a deeper understanding of *A Question of Power* and thereby help to explain the whole force of Head's artistic resolution. So in 1995 I traveled to Serowe and, staying in the accommodation provided at the Khama III Memorial Museum, read for three weeks through the Bessie Head papers.

Total immersion in these letters moves the reader into a world that is less controlled, more arbitrary, than the greater part of her fictional writing. Her feelings move between anger and love, joy and despair. Desperate poverty compels her to plead with literary agents for payments of royalties that she feels are outstanding; she haggles over book advances that will pay for repairs to a leaking roof or worn-out plumbing. There are angry outbursts to correspondents whom she feels have criticized her or her writing, and there are passionate avowals of love and everlasting friendship. Many letters reflect the insecurity and emotional instability from which she always suffered, her fears of being used by those in possession of powerful academic positions. Other letters record her attempts to find an alternative country in which to settle. But there is also her courageous attempt to make light of her isolation: "I have lived here for 18 years and those are the only three black people known to me. I seek no one . . . I have a big international world. The whole world has bought my books and the whole world walks to my door" (Appendix 20).

Letter writing, and the contact it provided with an outside world, became an immensely important part of her life. The effusive gratitude she expresses at the gift of a copy of *Mhudi* (Appendix 15) is also a heartfelt response to the overtures of friendship that the gift signifies. It was to friends whom she had never met, but who had contacted her on reading one of her journal articles, that Head disclosed the nature of her fantasies and delusions.

One of these letters (reprinted in Appendix 1) was written at a time which Head later describes as "three years or more [of] a strange journey into hell and darkness." In a later letter she explains that "it was the darkness [she] did not grasp because at the same time [she] saw the light" and believed that "an inner heaven could make a heaven on earth" (Appendix 4). The context of this "inner heaven" is the fantasy she creates surrounding her relationship with an important figure in Serowe. It is clear from the scenario described in this earlier letter that Head is expressing, in an unmediated form, the nature of the delusions that were to be turned into the material of *A Question of Power*:

> It has taken me thirty-one years to know who I am. It has taken my God 47 years. The two of us only finally knew each other in these past four or five weeks, though when he was born in Botswana a number of prophesies were made about him. I was included in them because the two of us have always been a team together. (Appendix 1)

She later revealed the identity of this man: "he was Seretse Khama, the first president of Botswana" (Appendix 20). That

Head should have fantasized in such a way is indeed evidence that at one period of her life she held only a tenuous grasp on reality — and her early letters, like *A Question of Power*, reflect her belief that as the soulmate of a powerful figure she has a momentous destiny to fulfill. Although Head was cured of her mental illness, nonetheless the resolution in her literary writing always depends upon the achievements of a dominant protagonist, one who embodies the characteristics of the hero of her early delusions. Indeed, it is Head's individualistic creation of the "hero" that ensures that her egalitarian "brotherhood of man" can only be brought into being by the most masculine, most explicitly male heroes—archetypal figures with the power to redress the wrongs of society.

The origin and significance of fantasies or hallucinations has long been contested. They have been seen as derangement or as prophetic wisdom, as the result of inherited genes, or as acquired cognitive experience. Whatever the cause or nature of Bessie Head's psychotic disturbance, in her letters she consistently refers to herself as a "learner," saying that she had endured "systematic and insistent" learning (Appendix 8). It was her experience of "basic suffering" that, as she wrote, turned her "inwards." She explains that whereas "all writers are first Russian, British, French, American and only after that universal humanity," her own "position is different." Her "preoccupations are all within" (Appendix 5). Most often she records the horror of this experience: "Half of me reels towards death, half of me reels towards life. I am so uncertain, except that the clamour is over. Sometimes one emerges from a darkness, bombed full of holes and very broken down" (Appendix 4). But she can—as in a letter that closes with the words "I have been enjoying a new lease on life"—also enjoy a wryly ironic acceptance of her experience:

> I am that much richer by having lived for a while in a death-grip of darkness and having been cursed and mocked by a vehement version of Satan. I know it took Jesus only 40 days to have a conversation with Lucifer. I hadn't expected my conversation to go on for three or four years and he was luckier than I. He did not seem to be scared at the end of it. I am. (Appendix 5)

This retrospective comment, however, reflects a mood of ironic detachment that is never within the parameters of the experience of Head's fictional protagonist, Elizabeth. There can be no doubt, from reading Head's letters, that she did experience the hallucinations that Elizabeth suffers. It is also clear that the "brotherhood of man," envisaged as an antidote to Elizabeth's problems, is a literary artifact, a more elusive version of the Utopia that Head's character Makhaya in *When Rain Clouds Gather* sought to build, and that had already utterly failed to provide Head with a sense of community she so urgently needed. This "universal brotherhood" defies description; it is the hard-earned prize of Head's heroine, who "rises at the end to a brilliance of soul as extreme as the degradation [Dan] inflicts on her" (Appendix 6). Moreover, this literary resolution is one that is stated in a letter that Head wrote in 1968, a time that marked the onset of her delusionary experiences:

> My life and history has been that of the suffering of the common man and with me he comes into his own. With me too comes into fulfilment this new age of universal brotherly love. For while I am the symbol of the common man I am also the symbol of love. That's what I have always expressed and died for whether as the Buddha, David of the psalms or Moses fighting for the freedom of the human soul. Those dramas are mine. (Appendix 1)

It is also a delusion that she later wished to "cancel," part of "a jumble of wild impulses, error and error and an arrogance of the soul that was submerged" (Appendix 4). And, Head, for the most part, shows in her letters that she had an astute grasp of reality. She parries the suggestion of the likely success of a "second coming" with the comment: "You know people really hate the being coming down on clouds of glory and they'd shoot at it in case it disturbs the stock market" (Appendix 17). It was, indeed, her apprehension of reality that directed her literary work. She is uncompromisingly direct in her portrayal of the oppressions that she has encountered within South Africa and Botswana. As Jacqueline Rose suggests, if we charge Head with proclaiming some kind of "universal humanism," we must also recognize that she is more often revealing its "deranging unacceptable side" (1994, 416). But Head is drawn by the compulsion of opposites, the "two pivots" that were "absolutely necessary" for her creativity. As she comments, "I live on a very violent cycle. I tend to crash right down to rock bottom where nothing exists and suddenly take a violent and unexpected upward swing. . . . Sometimes I have to wait and wait until I can control my material" (Appendix 26).

On the basis of this admission there might be a danger of reading Head's romantic resolution, this "upward swing," as a meaningless, albeit understandable, escapism. There need be no intrinsic connection between the suffering, the "learning" she endures and the artistic solution she offers. But even Jacqueline Rose's suggestion that "universal humanism" has its "deranging, unacceptable side" assumes that, indeed, as its naming implies, it also embodies a code of acceptable human principles. Head shows that this code is instinctive. Her interrogation of the psyche might reveal the struggle for power at the heart of all human relationships, and, as a consequence of this, the disproportionate risks inherent in the formation of egalitarian I/You relationships. Nonetheless, it is this interrogation that also reveals that the deepest impulses of the psyche *do* contain the possibility for humanism, that, as Head writes in a letter, "mankind did not really disagree at the level of intuition" (Appendix 17). Thus the "Dante's inferno" of Elizabeth's hallucinations, like the apocalyptic underworld of many visionary artists, is what Frye calls an apocalypse of the imagination. It is a voice of prophesy, the heroine "fighting for the freedom of the human soul" (Appendix 1). Perhaps then it is no paradox that this pursuit of humanism, this hazardous soul journey, becomes an esoteric, individualistic, and isolating quest, the prerogative only of solitary heroes and heroines.

For humanism is only *potentially* universal. This, then, is the connection between the knowledge gained from Head's hallucinatory experience and the utopian solution she portrays, the "two pivots" upon which she functions. She portrays only what could be and should be. In a letter she laments that "hatred and turmoil" are caused because "people could not see their souls, they do not know they are divine" (Appendix 1). Maru's archetypal psychic journey reveals the naturalness of this divinity. In Head's case, the creative act and psychic revelation are closely interwoven, sometimes even inseparable. For Head, the function of creativity is to challenge the escalating alienation of society, the power of her own creativity is portrayed in the revelations of Elizabeth's soul-journey.

From within a political and social context that invites committed social realism, Head's choice of artistic resolution may seem somewhat irrelevant. But as Caroline Rooney points out:

> In [Head's] terms, spiritual matters pertain to ethical matters—questions of compassion, equality, fellow-love—and to creative, life enhancing powers. These ethical and creative issues, though the terms may yet be inadequate, have crucial bearings on sociopolitical realities and aspirations. (1991, 122)

Significantly, *Maru*, arguably the most unreal of Head's narratives, is proposed by D. R. Beeton to be an example of the kind of artistic realization that is needed to help South Africa confront the foreseeable difficulties of national and cultural cohesion. Beeton argues that "the dark forces" inherent in society conceive of their own particular artistic solution, and thus, "society and culture have been given the articulateness and power to interpret the challenge and the wonder of those forces" (1980, 8). Head's narratives grapple with the challenge of these dark forces. In a letter she explains this process as the way in which she uses her

> intuition to interpret events, not the facts on the surface but the long term planning of the future and how it ought to be. That means I would mostly be concerned with the soul of man, the inner part and say that if that were not right and beautiful, then how could politics be? Or how could life be? And where do we go if we are just mindless guzzlers. (Appendix 3)

Giles Gordon, one of Head's literary agents, considered that the best of her writing was produced in her letters for their "sheer prose and perceptions" (Gordon, 1981). Head, however, stated that her creative writing was "better off than the letters because they are sort of pushed away from the immediate sorrows of my life and therefore have a wider perspective" (Appendix 3). In her biography of Head, Gillian Stead Eilersen describes how, at Head's funeral, Patrick van Rensburg (Eugene in *A Question of Power*), in his eulogy for Bessie Head, tried to explain how she was a different person when she was writing. When she withdrew to her typewriter her "fears, anxieties and physical needs were pushed to one side. . . . [I]t was here the realist and the dreamer achieved a brief communion" (1995, 294). One can fairly assume, from Head's own comments on the distinction between her personal and public work, that it was when she was engaged in her more literary pursuits that the freedom to create order out of chaos was most firmly established. Acquaintance with Head's personal correspondence shows the turmoil that her creativity attempted to rectify. The creative work takes on new meaning; it is part of and yet separated from its creator in the relevance it has for mankind. Creativity reveals the power of the psyche to rise above personal trauma. It seems apt that one of the last letters that Head wrote during the troubled period before her death seems to imply that it was the written, creative word that could provide her with the greatest comfort. She speaks, with delight, of her discovery of Doris Lessing's *An Unposted Love Letter*. Significantly it is in *A Question of Power,* her most personal narrative, that a complete synthesis of the individual and the universal is achieved. For Elizabeth perceives that "soul-power" is "linked in some way to the creative function, the dreamer of new dreams; and the essential ingredient in creativity is to create and let the dream fly away with a soft hand and heart" (*QP* 42).

Eilersen used the Bessie Head papers (available to all researchers) to piece together the story of Head's life. This became the biography published as *Thunder Behind Her Ears* in 1995. Interested readers could do no better than to turn to this volume for a perceptive and sensitive account of Head's life. Apart from the brief quotations in Eilersen's biography, the letters and articles reproduced in the Appendix in this book have, at the time of the completion of this writing, never been published, although readers will notice that many of Head's letters are concerned with the same themes that resonate throughout her nonfictional, published articles.

The letters and extracts of letters from the Bessie Head papers that I photocopied in Serowe were those that I believed helped to explain how the social context of Head's life was a departure point for her novels and short stories, the reason for the artistic resolution at the heart of her work. Three years on, I still think that it is this which is important about her writing, this curious, elusive romanticism that, in spite of its more obvious correspondence with unreality, has evolved from a confrontation with a very real and harrowing experience, and which provided Head with her faith in innate, instinctive, and natural human qualities. Access to these letters will, I hope, convince the reader that I have not embarked on a critical appropriation of Head's work, but hopefully have shown that Head's concerns were not only her concerns, but that they might also be our concerns (Rooney 1991, 102). Thus, this book proposes that, individual though Head's particular problems were, literature provided her with a body of symbols and images through which she could articulate her vision and render it eternally and universally relevant.

1

The Literary Context of Head's Writing

BESSIE HEAD DIED IN SEROWE, A VILLAGE IN BOTSWANA, IN 1986, aged forty-eight. During her lifetime six of her literary works were published: three novels (*When Rain Clouds Gather*, *Maru*, and *A Question of Power*), one collection of short stories (*The Collector of Treasures*), one "portrait" of a village (*Serowe: Village of the Rain Wind*), and a work of historical fiction (*A Bewitched Crossroad*). Since her death, separate volumes of her short stories and articles, *A Woman Alone* and *Tales of Tenderness and Power*, have been compiled and edited, and a collection of letters, *A Gesture of Belonging*, has appeared. More recently a short novel, *The Cardinals*, came to light and has now been published. It is the earliest of her novels and one of the very few pieces that she wrote before leaving South Africa.

Head spent the first twenty-seven years of her life in South Africa before leaving for Botswana, and so, as the reader might expect, Head's books reflect the uncompromising oppression of the apartheid victim: "It was like living with permanent nervous tension, because you did not know why white people there had to go out of their way to hate you or loathe you" (*QP*, 19). But, as Head shows, racism is not simply a pathological result of colonialism. In Botswana there are also victims—the Masarwa. They are addressed as "Bushman! Low Breed! Bastard!" (*M*, 11). As Head laments, "How universal was the language of oppression!" (*M*, 109). By widening the perspective from which racism is observed, she makes clear that the fight for national liberation would not eradicate oppression, for there would always be the "stronger man" who "caught hold of the weaker man and made a circus animal out of him" (*M*, 109). Thus, all Head's protagonists question the nature and source of victimization. As a way to transcend chaos, isolation, exclusion, and despair, they search for "a new dawn and a new world" (*QP*, 205).

Head's account of her origins first appeared in an article called

"Witchcraft," published in the magazine *Ms* in 1975, after the publication of *A Question of Power:*

> I was born on the sixth of July, 1937, in the Pietermaritzburg Mental Hospital, in South Africa. The reason for my peculiar birthplace was that my mother was white, and she had acquired me from a black man. She was judged insane, and committed to the mental hospital while pregnant. Her name was Bessie Emery and I consider it the only honour South African officials ever did me—naming me after this unknown, lovely, and unpredictable woman. (72–73)

These are the biographical details that Head, throughout her life, claimed to be hers. In 1984 she wrote in a letter that she was "acquired" because her mother had "sought some warmth and love from a black man who tended the family race horses" (Appendix 22). However, in her meticulously researched portrait *Thunder Behind her Ears*, Head's biographer Gillian Stead Eilersen shows that Bessie Emery had already spent some time in the asylum prior to her pregnancy. No information was ever forthcoming as to the identity of the father. Although the exact account of her mother's illness given to Head will never be known, what she is doing by rewriting her autobiography is denying the actuality of real madness for her mother, and thereby avoiding the "stigma of insanity" (*QP,* 17) that might extend to herself. As Teresa Dovey cogently points out, it is possible that "Bessie Head's ability to survive, and to transcend in writing, the suffering she endured growing up in South Africa" was "in some sense made possible by the autobiography she constructed for herself" (1989, 37). So autobiography can be a defensive response to victimization, presenting an opportunity for the writer to "authenticate [her] self-image" (Jelinek 1980, 15). Thus, Head depicts herself as not only a racial outcast but also a central victim of an apartheid system that, since 1927, had made extramarital sexual intercourse between blacks and whites illegal.

Head's fourth novel, *A Question of Power*, is, by her own admission, autobiographical—"Elizabeth and I are one" (Adler et al. 1989, 25). The description of Elizabeth's origins is close to the details Head gave of her own life. The core of Elizabeth's life is isolation: a broken marriage, minor participation in antiapartheid activity, an exit permit that "held the 'never to return' clause" (*QP*, 19), which brought Elizabeth and her young son to Botswana. It is here that Elizabeth suffers a severe mental breakdown. She is hospitalized but miraculously emerges from

her nightmare world—battered, bruised, but spiritually whole
and ready to declare her belief in a "brotherhood of man" (*QP*,
206). This resolution is implicit within all Head's writing, but
the writing that succeeds *A Question of Power* confronts more
directly, and at a more realistic level, the structures of society
that impede the formation of satisfactory "human" relationships. Her personal quest is to reimagine "community," to extend the real so that it can embrace her pursuit of the ideal.

POLITICAL AND FEMINIST READINGS

Although critics are conscious of the danger of drawing too
closely upon an author's life in order to interpret his or her work,
it is nonetheless to the autobiographical *A Question of Power*
that critics turn to establish the "political" impetus of Head's
writing. Elizabeth is the absolute victim. As Margaret Tucker
observes, as "stranger, exile, bastard, and woman, she is the
Other, the dispossessed" (1988, 170). So, critics have not failed
to point out that the context of Head's/Elizabeth's experience is
one ideally suited to provide a critique of postcolonialism and patriarchy—the voice of a black woman "talking back," or subvert-
ing a racially prescribed and gendered identity. Huma Ibrahim,
in her book *Bessie Head: Subversive Identities in Exile,* begins
her critique of Head's work by taking issue with "Western feminists" who see Head as their "icon—a Third World woman writer
who is interested in women's issues" (1996, 3). Ibrahim herself
wishes to "relocate that assumption" by reasserting the context
of postcoloniality. She argues that:

> Each woman character in Head's narratives resists being dis-
> missed or misused just "because she became" a woman or because
> there was no place for her in the phallogocentric economy. These
> women claim a space within the equivocal boundaries of neocolonial-
> ism. Resistance becomes part of the dialectics of women's identities
> in exile, which become subject places "negotiated as strategies."
> They not only claim a place for themselves in the postcolonial econ-
> omy but they have to define themselves within that sphere. (1996,
> 10)

One of the challenges that arise when confronting this kind of
argument is to try and decide how helpful it is towards an understanding of Head's writing. Other than Elizabeth, it is difficult
to find evidence that exile places such a burden of identity on

Head's characters. In *When Rain Clouds Gather,* Head creates females, who by virtue of their status as newcomers to the village, are more likely to accept innovations, which are also introduced from outside. Head emphasizes not only how these changes increase prosperity for the village, but how they are instrumental in making the village more of a community, and this is what is of paramount importance. Time and place are immaterial to the kind of utopia of Head's vision. That Head creates this utopia also allows her to define the terms by which men and women will begin to live together, terms that open the way towards increased equality between male and female, but are nonetheless dictated largely by the male. The consciousness that defines most of Head's female characters is one preoccupied by their overriding concern to find husbands and establish homes. In order to secure these goals, "resistance" is not offered because it is not needed, for Head also creates the "new" men to negotiate these improved relationships.

Elizabeth does offer resistance. Elizabeth in order to survive has to resist the "inferno" of her hallucinations in order to believe in the possibility that goodness exists. Doubtless "postcolonialism," "neocolonialism," and "phallogocentric economy" are all structures of the power apparatus included within the "question of power" that Elizabeth has to interrogate and resist. But the whole focus of Head's examination in *A Question of Power* is that it goes beyond the particular conspiracies of social and historical nomenclatures to the universal soul of man. Head is searching for first causes, the first reason why one should want power over another; thus her solution is also universal. Elizabeth may be socially and temporally placed, but her quest and its solution are most certainly not. Thus, issues of identity caused by postcolonialism or exile are only marginal in Head's concerns.

The critic Arun Mukherjee, writing from a political milieu similar to Ibrahim's, voices her unease at the supposition that she, as a postcolonial subject, will write from only one perspective—one that maintains an antagonistic or parodic relationship with the metropolis. Mukherjee condemns Rushdie's claim that postcolonial writers do not write out of their needs but rather out of their "obsession with an absent other," because, she argues, this theorizing leaves the writer with "only one modality, one discursive position" (1990, 6). In order to widen the scope of a writer's choice Mukherjee suggests that critics "should stop making and accepting homogenizing theories that create a 'unitary' field out of such disparate realities" (7).

Mukherjee is expressing her concern with the way in which the application of "external" critical schemata may lead readers to ignore all that is not relevant to their theoretical claims. Such an approach, she feels, encourages a limited perspective; or, as Rooney suggests, the literature under scrutiny becomes "one whose own creative originality is critically appropriated" (1991, 101). Head herself always refused to be labeled and voiced her suspicions of those tempted to label her: "If people wish to place one into certain categories they do so for their own purposes" (Adler et al. 1989, 7).

The very complexity of A Question of Power has, however, made it susceptible to a variety of readings. Head, in retrospect, was able to accept that the "uncertainty" of this novel was "an open invitation to the reader to move in and re-write and reinterpret the novel in his/her own way," that it "is a book that is all things to all men and women" (Appendix 18). Some critics, for instance, see the condensed and complex imagery that describes Elizabeth's breakdown as a highly structured literary convention symbolizing paradigms of oppression operating in an "insane" society. Thus, Kirsten Holst Petersen claims that "madness is an obvious metaphor for the kind of social organisation prevailing in South Africa, and the most striking use of this metaphor is made by the coloured writer Bessie Head" (1991, 131). Hence, madness in this interpretation is not literal but literary, a reading that endorses the primacy of the political, and in so doing suppresses the significance of the personal.

A similar kind of prescriptive reading occurs when some feminist critiques are applied to the symbols and imagery of Elizabeth's breakdown. Within the narrative, Head presents Elizabeth as forcibly compelled to observe Medusa's display of explicit sexuality and Dan's parade of his sexual conquests. They convince Elizabeth of her own inadequacy; she experiences intense distress and total despair. However, in order to identify Elizabeth as a radical feminist, Ibrahim interprets Elizabeth's response to Medusa, and to Dan's use and abuse of his "nice-time" girls as one of defiance. She argues that Head's writing illustrates Hélène Cixous's contention that women "write through their bodies." Elizabeth feels "an exile's urgent need . . . to reclaim her body through language in order to seek her lost, primary fundamental 'home'" (1996, 130). But the text contradicts this reading. Elizabeth prefers to believe in the idea of romantic, ideal male/female relationships that prioritize spiritual union and thus deny the importance of sexuality. It is a resolution that has evolved from Head's own particular experience and her self-perception of her lack of physical attraction—"I am so ugly to look at that I don't think too much about these things" (Appendix 2). Elizabeth is, initially, far too vulnerable "to reclaim her body." She is tormented by the contrast implied between herself and the succession of women Dan parades before her eyes.

Although Head, especially in her short stories, offers a critique of the domination women often suffer, she never suggests that emancipation for women can be achieved by their remaining single, free, or otherwise liberated. In a personal letter she expresses the specific nature of her own anxiety: "There is a horror somewhere in my mind Jean, a long story about a long string of gentlemen who always belonged to someone else, so my subconscious produces all kinds of people in advance whom I don't know" (Appendix 2). For Head, "man/woman relationships are like some kind of turning point in our age and time" (Appendix 8). Thus, whereas feminist critics choose to parallel the oppressive colonial regime with the structures of power implicit within patriarchal institutions, and thus seek autonomy and empowerment for their female protagonists, Head's portrayal is much more multilayered, negotiating as it does the political and gender implications of her social context with more urgent, personal preoccupations. Significantly, especially in Head's earlier work, these urgent personal preoccupations are resolved, for her heroines, by the creation of successful relationships with powerful male figures.

Head was always acutely aware that the urgency of political solutions for apartheid-torn South Africa did create a particular form of "protest" literature, a writing that dealt directly with committed revolutionary participation. Many critics noted the sheer inevitability of this development. The South African situation became what Ezekiel Mphahlele, in *Down Second Avenue*, defined as "a terrible cliché as literary material" (1959, 210). Writing thirty years later, critics were still claiming that it was impossible to write in Southern Africa in an unpolitical way. "Political" meant "marching shoulder to shoulder with others or breathing in and out the stink of prison cells" (Sepamla 1988, 190). For women, solidarity with the cause for liberation was also a priority. Feminist issues were not foregrounded, and although Ellen Kuzwayo contends that every black woman, particularly in Africa, has "an extra burden, as a black and as a woman" (James 1990, 55), these problems became peripheral in Third World writing, where matters relating to national politics, religion, and economics were prioritized over sexism, real or imagined.

Because it was expected that writing out of South Africa would closely reflect urgent social and political concerns, Head often felt compelled to defend her own literary position. She was conscious of the need for South African writing to be "functional" but recognized her own inability to "cope with the liberatory struggle—a world of hot, bickering hate, jealousy, betrayal and murder" (WDIW, 1). Head's interpretation of the struggle within South Africa totally negates the idealism of comradeship expressed by the poet Lindiwe Mabuza. His lines "We would love less / You and I / If we loved not freedom more" (1988, 197) expresses the idea of solidarity in the face of acute oppression that is a central theme of much South African writing. The poet addresses his reader as "comrade"; his desire for freedom intimates both a freedom from the oppression of the apartheid regime and a freedom to share with another the camaraderie of cultural identity. It is this shared cultural cohesion that Head lacks, her feeling of nonbelonging. She had remarked on the significance of the absence of any known relatives. She had not even "a sense of having inherited a temperament, a certain emotional instability or the shape of a fingernail from a grandmother or great-grandmother." As she always insisted, "I have always been just me, with no frame of reference to anything beyond myself" (AWA, 3).

Head's biographer Eilersen has commented that although this "aloneness" often distressed Head, it also gave her the freedom to create as an individual. As Head stated in a letter, "My writing is not on anybody's bandwagon. It is on the sidelines where I can more or less think things out with a clear head" (Appendix 12). It is this feeling that underlies her refusal to be labeled, her avowed antifeminism, her dislike of the title "African writer." As she said emphatically in a letter to Randolph Vigne:

> What is an African writer? Too bad. B.Head is just B.Head now. See how grim you can get? Fighting like mad for your own integrity however worthless this may be to others. (Vigne 1991, 19)

She continued to defend her right to be "international," to create her own "highly original" portrayal of the "African personality" in order to avoid the "dark dungeon called the 'proper' and recognisable African" (WDIW, 3). Nevertheless, her writing originated from an impulse to "answer some of the questions" aroused by her South African experience, and the "human suffering" of people—"black people, white people, loomed large" on her horizon (*AWA*, 67). It was clearly her solutions to these problems, the way her characters ignore political participation as irrelevant to their philosophy that made "the black student," according to Head, a "hostile audience" for her work (WDIW, 2). In *When Rain Clouds Gather*, Makhaya renounces all political affiliation and chooses to work towards creating his own idea of community. Head's creative output is properly seen as the aesthetic realization of Makhaya's dream. But for some, Makhaya is "a traitor to the African cause" (*WRCG*, 81), for his ideal community will not be a paean to African nationalism. Head stressed that her "sense of belonging" was "not to the country" but to "the human race" (*AWA*, 10). Because of Head's determination not to see new societies emerging from cohesive revolutionary action but rather from the intuitive desires of individual heroes, this choice of emphasis, for some of her audience, implied too close an identification with "western civilisation" (WDIW, 3).

This response echoes the trend in the past few decades to make a clear distinction between the socially orientated and committed art of the colonized world and the more personal, autonomous "art for art's sake" of the Western world. As an isolated individual the Western artist is cast as a representative of the current malaise in Western philosophy, that leads to the questioning of the existence of "absolutes" such as Reality, Truth, Self, or even Author. Authors and characters reflect an existential angst, such as the nihilism of Jean-Paul Sartre's Roquentin. Another kind of alienated Western artist is represented by James Joyce's Stephen Dedalus in *A Portrait of the Artist as a Young Man*. Exiled from his society, Dedalus encounters the "reality of experience" in order to "forge in the smithy of [his] soul the uncreated conscience of [his] race" (Joyce, 1916, 253). Both Sartre and Joyce move from the individual, the particular, to the general, their protagonists" specific form of alienation suggestive of a contemporary and "universal" preoccupation.

However, this "universalism" is, to some Third World critics, an unwelcome Western import, and Ibrahim comments that the "theme of 'universalism'" is an "aspect of [Head's] writing that has come under considerable attack" (1996, 19). Many Third World critics and writers view the idea of universalism with some misgivings, because they fear that it might eclipse "important social and cultural determinants" of their own national writing (Nasta 1991, xxvi). Other critics and writers view the term "universalist" with more suspicion, feeling that when this label is applied to their writing it is a form of Eurocentric appropriation. Onwuchekwa Jemie Chinweizu, one of the most extreme advocates of this view, argues that universalism is "a cloak for the hegemonic thrust of Anglo-Saxon cultural nationalism" (1983, 150). This critical perspective implies that there is a particular African experience that ought to be the priority of its writers, and indeed a particular experience that should be the priority of women writers. Thus Ibrahim, even after she has conceded Head's universalism, and accepts the implications of Elizabeth's "soul-searching" for "all individuals in all societies" (1996, 19) still finds it difficult to prioritize the breadth of Head's perspective, and interprets Elizabeth's healing as the securing of "her own salvation, as well as the salvation of all of womankind" (19). But Elizabeth has achieved more than this; she has "fallen into the warm embrace of the brotherhood of man" (*QP*, 206). Nothing could state more clearly than this the nature of Head's cause and the enduring passion of her protagonists.

Craig MacKenzie, in *Bessie Head: An Introduction*, points to the way in which Head's heroes and heroines have similar preoccupations and an identical goal shaped as they are by the desires of their creator:

> The central characters in the three novels, Makhaya, Margaret and Elizabeth, all share some aspects of the author herself and move sequentially closer to her own experience. This progression has a direct bearing on the shape each novel takes. (1989a, 19)

The writing that portrays the experience and concerns of her main protagonists in Head's earliest writing bears a greater affinity to what Northrop Frye defines as "literature of process," than to "literature of product" (1990, 66). It records a process of becoming rather than a product of being. There is, within each of the longer narratives, a discursive element that examines the developing thoughts, the desires and the evolution of the philosophy of her main characters. This discursive element is, as Frye explains, a literary convention in which "a state of identification" (67) occurs between the reader, the literary work, and the writer. During this process "the external relation between author and reader becomes more prominent, and when it does, the emotions of pity and terror are involved or contained rather than purged" (66). It is at this level that the reader engages sympathetically with the line of inquiry that the protagonist is following. The discourse, the fact and argument control the portrayal of the social situation out of which her protagonists emerge, their confrontation with the racism and oppressions with which they are familiar. It is this area of the narrative that portrays the author's own social context, her critique of society. The authorial voice is never absent. The resolution never depends on the historical or social contingencies of political change (and this makes her writing very different from other South African writing of the sixties), but on the creation of asocial and ahistorical utopias.

In many of Head's short stories she employs a different authorial stance, developing a clearer aesthetic distance. Christopher Heywood's comment that Head's novels "have the consistency and mathematical balance of ballads" (1976, xiv), applies more obviously to the style of her short stories. The poise and assured ease of these short pieces suggests that the writer enjoys here a less compulsive and more detached regard for the dilemmas she is recounting. After reading "Witchcraft" the reader does not feel that the author has personally been intimidated by the superstitions of her adopted country, even though they exist as a frightening reality for the character she is portraying. The irony and humor that Head employs to emphasize the inevitability of the human folly she describes in her short stories are not at her disposal when it comes to the portrayal of her own subjectivity in her earlier writing.

The discursive style of Head's longer pieces and the more aesthetic coherence and control of her short stories both describe the social, political, and temporal contexts within which her characters live. The reality she describes is often a grim world of experience. The antithesis to this, usually the province of the artists, dreamers, or unreal heroes of her longer narratives, is an imagined world defined by the writer's perception of what should be. Although some of the short stories, in their concentration on individual dilemmas, are more "real," thus denying the protagonists the expectation of romantic fulfillment, the role of the story teller is dramatized and universalized; it becomes her responsibility to find "gold amidst the ash" (*CT,* 91). This reflects Head's view of art, her role as a writer, to discover within the heroes she creates the power to dream of other realities. With the portrayal of Elizabeth and Maru, the idea of dreaming has an added significance, with which the author is also implicated. Head's resolution becomes an act of writing that no longer depends upon the discursive, the fact or the argument, and is, as Frye contends, an act of "creation, whether of God, man, or nature," that "seems to be an activity whose only intention is to abolish intention, to eliminate final dependence on or relation to something else, to destroy the shadow that falls between itself and its conception" (1990, 89). Frye's contention helps to explain the origin of Maru.

THE ARCHETYPAL READING

It was in Botswana that Head chanced upon the "stage props" that were to portray what she described as the "harmonious correspondence between me and my life here" (Adler et al. 1989, 21). Her initial apprehension of the dark Botswanan nights, the vast empty landscape, soon developed into a feeling of intimacy with "the powdery dust of the earth, the heat, the cattle with their slow, proud walk—all this has fashioned our way of life" (*TTP,* 46). It provided a haven: "I took an obscure and almost unknown village in the Southern African bush and made it my own hallowed ground" (*AWA,* 28). That these "props" bear only what she calls an "unfactual and intangible" relationship to reality (Adler et al. 1989, 21) confirm their status as archetypes, enduring symbols out of which she can fashion her ideal world.

It is for this reason that Frye's contention that art can have "a relation to reality which is neither direct nor negative, but potential" (1990, 93) has direct relevance to Head's creative enterprise. In the imagining of this potential world, the fiction—hypothesis and the imaginative—take precedence over the fact, the assertion and argument of discursive writing. And for Frye it is the archetype that contains the power to present the tentative, the elusive, or in Head's words the "unfactual and intangible" relationship to reality.

Frye defines an archetype as "an element in a work of literature, whether a character, an image, a narrative formula, or an idea, which can be assimilated to a larger unifying category." However, as he explains, "the existence of such a category depends on the existence of a unified conception of art." And for Frye this "conception of art" (1975, 68) would emphasize "the existence of collective human patterns, not confined to particular times, places and biographical facts" (Kugler 1990, 309). What is implied is a belief in universal humanism. As Paul Kugler shows, it was the New Criticism of the forties and fifties that stressed the "autonomy of the psyche, the focus on the emerging image patterns, the move to the deeper collective themes, the discovery of paradox and reconciliation, and the belief in the ultimate unity and coherence of the psyche" (309).

The usefulness of this as an interpretative method has been seriously undermined by a marked decline in the belief in the existence or authority of Absolute Truths, and the emergence of poststructuralist theories furthered the move away from what Caroline Rooney describes as the "legitimacy of a creative cognizance" (1991, 102). Aware of the prevailing ideology, Arun Mukherjee argues for the existence and relevance of texts that contain "truth claims" (1990, 4), which "are different from postmodernist texts that 'use and abuse' everything" (5). Rooney feels that "the erasure of textual authority and the dissolution of the classical text of knowledge into the generalised fictionality of all texts" is one of the "problematic side-effects" of poststructuralist rationalizing (1991, 124), and she contends in her own analysis of Head's *A Question of Power* that there is a place for a critical approach that does not deprive Head's writing "of its estate" (102). The discursive and thematic dimension of Head's didacticism shows clearly her predilection for values and moral codes. Makhaya needs "a few simple answers on how to live well and sanely" (*WRCG,* 71). These issues become the focus of "the conflicts and resolutions in the text" and "the unity and coherence" (Kugler 1990, 309) of the resolution is provided by a coherent body of imagery, Head's "stage props," that presents her idealistic worldview.

In Golema Mmidi, Makhaya discovers the raw material, the "stage props," with which to shape a community that will provide him with a haven after South Africa, from which he has fled. It is an "innocent vision," offering the means by which society can regain its "human form" (Frye 1975, 57) and invalidate the awful world of experience to which Makhaya has been a victim. Cooperation, generosity, the security provided by a home, and the building of community are set in the context of a numinous natural world that shares in the divinity of its creator. For Makhaya, the qualities necessary for a human community echo the "Mercy, Love, & Pity" of Blake's "Divine Image." It is Head's heroes and heroines, those characters more clearly in touch with their essential natures, who are guaranteed possession of these human qualities.

When Rain Clouds Gather ends on a note of optimism: Makhaya and Paulina having no fear of the "uncertain, new and strange and beginning from scratch" life they will share together (*WRCG,* 188). Frye argues that it is the imagery of the "mode of romance" that "presents a human counterpart of the apocalyptic vision," which he defines as "the analogy of innocence" (1990, 151). Makhaya, like Head, believes in the potential humanity of this small community. However, Head was later to express her disillusion with the authority of "pathetic little rural industries and cooperatives" to "expand the world and open new doors" (Sarvan 1990, 15). Her innocent vision lost to experience, Head can no longer believe in the possibility of the real, the social, or the material to provide a context for humanization to take shape. The innocent vision can only survive in an asocial world. Geoffrey Hartman contends that Wordsworth's "sense of apocalypse is simply his pre-vision of the failure of that process of humanization." Hartman concludes that with this failure "the imagination . . . more homeless than ever, falls back into itself. . . . It becomes solipsistic or seeming mad" (1975, 132). This has special significance for Head's next two novels, the inward turning that produces *Maru,* and which in turn becomes the context of *A Question of Power.* For the essentialism that always determines the nature of her heroes and heroines is all that can be depended on in a world that utterly fails to nurture. It is within the next two novels that Head interrogates the meaning and the potential of this essentialism, its acute vulnerability within the world of experience fraught with circumstances that threaten "the unity and coherence of the psyche" (Kugler 1990, 309).

It is at this point that the meaning of "archetype" has great significance for Head's writing. It was from Carl Jung that Frye borrowed the term "archetype," and the importance of the collective, universal themes to be discovered in literature were, for Jung (as they were for the critics of the forties and fifties), synonymous with Jung's conception of the structures and archetypes that determined the coherence of the psyche. Jung describes how within the individual psyche there is a submerged layer of the unconscious that he calls the "collective unconscious," and for which he offers the following explanation:

We mean by collective unconscious, a certain psychic disposition shaped by the forces of heredity; from it consciousness has developed. In the physical structure of the body we find traces of earlier stages of evolution, and we may expect the human psyche also to conform in its make-up to the law of phylogeny. It is a fact that in eclipses of consciousness—in dreams, narcotic states and cases of in-sanity—there comes to the surface psychic products or contents that show all the traits of primitive levels of psychic development. (1934, 190)

Jung used the term "archetype" to describe his conception of these "psychic products." Any reader familiar with Jung's theo-ries will not fail to see that the imagery, symbols, and hallucina-tory content of Elizabeth's breakdown, the meaning of which could not be fully known to her, bear a remarkable correspon-dence to Jung's description of such phenomena.

It is, moreover, Jung's analysis of the nature of specific recur-ring archetypes, their significance for the dreamer, that can also explain the complex, and what often appear to be conflicting im-pulses in the personality of Maru. Although *A Question of Power* is the novel that describes Head's breakdown, it was during the writing of *Maru*, when Head was ill, that she created Maru, whom she considered to be her greatest hero. Most readers will be familiar with Freud's application of mythopoeic allegories to explain psychic complexes (Oedipus, Electra), the way phobic be-havioral patterns of obsession or repression can be traced to early ill-formed affective relationships. Jung went much further than this, for in showing how "human consciousness" evolved, and how ancient myths can be seen to explain the evolution of human personality, his mythic archetypes, unlike Freud's, are not only representative of pathological states of being, but can also serve as compensatory measures or therapy: "they can bring a one-sided, abnormal, or dangerous state of consciousness into equilibrium in an apparently purposive way" (Jung 1934, 191). This is the responsibility that Maru, as archetypal hero, bears towards his society.

Critics invariably note the problematic nature of Maru, either as a fairy-tale figure or manipulative demi-god. His explicit mas-culinity causes readers to question Head's feminist position. But, in fact, what Head contrives in her portrayal of Maru is a much more careful analysis of the meaning of gender identity. For she takes the very notion of masculinity, and defines its meaning by making it the explicit driving force of the arrogant and domineering Moleka. Then, in a very subtle contrast, Head shows how the power of the "hero" Maru is grounded in the te-nacity with which he guards his essential nature against the claims of the social structure. It is by virtue of this essentialism, the superiority of the natural over the social that Maru becomes an archetypal hero. And the role of this archetype in *Maru*, as in all myths, is to secure the reconstruction and regeneration of society. A Jungian analyst might propose that as an archetypal image the artist in Head has drawn Maru from the depths of her unconscious in order to redress the way that human relationships have been formed, a way that has led to the dog-eat-dog fight of human society (*WRCG*, 156). The "hero" figure, in order to fulfil his role, also represents man at his highest evolutionary state, and Margaret, at one level, represents the anima of the hero, the perfect complement who shapes his humanity.

On another level—and it is here that the fairy-tale disintegrates—Margaret, as the all-too-human author herself, still longs for the masculinity promised by patriarchal domination. Elizabeth's breakdown traces in detail the result of an obsession that has also flawed the development of Head's first heroine, Mouse. With her interrogation of Elizabeth's relationship with Sello and Margaret's with Maru, Head shows the nature of flawed human relationships. Indeed, Elizabeth's healing is a manifestation of her ability to negate her obsessive dependency.

Joanna Chase argues that it is "a misrepresentation of the ordeal of the mentally ill to claim that it is creative and productive rather than a sickness like any other" (1982, 71). Other critics also stress the negative aspect of Elizabeth's experience. Jean Marquard quotes Head's claim that "a person with a nervous breakdown is co-operating with the forces that are destroying him" (1978, 54), and Sara Chetin, although she is referring in particular to Head's short stories, comments on the "self-destructive power that exists in a corner of the collective psyche" (1989, 129).

It is true that Head is describing an intensely disturbing experience, "a strange journey into hell and darkness" (*QP*, 190). But within the narrative Elizabeth recovers. Rescued "on a warm sandy beach," Elizabeth stares "back at the stormy sea that had nearly taken [her] life" (204). The writing of Elizabeth's story is proof of her survival. As writing subject, as the discursive authorial voice Head has employed:

> structures—myth, metaphor, symbol—which continually mediate between unconscious and conscious processes. [S]he is often a gifted explorer of what have been called the "*unlabelled* metaphors" of the schizophrenic, an interpreter . . . of hidden layers of psychic reality. (Feder 1980, 5)

Elizabeth can also name the *"unlabelled* metaphors," for healing always involves a turning to the external world. As Jung recognized, "A primordial image is determined as to its content only when it has become conscious and is therefore filled out with the material of conscious experience" (1967, 9i: par. 155, 79). So not only is Elizabeth's healing assured, the writer's creativity is empowered; "the image forces itself from formlessness into clarity and through the creative act the artist also transforms subjective experience into the realm of the universal" (Watts 1989, 47). By making the psychic illness of an individual a reflection of the psychic illness of a society, the personal healing process of Elizabeth synonymous with the healing of society, her "gesture of belonging" to a "brotherhood of man," she dramatizes what Lloyd Brown refers to as, "the central paradox of individualism and art: they are essentially self-conscious, even self-contained, but simultaneously committed in their ideal states to contact and harmony with others" (1979, 49).

Head provides an impressive clue to the nature of the content of the unconscious and its potential for the recreation of the individual and his place in society. The archetypal imagery that shapes the coherence of her psyche performs a similar function in its portrayal of her artistic vision. That these archetypes, literary and psychic, are invoked at times of crises shows clearly the nature of the artist's power and its value as a means to restore the psychic equilibrium of society.

APOCALYPSE

The function of art as commentary on society has long been recognized. Head was conscious of her responsibility as a writer: "In a creative sense I found myself left only with questions. How do we and our future generations resolve our destiny?" (*AWA*, 66). This concern for the future of the society is expressed by Lukacs as:

> a deeply felt need to go beyond the mere affirmation of existing conditions, to explore values not to be found in present society—values which come to be thought of, necessarily, as hidden in the future. Thus the utopian perspective serves a double function: it enables the artist to present the present age truthfully without giving way to despair. (1969, 61)

This was Head's project in *When Rain Clouds Gather*, and in any of her writing in which community is imagined, Head turns again and again to the motifs she uses in this early novel. The failure of political and social action to guarantee the success of Makhaya's Utopia makes it more imperative that it should live on in literary form, that setting infinite aims for finite man becomes the inevitable course for the writer.

Frye believes that art "as the creative root of civilization and prophecy" (1975, 58) can permit itself the portrayal of less tangible manifestations of reality, that it can deal "not only with the possible, but with 'probable impossibilities.'" He contends that:

> just as the controlling idea of civilization is the humanizing of nature, and the controlling idea of prophecy the emancipation of man, so the controlling idea of art, the source of them both, must be the simultaneous vision of both. This is apocalypse, the complete transformation of both nature and human nature into the same form. (58)

This is art at its most visionary, the envisaging of an ideal state in which "nature" and "human nature" become one and the same form. A principal prerequisite for the realization of this apocalypse is the hero, who, as a "god, whether traditional deity, [or] glorified hero . . . is the central image . . . trying to convey the sense of unlimited power in a humanized form" (Frye 1990, 120). Head is always emphatic about the pivotal role that her heroes play in her writing, the importance of her "grand" man (Adler et al. 1989, 16). From the most grand and spectacular, Maru, to the lesser heroes in her short stories, they all anticipate a form of human freedom rarely experienced in a civilization controlled by a law that has come to mean "to defend by force what has been snatched in self-will" (Frye 1975, 56). Their ability to resist "petty human hatreds and petty human social codes and values" gives them the freedom to become more attuned to the "natural." For Frye contends that in the apocalyptic vision, as "the goal of life, is the humanization of nature, there is a profound similarity between human and natural behavior . . . which . . . becomes identity" (67).

In Head's narrative, the natural landscape is nurtured rather than plundered. Makhaya would "treasure every green shoot" (*WRCG*, 160) and Gilbert's life was "like all the rivers and sunsets and the fish in the rivers and the trees and pathways and sun and wind" (86). Most critics of Head's work note the significance of Head's evocation of the natural world. Jean Marquard writes that it is a "mind landscape too, the storm clouds gather in the individual psyche" (1978, 61). Invested in it throughout, is a pervasive religious spirit that, in its denial of institutionalized Christianity, has "produced the god, the personalized aspect of nature, and a belief in gods gradually builds the sense of an omnipotent personal community out of nature" (Frye 1975, 67). Here the opportunity exists for the crystallization of personal creeds uninformed by the contingencies of time and place.

For Margaret, temporal and spatial reality is of little significance; her life and work in Dilepe is of no consequence: "she was not a part of it and belonged nowhere." Instead, "the rhythm of sunrise, the rhythm of sunset, filled her life" (*M*, 93). As Kenneth Harrow comments, "Dawn, nightfall, cusps of existence where existential decisions are made—these are boundaries given meaning by personal choice and not historical movement" (1995, 196). The concept of the infinite and eternal in the apocalyptic vision is not the eternal life of Christian redemption, but the infinity and eternity of the natural world with its recurring cycles within which man has his place. It is within this place that the divine will become human; the human divine and man will become holy to man. Elizabeth's courageous effort, in the midst of her breakdown, to hold fast to her belief that "God is people" (*QP*, 109) is recompensed on her recovery by the freedom she has secured from the constraints of orthodox Christian dogma. Now she can claim "There is only one God and his name is Man. And Elizabeth is his prophet" (*QP*, 206).

The possibility for personal choice, for human freedom anticipated in this vision, operates on different levels within Head's writing. In *When Rain Clouds Gather,* the idea of freedom is more overtly connected to the social and political situation of the hero. Exile in Botswana may mean political freedom for Makhaya, but it also means commitment to a communal enterprise. Thus, Makhaya has to negotiate how he can maintain his individuality and yet forfeit his separate and isolated ego in order, like Gilbert, to recognize the mutual interdependence of all human beings (*WRCG*, 134). Work becomes the means to establish shared aspirations. Work is never drudgery. It is always affirmative. For Elizabeth the garden is a lifeline. For Sebina the building of homes, the preparing of new lands, symbolizes the promise of the perpetuation and recurrence of life. And Maru imagines how he will cultivate a field of golden sunflowers that will mirror the sun of his love. In the apocalyptic vision, as Frye shows, "the work that, projected on nature, forms civilization, becomes, when projected on society, prophecy, a vision of complete human freedom and equality" (1975, 57).

All these motifs within Head's work invoke the vision of her "new dawn and new world" (*QP*, 205). As Cherry Wilhelm argues, the beauty of this literary realization "lies in its ability to rescue man from the disturbing and destructive effects of class society [or racist society] through the poetically direct portrayal of man's wholeness" (1983, 12). Clearly, the idea of freedom changes in Head's project. What begins as an intimation of the possibility of political freedom for Makhaya develops into an interrogation of the meaning of personal freedom as it affects human development. The question of man's wholeness, its correspondence with the idea of "both nature and human nature in the same form" is fundamental to the apocalyptic vision and is of particular relevance to Head's creation of Maru. The portrayal of all Head's main protagonists emphasizes their possession of essential qualities. For Paulina, in *When Rain Clouds Gather,* it means that she has preserved her vitality. For Maru, however, it means that he can "communicate freely with all the magic and beauty inside him" (7). In order to remain attuned to his "gods," Maru must live in a state of exile defined entirely on his own terms. The idea of human community is denied him. As Martin Tucker argues, "the artist, if he is successful in his constructs— that is, if he achieves the creations of his vision—will emerge without any home or history" (1991, xx). The idea of freedom loses any connection with sociopolitical issues that it may have held for Makhaya; Maru dreams of "a world apart" where "the human soul roamed free in all its splendour and glory" (67).

Clearly Maru is ahistorical and asocial, an archetypal hero who can emerge at any moment of history to redress and reshape human destiny. For Head he is the embodiment of the ideal personality. A Jungian analyst would argue that the evolution of mankind does provide for the possibility of this ideal state of evolutionary perfection, and that the potential for this affirmation resides within the human psyche. In a letter to a friend, Head wrote "when that new day [will have] dawned," "each man will have completed his cycle of evolution." It is then, she anticipates, "I could retreat to a way of life I love very much" (Appendix 2). Maru is clearly the personification of such a character. He is imagined, but, for Head, he is not imaginary.

Very early on in her writing career, Head wrote "I've just got to tell a story" (*AWA*, 8). About two years before her death, she was commissioned to write her autobiography. Letters to her publisher express her reluctance to write about her early life. In order to renegotiate the expectations of an autobiography, she expressed the wish to call her novel "Living on a Horizon." As a title, Head perceived it to be

> definitive of one who lives outside all possible social contexts, free, independent, unshaped by any particular environment, but shaped by internal growth and living experience. (Appendix 22)

Head's agent stated her preference for the guarantee of a more factual perspective. At Head's death, amongst her vast accumulation of private papers, there was no evidence that she had ever started on this endeavor. Her autobiography was not the story she wished to tell.

There is plenty of evidence to show the kind of story she wanted to write. What becomes clear is that her view of the value of literature is synonymous with the dreams of her heroes. Three of Head's main characters are artists, and their artwork denies the primacy of their lived experience in order to prophesy their dreams and visions. However, the latter would never have been achieved without the reality of the former. The vision counterbalances the nightmare. The apocalyptic vision, with its stress on the importance of nature, is the antithesis to a world in which the social is reduced to a manifestation to all that is corrupt, destructive, and oppressive.

Jung writes that the vision is "true symbolic expression that is, the expression of something existent in its own right, but imperfectly known" (1934, 187). This can explain the creation of Maru, and touches on the nature and function of Head's archetypal imagery. One of Head's minor heroes, Paul Thebolo, has "the power to create himself anew" (*CT*, 93). For Head it is the measure of his greatness. It is also the measure of hers. For "creativity does not lie alone in the production of great works of art. . . . It lies, essentially, in freeing the mind from its shackles, so that we create our world and ourselves anew, over and over again, in every moment" (Singer 1990, 172).

2

The Cardinals

BESSIE HEAD'S FIRST NOVEL, *THE CARDINALS,* PUBLISHED ONLY after her death, was dismissed by Head in later life as a "hotch-potch of under-done ideas, and, monotonous in the extreme" (Eilersen 1995, 55). But it is, at the level of projected fantasy, one of her most personal and unmediated pieces of writing, undertaken at a time which Head's biographer, Gillian Stead Eilersen, refers to as "a deeply painful period of her life" (1995, 54). Head always acknowledged the personal aspect of her writing. In her words, "Every story or book starts with what I need" (Fradkin 1978, 430). Thus, it is probable that the elements of romantic fantasy helped, at that time, to fill a void in her life.

There is often a deliberate design amongst critics to avoid drawing any parallel between the author's life experiences and her art. Annie Gagiano argues the way in which Head explains the meaning of her title—"The Cardinals in the astrological sense, are those who serve as the base or foundation for change"— is a caution to the reader

> not to mistake the novel for simple realism, unconscious autobiography, sociological portrayal of earlier apartheid conditions in the Cape, or erotic/neurotic wish fulfilment by its author. (1996, 50)

Instead, Gagiano contends, *"The Cardinals* has the dimensions of a parable" (50). But as any reader of this novel will discover, ideas and resolutions are only tenuously touched upon, the outcome elusive, the future uncertain, and the normal course of cause and effect (important in the structure of a parable) is immaterial in the irrational social context that is portrayed. All the features that Gagiano dismisses are fundamental to the psyche of the writer. That Head transmutes them into an examination of the foundations of the categories of power and the qualities that are needed to dismantle them, reflects the way in which the personal moves towards the general in her writing. Perhaps it is

41

in this way that *The Cardinals* has "the dimensions of a parable."

In the early 1960s, when Head wrote *The Cardinals*, she was newly married, expecting a first child and living in the colored district of Cape Town. She had recently worked as a journalist, but, like Mouse/Miriam, the protagonist of *The Cardinals*, Head was set on becoming a serious writer. Her first novel was the product of this resolve. There are obvious parallels between the early experiences of Mouse and her creator. There is the foster mother, the lack of a real father figure, the poverty, and the experience of racism. But the degree of deprivation to which Mouse is subjected is an imaginative revision of the author's own life. Within the narrative such deprivation retards Mouse's emotional growth: "Year by year she had become more and more silent and her inner retreat was almost to a point where no living being could reach her" (10–11). For her fellow journalist, Johnny, Mouse's refusal to be provoked out of her impassiveness is a source of irritation. It is he who is responsible for her harmless, if unflattering, nickname. His insults, though often cruel, are aroused by his frustration at Mouse's lack of response rather than by any malicious intent. The more she remains impassive under his taunts the more abusive he becomes: "Do you know what you are? You're just a screwball, oddball crank that the loony-bin overlooked" (21).

This uneasy abuse serves to emphasize the magnitude of Mouse's ultimate success in securing for herself the undivided love of Johnny, this much sought after, most masculine of male heroes. A charismatic male is central in all Head's subsequent writing, and Head conceded that Johnny became the model for all her heroes, "a mythical man" who "appeared everywhere" (Daymond 1993, xvii). In this way, much of Head's writing exploits the motifs of the popular romance; but what is highly significant is that the conventional formula that sees the heroine finally safe in the arms of an adored and powerful father figure is, in *The Cardinals*, crudely reinforced by the fact that Johnny is, in fact, Mouse's biological father, although this fact is unknown to either of them.

So, whilst *The Cardinals*, like all popular romances, is concerned to record the progress and ultimate success of the heroine in winning her man, Mouse's triumph encodes Freud's description of the most primal and elemental force of sexual gratification, the unconscious desire of the female for her father. Most feminists, however, resist the totalizing implications of the Electra complex and are thus opposed to the idiom of the popular romance with its tendency to endorse the desirability of such patriarchal compliance. Some feminists, however—Alison Light for instance—concede that romances can be compensatory, that as fantasies they make space for "the explorations and productions of desires which may be in excess of the socially possible or acceptable" (Light 1990, 142). This is indeed what is happening in *The Cardinals*. It explores the ultimate expression of female passivity, the fantasy of permanent foreplay. Whilst psychoanalysis will interpret this need as manifestation of a profound emotional dysfunction, the ultimate "love pact" that concludes these narratives assumes the transfer of power from the male to the female.

This ensures that Head can explore the fundamental role played by love in the disruption of the structures of power and social taboos. The relationship between Johnny and Mouse presents a challenge to the unequivocal rightness of the incest taboo. Thus, what is foregrounded in Head's portrayal of her heroes and heroines, in a startlingly radical form, is their ability to transcend their social conditioning. Indeed, it is this characteristic that manifests their difference from the other characters. Mouse is simply a "beautiful soul . . . nurtured on a dung heap" (24), but whilst Johnny's attraction for other women lies in his reckless contempt for social convention, he must, to gain parity with Mouse, rediscover links with his essential nature. The development of his relationship with Mouse is the key to this process. Love is seen to be both the function and the product of this endeavor. In its transcendence of "the petty transactions of life" (91), it offers a promise of freedom from oppressive forces. It is the knowledge of this that sustains Mouse as she begins to write.

Love as Romance

The central theme of *The Cardinals* is courtship, its plot encoding the simple formula of popular romance: the heroine against all odds is finally safe in the arms of the attractive, previously unattainable male hero. As a hero Johnny receives double exposure. He is in his youth the lonely idealist, the lover of Mouse's mother, who by day does battle with the sea and by night lies beneath the stars. As the older Johnny, he is the cynical, worldly-wise journalist who makes the unlikely commitment to the waiflike Mouse. Eilersen comments that Johnny is probably the least romanticized of Head's heroes. He certainly does not possess the mystical aura of Maru, the spiritual goodness of a Paul Thebolo or a Jacob. He is dominating, aggressive, and even brutal, but it is in fact just these qualities that define him as the archetypal romantic hero. Critics of the popular romance define its single most vital factor as the character of the hero. As Ann Snitow writes:

> He is the unknowable other, a sexual icon whose magic is maleness. . . . Male is good, male is exciting, without further points of reference. Cruelty, callousness, coldness, menace, are all equated with maleness and treated as a necessary part of the package. (1990, 134–35)

Indisputably, within Head's novel, all these qualities are to be admired. In *The Cardinals*, Ruby says to Johnny, "You are very rough with me . . . but I like it" (53). The women with whom he dallies are drawn by his "devastating physical magnetism" (112). Head has poured much imaginative energy into the creation of Johnny; he becomes the projection of the needs of Ruby, Miriam's mother, Mouse, and of the author herself.

The character of Mouse does not present such a recognizable stereotype, but she does in Snitow's analysis qualify as a suitable heroine simply because of the apparent gulf that separates her from the hero. The romance formula glorifies this difference between the sexes:

> Distance becomes titillating. The heroine's sexual inexperience adds to this excitement. What is this thing that awaits her on the other side of distance and mystery? Not knowing may be more sexy than finding out. Or perhaps the heroes are really fathers—obscure, forbidden objects of desire. Whatever they are, it is more exciting to wonder about them than to know them. In romanticized sexuality the pleasure lies in the distance itself. (1990, 136)

This analysis might well have been written as a description of the sexual relationship that Johnny initiates with Mouse, which is different from his sexual experience with Ruby, and different again from his sexual adventures with his other admirers. The avowals of love that Johnny makes to Mouse are constantly interrupted by threats of violence, which, like Mouse's inexplicable plunge into the sea, act as a crude deferral of the inevitable moment of union. As Snitow explains:

> Perhaps there is pleasure, too, in returning again and again to that breathless, ambivalent, nervous state before certainty or satiety. In-

sofar as women's great adventure, the one they are socially sanctioned to seek, is romance, adventurousness takes women always
back to the first phase in love. (136–37)

This common fantasy of popular romance is interpreted by Rosalind Coward as regressive: "In the adoration of the powerful
male, we have the adoration of the father by the small child"
(1990, 145). Thus, both Snitow and Coward point out the importance of the father figure as a common element of romantic fantasy. That Johnny actually is Mouse's father does identify him
as the "forbidden object of desire," and this desire, is, in Coward's view, a form of regressive infantile fantasy born of inadequacy—indeed, the kind of fantasy to which one such as Mouse,
or indeed her creator, would be highly susceptible.

The role of the female as passive, narcissistic, and submissive
in the popular romance is problematic for feminists, who sometimes prefer to avoid an analysis of its cause, refusing to accept
that women can be complicit in their own domination. An extreme example of this attitude can be seen in a theorist like
Sheila Jeffreys, who defines all forms of heterosexual desire as
eroticized power or submission. It is impossible to imagine
equality, she writes, because "we are born into subordination
and it is in subordination that we learn our sexual and emotional responses" (1990, 302).

Such a totalizing reduction of the development of gender identity obscures the real complexity of the issue. Coward explains
the persistence of "passive" heroines as the failure of the child to
reconcile her adoration of the parent with her desire for autonomy; thus, the development of her separate self is thwarted. Jessica Benjamin's analysis, however, tries to explain why
domination can offer a form of masochistic satisfaction for the
woman. She feels that domination and submission "result from
a breakdown of the necessary tension between self-assertion and
mutual recognition that allows self and other to meet as sovereign equals" (1990, 12). What is important in Benjamin's account is that affective interchange between child and parent
means that a child's sense of self needs for its confirmation the
knowledge that it is recognized as an individual by its parent.
When such needs are not met, the thwarted child, in a compensatory search, will find recognition only through another individual powerful enough to bestow this recognition. Herein lies
the theory of masochism, of pleasure in submission. The Electra
complex, the desire of the female for her powerful father, is re-

vised, to have lasting relevance only for those individuals suffering impaired emotional development.

As the passive heroine, Mouse submits totally to Johnny's bidding, whether it be to turn up the hem of her skirts, to walk on a different side of the road, or to move into his house with him. That she is prepared to exchange her state of independence for one of submission is evidence that Johnny's attentions, in whatever form they take, are welcomed. She is sexually aroused by him: "Her gaze was drawn to the magnetic, hollow curve of his back and at the same time she felt a strange sensation in her hands as though they wanted to reach out towards it" (128). She does not allow herself to respond but presses her hands "firmly on the ground" and thus maintains her passivity. Johnny is often physically violent; Coward, commenting on the frequency with which this kind of scenario occurs in popular romantic fiction, argues that the hero's "uncontrollable desire has close resemblances with descriptions of rape" (1990, 147). Active female desire is projected from the heroine to the hero, and his position of dominance absolves the heroine from all responsibility for sexual engagement. Her passion is always forced out of her. In Head's novel, the crudity of Johnny's words to Mouse emphasizes this aspect of their relationship. After Mouse kisses him for the first time, Johnny comments, "To get you to do such a simple and uncomplicated thing I have to put you on the torture rack" (133).

Nevertheless it is, as Coward shows, at this extreme point of submission that a transfer of power takes place, for the romance formula insists that sexual engagement is only anticipated or tolerated on the understanding that the heroine has won the undivided love of the hero. For Johnny needs Mouse to "complete" him "in some vital way" (100). It is only his feeling for Mouse that justifies his "love and faith in some living thing" (136). Thus the heroine's submission also gives her access to power. The child has finally gained the recognition of the father.

ROMANCE AS LOVE

The importance of love is always explicitly acknowledged in *The Cardinals*. It is not only seen as the fulfillment of romantic yearning, symbolized by birds "with sunset on their wings" (72), but, more seriously, as the life-affirming quality that will deliver Mouse from what Johnny sees as her "remote, unapproachable, inhuman and eccentric" persona (29). It is Johnny who is to be responsible for this deliverance. This is the role that Head envisages for all her heroes: "everytime I need to say something about love—he's always there—so conveniently" (Daymond 1993, xvii). A similar pattern is seen in the case of Makhaya in *When Rain Clouds Gather*, and also in *Maru*. The fulfillment of their destinies as enlightened reformers cannot be isolated from their personal relationships. *A Question of Power* proposes a movement from the exclusiveness of love, symbolized in Margaret's portrayal of the embracing lovers in *Maru*, to a world in which "personal love had died in them" (*QP*, 202). It offers in its place human connectedness that can envisage a "brotherhood of man" (*QP*, 206). This utopian vision avoids the responsibility of personal love. Personal love may be "moonlight and rosy sunsets" (103), but can also, as Johnny says, be "brutal, violent, ugly, possessive and dictatorial" (103). In *Maru*, these aspects of love have defined Maru's control over Margaret. A guarantee against absolute surrender to Maru's power is Margaret's love for Moleka, a constant element within her subconscious dreams. Johnny anticipates the arbitrary nature of existence when he says, "Life is a treacherous quicksand with no guarantee of safety anywhere" (137).

Nevertheless, love for Head always acts as an antidote to the impoverishment of society, providing a source of human bonding that will create a society that is not regulated solely by the operations of power. Head, like Freud, sees the restrictions of culture as painful, but whereas Freud sees the rule of authority as preferable to the willful anarchy that would otherwise exist, Head sees the social order as a system that dangerously represses one's better nature. As Jessica Benjamin points out in *The Bonds of Love*, this view may appear to be naive in its assumption that power and authority can only mean prohibition. Certainly Benjamin is right, but, in order to be benign, the exercise of authority must operate on the principle of equal rights between individuals. And this, at the time Head was writing, was not the case in South Africa. Mouse at a very early age has not only learned how circumscribed her rights were but also that their continuation demands total acquiescence:

She learnt the lessons every unwanted stray has to learn: "Work hard. Do not answer back no matter what we do to you. Be satisfied with the scraps we give you, you cannot have what our children have. Remember we are unpredictable, when the mood gets us we can throw you out." (10)

To read *The Cardinals* as first a protest against apartheid, the system that legalized the way of life endured by Mouse and the majority of South Africans, would be to agree with most critics of African literature, who regard the critique of colonial and postcolonial society as the single most consistent preoccupation of African writers. Abdul JanMohamed asserts that the structure of colonial society is the source of "such a powerful socio-political-ideological force field that neither colonial nor African literature is able to escape or transcend it" (1983, 277). Head herself seemed to be confirming the difficulty in seeing beyond the racial bind when she wrote, "I would just like to say people is people and not damn White, damn Black" (*TTP,* 17).

Yet, in *The Cardinals*, it is very significant that Head carefully avoids using race as the barrier that separates Johnny from Ruby, and which leads indirectly to the abandonment of Mouse and to Ruby's death. The race of each character in the novel is established within the text, but defined in such a way that their color is just one other feature that describes their physical appearance. Any mention of PK usually includes some allusion to his "long ginger beard." He is the token white, a liberal newspaper editor. The color of other characters is more subtly indicated. The reader learns that Ruby is not white because of the reference that is made to her "large black eyes," "her wild black hair" (50), and more definitively to "her dark brown face" (52). But the inclusion of these physical details is primarily to concentrate the effect of her attraction for Johnny. Given the fact that Head's own mother was white and her father black, Head had every reason to politicize Mouse's dilemma, to see it as a direct consequence of the current pathological taboo on interracial breeding. There could be a number of reasons why Head should choose not to do this. It might be that, at the time of writing, she was isolating a more immediate and compelling issue than apartheid. A clue to Head's concern at that time is given in a letter that she wrote describing her experiences in Cape Town:

> I have walked into some houses where the reception has been very cold. They seemed to pick out immediately that I had no class and sophistication, which is associated with being fair. . . . I have never thought of belonging to any particular class of society but most probably I belong to the low class because I feel so happy in their carefree unsnobbish society that I already have many friends among them. (Eilersen 1995, 40)

Clearly, in South Africa, race and class are closely affiliated, but class barriers can flourish in the absence of racial differ-ences. In *The Cardinals*, it is class that separates Ruby and Johnny. Ruby's father might well try to comfort Ruby by saying that "women were meant to have babies" (56), that it is a natural law. Ruby's mother, more concerned with the laws laid down by society, demands that Ruby remain hidden so that her pregnant state does not bring shame to the family. Their upper-class status also accounts for there being a woman to do the washing, Sarah, who can take Ruby's child when it is born and conveniently bring it up as her own, because she and the baby share the same color.

In other instances within the novel it is also class as surely as race that is the significant leveler. Mohammed, the shopkeeper, addresses a customer as "Sir" simply because "well-dressed people always made him feel obliged to put on his most polite manner" (35). It is James's obsession to "get the slum out of [his] system" (16) that earns him the greatest contempt from Johnny. Also, significantly, it is the influence of a colored family who "made one hell of a racket in court" (125), rather than PK's white face, that succeeds in having a case against him and a young colored girl dismissed. It would appear that absorption into the cultural milieu of the Cape Town colored community, where Head's mixed racial origins were the norm rather than the exception, directed her attentions to the conflicts and tension that arose from within the community rather than those imposed from without.

There is however, a more significant reason why Head resists the temptation to exploit the melodramatic potential of interracial liaisons. On the most basic imaginative level she is less concerned with the legalized injustices of the apartheid system than she is with the larger, more insidious, structure of discrimination and prohibitions that, even without laws to enforce them, dominate all societies. Her subject is not the historically limited situation of apartheid but the universal patterns of intercourse that define the nature of all human relationships.

It is within this context that an interpretation of power and authority as only prohibition seems justified. Head's fundamental message, that society corrupts, does also, in her later writing, extend to include an examination of traditional African communities untouched by colonial power. In all her books there are the heroes and the heroines, the victims and survivors. The victims become dehumanized, with "blind, brutal hearts" (4). The survivors, who are ruthless and corrupt, thrive on their acquisition of power: "the crudest expression of the power drive is in the gang-ster; the most subtle and disastrous in the politician" (87).

Thus, for Head, the abolition of power must be a priority; love as an oppositional quality is offered in its place. Because power, for Head, is the product of exploitative and manipulative traf-ficking, love is presocial. Johnny says that he possesses "sacred" ideas about women, ideas that owe nothing to what experience has taught him.

> No religion or person taught them to me. If I've ever had any kind of religious feeling in my life it was simply achieved by lying back and looking at the stars. Those many nights I spent sleeping out in the open on the mountain like this or by the sea, I found a kind of prayer of my own. It went like this: "In the still of the night my soul in free-dom soars." (101)

All the images that mirror Johnny's finer feelings—the moun-tains, the sea, the stars—are elemental; part of the natural world, constant, immutable, and immune to the hand of man. Here, in this very early piece of writing, Head touches on the power of archetypes to affirm the need for a fusion of the "natu-ral" with the "essential" human qualities. Love that is manipu-lated by society becomes the prerogative of "high-society glamour doll[s]" (94), with their "feminine tricks" (115) and "false voices" (95). In stark contrast, Mouse, with the innocence of a child, is, for Johnny, someone that he can "love and under-stand and can live with, and who loves and understands and can live with [him]" (84). Even Johnny's aggressiveness becomes in-terpreted as part of his indomitable personality, and is vener-ated as evidence of his honest refusal to acquire social skills. Ruby is attracted by his roughness, believing as she does, that, "often those who talk softly and sweetly hide a stabbing cruelty in that softness and sweetness" (53). For Ruby, Johnny, in the way that he holds up his "head so high and independently," and in the way that he walks, is a "king" (53). But in spite of Ruby's admiration for all that is free and unsocial about Johnny, she knows she must forfeit all claims to his love because she herself is tainted by the consciousness of her class. However, recogniz-ing for herself that a loveless, albeit socially acceptable marriage to Paddy, holds neither the promise of happiness nor fulfillment, Ruby chooses death.

It is within this larger context of the discrepancy between so-cial and natural law that Head situates her examination of the

South African Immorality Laws. In *The Cardinals*, these laws represent the obsessive ends to which the operators of power will strive to control and prohibit. As a product herself of an interracial relationship, Head has strong personal reasons to resist the deep-seated belief that miscegenation is either neurotic or pathological. In *The Cardinals*, Johnny's analysis shows that it is the white businessman who appears most often in court for contravening this law. Threatened by financial ruin as the most likely victim of an unstable economy, he stares down "in fascinated horror into the abyss," and, as though compelled to hasten on his own destruction, "he leaps over the edge" (115). But his liaison with a colored girl is destructive not because interracial sex is wrong but because the law teaches that it is. It is the breaking of a law created by the prejudices of an oppressive society that will bring about the ruin of the white businessman. Head is showing how the law, and the morality it preaches, is primarily repressive in its confounding of natural instincts with perversion and corruption.

Racist ideology propagated the myth of the biological superiority and purity of the white race. Sarah Gertrude Millin's uncompromising treatment of miscegenation in *God's Stepchildren* is designed to prove the genetic folly of mixed breeding, how pure white blood becomes irreparably tainted. In this way racism elected its own biological, and thus respectable justification for its separatist politics. Miscegenation became a social taboo. Most readers will have little difficulty in accepting, like Head, that the fear of miscegenation is pathological. They will comprehend the bewilderment of the young Norwegian sailor when confronted by the racist interpretation of his liaison with a black girl. Miscegenation is not, like incest, a universally accepted taboo.

But it is interesting, in Head's novel, that her portrayal of the incestuous nature of Johnny's and Mouse's relationship asks the reader to judge it with a similar disregard for society's laws that has guided their response to the portrayal of miscegenation. This does not mean that Head is insensitive to the biological justification that underpins the taboo on incest. Even within the novel she shows how the inhabitants of the slum in which Mouse grows up are victims of inbreeding and as a consequence of this are handicapped by "a facial structure and mentality that is like something inhuman" (28). But even this account condemns incest no more than it condemns all forms of human intercourse practiced by the brutalized inhabitants of the slum. With Johnny's description of his near-incestuous lovemaking to his sister, Head is moving towards an exploration of incest that demands that it be judged only in terms that consider the motives and needs of the participants. Clearly, when balanced against the exploitation that his sister has suffered as a prostitute, Johnny is seen to be offering her "the kind of love she wanted" (78).

When it comes to the relationship between Johnny and Mouse, any appraisal, if it is to sympathize with the circumstances and underlying principles of their love, must circumvent the law of the land. This does not mean that Head resolves the situation satisfactorily. The prolonged courtship serves not only to extend the anticipatory pleasure that is a feature of romantic fiction, but also avoids the actuality of sexual union. The author evasively defers responsibility for the literal consummation of an incestuous relationship and the risk of a genetically deformed child.

Perhaps it is at this juncture that the full force of the Electra theory holds true. The female's desire for her father cannot be socially sanctioned, the author is obliged to seek elsewhere, and Head, in her later writing, imaginatively creates a succession of masculine, powerful heroes who not only fulfil this need but who offer love that cannot be compromised by social taboo.

The element of protest found in *The Cardinals*, while it focuses on particular injustices, is clearly leveled at the whole question of coercion, control, and prohibition, as it defines and impedes personal freedom, as it perverts and corrupts natural development. With moral intensity, Head can reconstruct her romantic fantasy into a narrative in which love is not only the denouement of romantic desire but also the means through which society's ills can be ameliorated. Here supervenes the uneasy gulf between what the writer can envisage and the social realities around her. This is the essence of Mouse's dilemma. Head describes how Mouse escapes the slum and, untainted by the moral wasteland around her will, as "the living symbol of freedom," begin to write. As a writer she will insist in the face of all the evidence that contradicts it, that there is the potential for human freedom if it will recognize love as the ultimate form of human fulfillment. Yet, the very terms of Mouse's own deliverance belie this faith. The resolution at the end of this novel rests only within the scope available to any romantic fantasy. As Johnny says, "We can only try to grab what happiness we can before we are swept off into oblivion" (137).

3

When Rain Clouds Gather

In one of her letters, Head states that out of all her writing, she likes best the description of an early morning sunrise in Botswana. She quotes:

> As far as the eye could see it was only a vast expanse of sand and scrub but somehow bewitchingly beautiful. Perhaps he confused it with his own loneliness. Perhaps it was those crazy little birds. Perhaps it was the way the earth had adorned herself for a transient moment in a brief splurge of gold. Or perhaps he simply wanted a country to love and chose the first thing at hand. But whatever it was, he simply and silently decided that all this dryness and bleakness amounted to home and that somehow he had come to the end of a journey. (Appendix 13)

This extract is from *When Rain Clouds Gather;* it describes Makhaya's response to his first dawn in Botswana. *When Rain Clouds Gather* was the first novel that Head wrote in exile in Botswana. There is sufficient evidence in Head's written accounts, both published and private, to show that Head grew to love the Botswanan landscape, and throughout her writing her evocation of the natural world is an affirmation of her belief in the restitutive quality of the natural as an antithesis to the social and the material. In *A Question of Power*, Elizabeth's first home in Botswana is a mud hut, and Elizabeth becomes intensely aware of the closeness of the living earth. Her work in the garden, like Maru's plans to grow his sunflowers, and like the General's dreams to be allowed to work his land (*TTP*, 102) are all means by which these characters seek redemption from the demands of an alienating world. Even in *The Cardinals*, a narrative dense with the imagery of the poverty of the slum dwellings of South Africa, Johnny and Mouse seek consolation in the margins of their urban environment, in the sky, the sea, and the mountains.

Thus, although there is no doubt that Head is describing the real, the visual, she is also providing what Jane Wilkinson defines (in her explanation of the South African landscape in Olive Schreiner's *The Story of an African Farm*) as a "moral landscape" (1991, 118). Makhaya, captivated by his first dawn in Botswana, is responding subjectively to the Botswanan landscape. This subjective response to the natural world has always been a characteristic feature of romanticism. It is explained by W. K. Wimsatt (using Samuel Taylor Coleridge's term) as the "*esemplastic* power which reshapes our primary awareness of the world into symbolic avenues to the theological" (1975, 25). So it is with the stress on the animism of this new environment that Makhaya can begin to "undo the complexity of hatred and humiliation that had dominated his life for so long" (71) and reflect on the meaning of community in its displacement of his South African experience.

As a refugee from apartheid in South Africa, Makhaya is seeking "peace of mind" (20) in rural Botswana, and it is here that he chances upon the experimental farming projects initiated by Gilbert, a British agronomist. The details of Gilbert's work are (as Head insists) all securely founded on practical, scientific knowledge, schemes that reflected not a "fancy or pretty-pretty, but a practical, busy world where people are planning for the future" (WDIW). It was this care taken to provide an accurate account of farming procedures that made *When Rain Clouds Gather* suggested reading for international volunteers intending to work in Botswana.

For his schemes to work, Gilbert needs the cooperation of the local inhabitants, their willingness to engage in communal enterprises:

> you had to start small, and because of this small start, co-operative marketing was the only workable answer, and its principle of sharing the gains and hardships would so much lessen the blows they had to encounter along the way. (115)

Thus, communal farming is perceived by Gilbert to be the most efficient way of developing the natural resources of Golema Mmidi. He surveys the newly fenced pasture lands, the irrigation dykes, the fresh growth of grass on drought-stricken land, and declares to Makhaya, "'This is Utopia, Mack. I've the greatest dreams about it'"(31). Nonetheless, in spite of this caveat, Gilbert's "long discussions on the marvels and wonders of the earth" (80) are primarily to convince his audience of Botswana's potential as a "farmer's heaven" (155), and the opportunity this presents to improve the living conditions of the community. Head, in a letter, recognizes that physical and material considerations are a priority: "I bow to Marxism and stand close to it in the sense that it is important to feed and clothe and house mankind" (Appendix 17).

But utopia for Makhaya means much more than this. Communal farming stresses "human" community; cattle farming near at hand strengthens family bonds and removes the necessity of enforced isolation for people who lived "like trees, in all the lonely wastes of Africa, cut off even from communication with their own selves" (166). Indeed, Makhaya makes "a religion out of everything he found in Golema Mmidi" (122):

> Golema Mmidi seemed a dream he had evoked out of his own consciousness to help him live, to help make life tolerable. But if it was a dream, it was a merciful one, where women walked around all day with their bare feet and there were no notices up saying black men could not listen to the twitter and chatter of birds. (137)

In her first draft of the novel, Head used a first-person narrative voice, but with a male persona. When her publishers complained that the male narrator sounded too much "like a woman," Head resorted to a third-person voice in order, she explains, to "widen out the range and horizon" (Vigne 1991, 50). Nonetheless, as Huma Ibrahim argues, Head's letters attest to the fact that her exile is defined, just as it is for Makhaya, by the desire to find a home. Thus, she continues, "*When Rain Clouds Gather* is characteristic of an early stage in the development of an exile's system of desires and the consciousness out of which they emerge" (1996, 54). It is in this way that this early novel, "Makhaya's personal odyssey" to find "a few simple answers on how to live well and sanely" (*WRCG*, 71), is the author's portrayal of her own needs; Makhaya's "psychic power is analogous to the artistic imagination itself" (Brown 1979, 48). The narrative closes with Makhaya secure in his newfound home, having discovered, as Lloyd Brown suggests, "his own inner peace and sense of fulfilment" (46).

However, because in this novel, Head is describing her own firsthand experience of an experimental farm near Serowe—facts that Head claimed were drawn from reality, the "development of rural projects" (Appendix 29)—there is a danger that this novel might be read as an attempt to imitate reality. It is this assumption that leads Elaine Campbell to her conclusion when she argues that "these agricultural matters are not Eliot's objective correlative: external equivalents of inner emotional reality. Instead, they are subjective correlatives of the human lives with which they are intertwined" (1985, 82). This analysis might accurately describe Gilbert's relationship with his work, and indeed even explains why he seems more real than the other characters. However, the whole context of the narrative, including the other characters, serves for Makhaya, and his creator, as an objective correlative, an expression of acute and personal emotional need.

So Golema Mmidi is never a "real" community. It is "a place [God] had especially set aside to bring all his favourite people together" for "there was not anything he would not do for a village like Golema Mmidi" (187). What is significant about this conception of community is that it has emerged from the same subjectivity that created the hero; Makhaya discovers his peace of mind simply because Head contrives to create a community in which he can do so. The other characters in the narrative, with the possible exception of Gilbert, only exist so that they can substantiate Makhaya's heroic stature and this often leads to what some readers may feel is an uncomfortable and somewhat mawkish adulation of the hero. Dinorego, one of the oldest residents of Golema Mmidi, immediately adopts him as his son; for Mma-Millipede, her friendship with Makhaya means that "a rich treasure had entered her life" (132); the women whom he teaches watch him with "thrilled eyes" (110).

Lloyd Brown argues that Makhaya "grows into a dual perception, a complex synthesis of idealistic and realistic awareness that reflects the highly effective tension . . . between the visionary and the skeptic" (1979, 46). As literature of "process," the discursive style in which the novel is written does depend upon a frame of reference that defers mainly to the consciousness of the protagonist. But most readers would argue that even though Makhaya's consciousness portrays his disturbed reflections on past suffering, it does not necessarily follow from this that the developing consciousness is characterized by conflict or indeed tension, for the village that Makhaya "evokes out of his own consciousness" guarantees fulfillment for the hero. For Head, in this novel, usually tells and rarely shows. It is when she shows the consequences of the interaction of her characters, as she does in her short stories, that complexities and contradictions are allowed free play and tensions remain unresolved. This kind of autonomy for minor characters is never a possibility in those of her narratives that are dominated by the aspirations of a hero figure. So, after the routing of the chief villains, there is little to undermine the code by which Makhaya chooses to live, so completely are the subsidiary characters an extension of his needs. Within Golema Mmidi he discovers a surrogate mother and father, a woman eager to become his wife, and a white man with whom, through mutual understanding, Makhaya can forge a link between the black and white races, to combine "the good in Gilbert with the good in his own society" (135).

Utopian writing has always been vulnerable to the charge that, as fantasy or chimera, it can have neither practical nor literary value. But, as Martin Buber explains, utopian writing is a response to "suffering under a social order that is senseless." If, Buber argues, this suffering should arouse the critical faculties of a writer, his/her recognition of "the perversity of what is perverted" endorses the creation of a Utopian picture of what should be and the "longing for that *rightness* . . . is experienced as revelation or idea, and which of its very nature cannot be realized in the individual, but only in human community" (1949, 7–8). Makhaya's dreams in *When Rain Clouds Gather* are a reaction to the "torture and torment" (128) of human relationships within an oppressive society. As Buber suggests, the antidote to this is the realization of a "human community." Makhaya discovers that he "could run so far in search of peace, but it was contact with other living beings that a man needed most" (166).

It is at this point that Head must romanticize, for these "living beings" must be of a certain type if they are to compensate Makhaya for the bitterness of past experience. This thematic, discursive style of writing that characterizes *When Rain Clouds Gather* is one in which the reader sympathizes with the needs of the protagonist; this means, in Frye's view, that pity is "involved or contained rather than purged." The implications of this are, as Frye argues, that "pity without an object" is "an imaginative animism which finds human qualities everywhere in nature, and includes the beautiful, traditionally the corresponding term to the sublime" (1990, 66). It is within this perspective that the characters in this narrative function; for Makhaya, and for the reader, they belong in a context that can provide significant meaning. Embodying this animism, which Rooney refers to as a "creative mode of knowledge" (1991, 118), are Head's archetypes and motifs that define her good characters and the world they inhabit. They belong in a world that celebrates the consciousness of the child, the exile, the primitive, the asocial hero and heroine. It is a consciousness still attuned to a natural world, and it is with the development of these archetypes that Head can justify her implicit belief in the existence of human qualities and also assert that they are instinctive, natural, and essential. In *A Question of Power,* she shows the vulnerability of these instincts, how easily they can be flawed by socialization. But it is precisely this vulnerability for which the artistic imagination must compensate.

When Rain Clouds Gather marks the first stage in this process. If it is beset by romantic escapism, it is so because its author, persuaded by her own emotional insecurity, still hopes for the possibility of her human community. This really is the value of *When Rain Clouds Gather*. It is an introduction to the development of Head's artistic imagination. It may fail to convince the reader, or prove true for its creator, but this compels the author—literally and literarily in her later books—to delve more deeply into human consciousness. Makhaya is the hero who feels there is a world he can live in; Maru, the hero of Head's next novel, knows there is not.

POLITICS

As Buber claims, utopian writing is a response to "suffering under a social order that is senseless" (1949, 7). The social order that dominated Makhaya's life in South Africa was apartheid, and in order to escape this oppression Makhaya seeks refuge in Botswana. In Golema Mmidi Buber's criterion is also relevant, for it is struggle that makes "true comrades" of the local people: they "would not ever have clarified their ideas had they not lived under the shadow of blind opposition" (*WRCG* 187).

Makhaya's own minor participation in antigovernment guerrilla activity in South Africa had been cut short by premature arrest, and it was in prison that he formulated his ideas on the wider implications of power and oppression. He decides that "Violence breeds hatred and hatred breeds violence. Hatred can only be defeated by love and peace" (134). But Makhaya is also aware of the irrelevance of this as a weapon against oppressors, for "had Hitler been defeated by love and peace? Six million Jews had quietly died before Jewish people earned the right to live on this earth" (134). In her personal letters, Head is also astutely realistic about the political situation within South Africa, and she laments what appears to be the invincibility of the South African government: "If you protest and make one gain against apartheid, the South African government, possibly in terror, has to pass two more repressive laws to liquidate your gain and you end up by increasing the suffering of the people in the country" (Appendix 12). Nevertheless, it seems that an effort of concerted violence will be the only way to break the deadlock of oppression in South Africa, and Makhaya believes "that one day all those millions of unarmed people would pitch themselves bodily on the bullets, if that was the only way of ridding themselves of an oppressor" (134). Many South African writers stress the impossibility of nonparticipation in the liberatory struggle, even if, with Bloke Modisane, they are disillusioned with the self-serving acts of political leaders. As Modisane states, "because I am black I was forced to become a piece of the decisions, a part of black resistance. . . . There was no choice, during riots the police shot their rifles and sten guns at anything which was black" (1963, 140). The only solution for Makhaya is to find a place apart where he can "dream dreams a little ahead of the somewhat vicious clamour of revolution and the horrible stench of evil social systems" (*AWA*, 28). Makhaya has to come to terms with the fact that his escape makes him "a traitor to the African cause" (81), but Head makes it increasingly clear, as her work develops, that it is only her protagonists' experience of impoverished and oppressive social systems that determines their quest to seek an alternative way of life.

Golema Mmidi has also suffered from tribal oppressions and corrupt politicians. For Gilbert, the main problem to be overcome is not the inauspicious climate, but "the African way of life, which seemed to him a deadly, chilling society which kept out anything new and strange" (100). Politically, Joas Tsepe, a self-seeking opportunist, represents the "nightmare side" of Pan-Africanism. He exerts his political power to his own advantage, and willingly conspires to "plunge the African continent into an era of chaos and bloody murder" (47). Chief Matenge, the most powerful man in Golema Mmidi and crony of Joas Tsepe, is interested in politics only in so far as it can preserve his power. As a tribal leader he represents the "diehard traditionalists" (44) with their "clinging, ancestral, tribal belief[s]" (15). To preserve his power he becomes "involved in the political ideologies of Africa and the cauldron of hatred" because "it was the last camp that reflected his traditional views" (45). As Makhaya believes,

all power is corrupt; for even Pan-Africanism—which, he concedes, to many is "an almost sacred dream" (47)—can become
another variant of the aggressor; it can fall "prey to all the hate-
making political ideologies" and "a whole new set of retrogressive ideas and retrogressive pride" (80).

The destruction of the corrupt Chief Matenge, the most powerful adversary to Gilbert's schemes, is portrayed as a concerted
action that highlights the cohesion of the community and liberates it from the unhealthy influence of tribalism and politics.
The new political leader of Golema Mmidi will not be Joas
Tsepse, but Mma-Millipede, "who mixed up spiritual counselling
with practical advice" (187). It is only with the emergence of an
apolitical community that it becomes possible to show that "all
the tensions, jealousies, frustrations, and endless petty bickering which make up the sum total of all human relationships
were in reality unnecessary" (135). In this narrative, Head portrays a community for which the implications of all political systems, both past and present, can be avoided.

THE INNOCENT VISION

Within the narrative, many motifs suggestive of innocence
and childhood portray the analogy that is drawn between the
model village that Paulina's young daughter is building out of
mud and the model village of which Makhaya and Gilbert both
dream. The idea of protection is paramount in this realization.
The model built from mud is a "sanctuary of genius" (107), with
the needs of its inhabitants carefully attended to. Whilst Makhaya and Gilbert plant trees on the child's model, they discuss
the improvements that will turn Golema Mmidi into a paradise:
"Each household will have to have a tap with water running out
of it all the year round. . . . And not only palm trees, but fruit
trees too and flower gardens" (113).

By implementing crop-growing within the village instead of
miles away at the "lands," and by bringing cattle-grazing close
at hand, the opportunity for permanent settlement is also established. Makhaya decides that the benefits of this, the possibility
for "some real family life" (115) will ensure that children will
not, like Isaac, be compelled to "carry burdens beyond [their]
age" (163). Makhaya's commitment to Paulina is precipitated by
the death of Isaac, and is an acknowledgement that marriage
holds within it a prime responsibility towards protection and

nurturing. Paulina is particularly impressed, that in a society where it is commonplace for men to neglect their paternal responsibilities, Makhaya is concerned about the welfare of her children. The emphasis on the male's role as "protector," exemplified by Makhaya's intention to bear all Paulina's burdens, whilst it may leave, as Dorothy Driver recognizes, "standard gendered role divisions otherwise unchanged" (1990, 246), is an indication that care and protection is, above all else, a priority for the new community that Makhaya envisages.

Nevertheless, feminists who feel that female dependency is inimical to the formation of equal female/male roles may wish to query the fact that Paulina's happiness depends so much on her securing Makhaya's love. An example of this kind of criticism is Ibrahim's interpretation of Makhaya's decision to take charge of the disposal of Isaac's body, as "phallocratic," denying Paulina "the last farewell" (1996, 83), rather than as the manifestation of Makhaya's understandable concern to spare Paulina further, unnecessary pain.

The need for parental protection is emphasized by Isaac's death. Seriously ill at his lonely cattle-post, for Isaac "the thought of his mother and her surprise and concern filled the small boy's heart with warm comfort" (151). It is only when such protection is guaranteed that the child can not only survive but also maintain its "innocent vision." The child whom Makhaya encounters after crossing the border into Botswana, and who offers herself to him for sex, is "very unchildlike" and has a "full bold stare" (13). Her relationship to the old woman with whom she lives is not disclosed, but in the way that the child has been exploited, it is clear that the old woman has failed to protect her. As a result of this, the child has been compelled to sacrifice her innocence, to develop instead "her awful, unchildlike stare" (14). The implication of this loss of innocence, using Frye's explanation, is that the child is no longer able to "assume a coherence, a simplicity and a kindliness in the world that adults have lost and wish they could regain" (1975, 57).

It is this simplicity and kindliness as a characteristic of the new community that is reiterated by the analogy drawn with the child's mud village; it is Gilbert who seems to fit most naturally into this world. As Makhaya can see, "Gilbert's views on Africa and world politics [are] extremely naive and childlike" (82). Maria also recognizes this aspect of Gilbert's personality, that she must protect Gilbert from his ignorance that the world is "full of danger" (89). It is however, this naivete that helps to explain the single-minded and uncomplicated determination with which Gilbert tackles his work. He is "intent only on being of useful service to his fellow men" (81). His first objective is to raise the production of food above subsistence level; to do so he needs to forge a "desirable human shape" out of the barren desert landscape (Frye 1975, 57). The growing of crops and the protection of the soil go hand in hand, and it is this idea of nurturing that is paramount in Gilbert's attitude to the land. He coaxes into growth "the long, frail, feathery stalks of the wind-blown eragrostis, a lush sweet grass" (36), the "miracle" that had "lain dormant for years and years in the soil" (37).

With the concentration on "the details of life" (136) the importance of the present is emphasized. It is, as Frye explains, to the capacity to live in the present that "man returns when his conception of reality begins to acquire some human meaning" (1975, 59). The importance of the present, its value over some immeasurable infinite time, is constantly reiterated throughout the narrative. After Isaac's death, Paulina can find no comfort from Mma-Millipede's suggestion that "this earth was not the final abode of man. It was a place of sorrows, a wilderness in which his soul wandered in restless torment" (169). For Paulina, living was "firmly attached to love, child-bearing, child-rearing, hunger, struggle, and the sunrise of tomorrow. Life had to flow all the time, for the living, like water in a stream" (169–70).

Gilbert discovered that "the leaden winter skies" that "looked like great swathes of eternity which were there to stay, forever and forever" represented not eternity, for there was "no eternity: only the ever changing pattern of life" (103). It is in this way that Gilbert has defined the importance of the here and the now, the priorities of the "workaday world" (86). The "hurricane of activity" (184) that defines Gilbert's lifestyle is never compromised or interrupted by speculative doubts as to the value of his work in this "quiet backwater" (103). His approach is straightforward and uncomplicated: "progress was as easy as learning to drive a tractor" (187).

Although Makhaya's discovery of a "haven of security" (142) where present needs, "ordinary things like cups, brooms, pots and houses . . . anchor him firmly to the earth" (165), he is more detached. He is aware of the curious anachronism that this rural village presents to a modern world. Unlike Gilbert, he strategically and consciously turns to "agriculture for his salvation" (81). Makhaya's conscious resolve to exploit the therapeutic qualities presented by Golema Mmidi symbolizes Head's imaginative cre-

ation of it. To use Frye's definition, it is Gilbert's more uncomplicated vision that defines for Makhaya the nature of this
community and its relationship to the real world. For Gilbert,
his work is "the realization of a dream," a dream "descended
from the child's lost vision of a world where the environment is
the home" (Frye 1975, 57). Gilbert is shown to have experienced
a childhood in the charge of a "stupid, neurotic mother" (102),
wholly insensitive to the needs of a child. Just as Isaac believes
implicitly that the presence of an absent mother can save and
protect him, Gilbert's contribution towards the establishment of
the more human community of Golema Mmidi can be read as an
unconscious compensation for the deprivation of his own childhood, his desire to make possible a society in which the innocent
vision of the child is allowed to flourish.

For the inspirators of romanticism, it was always childhood
that was perceived to be closest to divinity. But whereas in
Wordsworth, as for Freud, the child must be humanized, this is
a process that the world of experience rarely guarantees Head's
characters, likely as they are to become victims of "the living
death" (136) into which they are born. It is for this reason that
the term "society" is rarely positive. Makhaya refuses "a stake"
in any man's society, for "no human society was sane and normal" (164). Whereas Hartman comments that for Wordsworth "a
man's sense of the light that was can be his greatest obstacle"
(1975, 131), the conception of Golema Mmidi would not have
been possible without it. In Head's writing, it is the ability of her
heroines and heroes to maintain a close guard on this "light that
was" that defines them. As Mma-Millipede explains to Makhaya, "people who err against human life . . . do so only because
they are more blind than others to the mystery of life" (131).

EXILE

Makhaya is Head's first exiled character. As well as searching
for political freedom, Makhaya is also anxious to free himself
from the constrictive tribal ties that, ironically, insinuate their
claim in the very name he bears. As Makhaya explains, his name
means "home-boy," "for one who stays home," and yet he had
"not known a day's peace and contentment in [his] life" (9). The
kind of society that Makhaya needs in order "to develop freely"
is one in which "some inner voice" becomes the guide, instead of
the necessity of conforming to some "precious prejudice" or "tra-

dition" (80). What Makhaya needs is a place like A. C. Guthkelch's description of More's Utopia, a "far-off new world" where "everything was possible" (1914, xxii).

Because of the kind of opportunity that their new society presents to Head's exiled characters, she describes a form of exile experience that differs entirely from the body of autobiographical writing that emerged from South Africa as a result of the mass exodus of writers in the fifties and sixties. The homeland that is usually a poignantly invoked presence in most South African exile writing is absent in Head's portrayal of Makhaya's experience; never is his integration into the life of Golema Mmidi jeopardized by nostalgia for a lost homeland or family. The sense of rootlessness is an important condition for Head's protagonists if they are to imagine new communities; but (as James Olney shows) for many other exile writers this rootlessness is portrayed as a negative psychological burden for their protagonists, compelled as they are "to wander, forever and aimlessly" as aliens (1973, 250).

For Head, exile is "not a prison house: it is in exile that a writer is most at home" (Parthasarathy 1989, 2). It is only within the new freedom offered by the exile experience that past traumas can be rejected and a new society fashioned in which cultural and racial diversity holds the key to harmony and cohesion. It portrays, as Marquard recognizes, a "composite extranational humanity" (1979, 306). So Golema Mmidi is "a unique place" (22) whose inhabitants are "a wayward lot of misfits" (23), exiled characters, who, as Martin Tucker argues, can never be "at home till they travel beyond their home communities" (1991, xv). The backgrounds of these exiles are all different. Makhaya's is South Africa and prison. Paulina, from the north of the country, has endured the suicide of her husband and the loss of her home. Gilbert is escaping from "upper middle class" England, where you "could not tell friend from foe behind the bright brittle smiles" (102).

Just as Makhaya believes in the integrity of his inner voice, it is the essentialism of her main characters that has provoked, and is also protected by the experience of exile, and which determines their individuality. This individuality assumes a greater dependence on natural qualities; everything Makhaya needed

seemed to be needed by no one else in his own environment, among his own people or clan. . . . [T]here was nothing in his own environment to account for all the secret development that had taken place in him. (124–25)

Mma-Millipede is also different, "one of those rare individuals with a distinct personality at birth" (68), and it is Paulina's undaunted spirit that distinguishes her from the rest of the women, "even though her circumstances and upbringing were no different from theirs" (94). In Golema Mmidi it is these personalities who become the leaders of the new projects that are designed to improve the living conditions of the people and to create firmer foundations for the realization of home. In Caroline Rooney's analysis, for such characters their land of exile represents motherland, they have a "non-appropriative" relation to the land, one that recognizes that their adopted country is "subject to the land or nature, an acknowledgement of a certain vital dependency" (1991, 100).

THE PRIMITIVE

The manifestations of the apartheid regulations in South Africa have convinced Makhaya that the very meaning of civilization is suspect: "It was hard to be charitable towards a civilisation like this. It was hard to sit back and contemplate the real wonder of the white man's world which was this civilisation" (133). Head's solution to this conception of civilization is her imagining of "the man with no shoes," a figurative symbol that occurs throughout all her writing. He represents "uncivilized" or "primitive" man. He must not, however, be confused with the old woman and child, who, like the "lurid" people who dwell in the slums in *The Cardinals*, have been disfigured by the world they have experienced. The "man with no shoes" belongs to the cycle of nature that, harsh though it sometimes can be, promises cyclical renewal and return. Such primitives are, in Head's conception, "a complement to the earth"; sometimes it becomes impossible to tell "where man ends and nature begins" (*TTP*, 48).

In *Maru*, Margaret's biological mother, a Masarwa, is seen by the artist who sketches her as a "goddess." The primitive Masarwa tribe is described as possessing the "true vitality" of Botswana (*M*, 109). In *When Rain Clouds Gather,* it is primitive people who likewise are spiritually blessed, for "the God with no shoes continued to live where he always had—in the small brown birds of the bush, in the dusty footpaths, and in the expressions of thin old men in tattered coats" (185). As Christopher Heywood explains, Head is here favoring the "Primitive as a worthier manifestation of the human spirit" (1991, 35). Like Olive Schreiner, Head is reacting against the scientific positivism of the latter half of the nineteenth century and the doubt it cast on the existence of any phenomenon not directly perceived by the senses. It was this scientific "progress," as Heywood explains, this faith in the superiority of scientific accomplishments that implied the superiority of the "civilized" races. Paul Rich discusses how scientific progress also supported the Calvinist creed of the Boer trekkers and the British evangelical missionaries in their assertion of "technological control over nature." Rich argues that to this was added an "imperialistic spirit of domination and manipulation of alien and non-Western cultures" (1984b, 370). From this perspective of appropriation, development is "maldevelopment in that the land is destructively treated as merely an exploitable resource, while other forms of development and knowledge, the local and ecological, are not recognised" (Rooney 1991, 100).

In *Maru*, Head indicates the way in which psuedo-scientific data justifies discriminatory practices against the Masarwa: "Ask the scientists. Haven't they yet written a treatise on how Bushmen are an oddity of the human race, who are half the head of a man and half the body of a donkey?" (11). For Head, the primitive mind is still proof against the alienating experience of modern technology. Like "maniacs, children and women," he is still in touch with "the world of dream and myth." It is this world that is, as Heywood argues, "seen by writers in the tradition of symbolic interpretation as the well-spring of regeneration in society and in the life of the individual" (1991, 26).

It is this interpretation that most adequately explains the relationship that Head's characters have with the land. The hard work that is celebrated is that which emphasizes belonging rather than dispossession. It reflects what Head describes as "the passion we feel for this we love" (*TTP,* 46). It is in this light that the work of women as cultivators of the soil is inseparable from the organic productive cycle of the natural world. For Sebina in *A Bewitched Crossroad,* this relationship represents continuity and mutuality:

> Her form swayed to and fro with the rhythm of her work, her face closed and withdrawn in concentration. The warm slanting rays of

the late afternoon sunlight seemed to transfix that timeless moment
in his memory like every other moment of happiness for him. (100)

A feminist may well express misgivings at such a romanticized portrayal, which overlooks the real hardships of women's
work and, in so doing, fails to offer a feminist challenge to oppressive female roles. It becomes, as Rita Felski explains, an
avowal of "a mystical secret knowledge residing in the inner
worlds of women, a position which brings with it all the atten-
dant dangers of quietism" (1989, 76). For socialist feminists the
danger of quietism is its refusal to engage in the public sphere
and to see a narrative model of history as one of progress. But
this indeed is exactly what Head is doing, especially in *When
Rain Clouds Gather*, when, in order to challenge the exigencies
of the world of experience, she loses interest in the feminist
movement that "point[s] outward and forward into social activity and political emancipation" but chooses one that looks "back-
ward and inward, into myth, spirituality and the transformation
of subjective consciousness" (Felski 1989, 128).

So whereas white South African writers may emphasize the
malevolence of the natural world—for example, the encroaching
bush that threatens the sanity of Mary Turner in Doris Lessing's
The Grass is Singing and the earth that refuses to take possession of the corpse in Nadine Gordimer's *The Conservationist*—
the natural world in Head's portrayal not only produces crops
and rich grazing, but also becomes an extension of the needs and
aspirations of its inhabitants.

An example of this is the description of the journey that Paulina and Makhaya make to the cattle-post to find out what has
happened to Isaac. The worst is feared, especially by Makhaya,
and the desolation and destruction is vividly evoked: the landscape cluttered with gorged satiated vultures and the corpses of
dead and dying cattle. Makhaya registers the full horror of the
scene, but for Paulina, overcome by her happiness at Makhaya's
love, the morning "seemed like an unreal and lovely spring
morning when life was just beginning anew again instead of
dying" (160).

The numinous and pantheistic landscape is one that most
often "bewitches," and this reinstates the relevance of "cosmic
oneness" that is identified an essential feature of primal religion:

all things share the same nature and the same interaction one upon
another—rocks and forest trees, beasts and serpents, the power of

the wind . . . the living, the dead . . . for all are one, all are here, all
are now. (Keen 1969, 63)

Makhaya, deeply suspicious of what he feels has been the institutionalized Christianity of "the mincing, squeamish little missionaries" (130), prefers to look for other evidence of the holy,
and he finds it constantly in a landscape that reaffirms the
"kindliness" of the innocent vision. He feels that the stars provide "all the conviction . . . that some quiet and good creator controlled and owned the earth" (169). For Head, the characters still
in possession of what D. H. Lawrence calls "the sixth sense," the
"natural religious sense" (Keen 1969, 200), are her heroes and
heroines, distinguished by their ability to transcend socialization. Thus, it is to an affirmation of natural qualities that Head
consistently returns, and in her narratives it is the "primitive,"
the child, the exile, the women defined by their "quietism" who
are attuned to the spirit of the natural world. Makhaya prefers
to believe in a divinity alive in the natural world rather than the
dogma of institutionalized religion.

Nonetheless, there is an aspect of orthodox Christianity that
has some bearing upon Makhaya's elected philosophy. As
Cherry Wilhelm suggests, Makhaya is "the most overtly Christian of Bessie Head's protagonists" (1983, 6). For Makhaya,
Mma-Millipede is the embodiment of this Christianity. She is,
however, excessively saintly, and Makhaya's initial reaction to
such saintliness may anticipate the reader's response: "He was
a little repelled at first by the generosity of the strange old
woman. It was too extreme" (71). However, because Mma-Millipede is, unlike the missionaries, portrayed as someone whose
"words match [her] deeds" (131), what she provides is an account
of Christianity that puts its faith in a God who is a loving protector over all. This means to Mma-Millipede that she "cannot put
anyone away from [her] as not being [her] brother" (131). Some
readers may regard these views as belonging only to the realm
of sermon and tract, to a world uninterrupted by the real complexities of human relationships. Head is using Mma-Millipede's
Christian philosophy to define an ideal world, a society that emphasizes human community. She takes pains to demonstrate
that the strange and rather melodramatic death of the corrupt
Chief Matenge can be accounted for by an act of communal solidarity and that the community shares an instinctive understanding that Matenge's death represents the demise of a
corrupt social order. In order however, to establish that it is the

"cohesion and singleness of purpose" shown by the local people (182) that rids them of their corrupt chief, she describes the result of this cohesion without explaining why it occurred in the first instance. In this way, what it effects is also taken to be the cause:

> People were being drawn closer and closer to each other as brothers, and once you looked on the other man as your brother, you could not bear that he should want for anything or live in darkness. (180)

Makhaya's speculative internal monologue on Mma-Millipede's beliefs is the discursive element of the novel, that part which examines the developing consciousness of the main protagonist. The problem with Makhaya is that he seems to be finding comfort in an act of faith that bears no relationship to the evidence of his own past experience. He is only able to believe in Christianity because it is defined in "a dream" that is "merciful" (137). Head wrote in a letter: "I have my development. It was first the dithering Makhaya. The dubious Maru . . . and from there a more or less shaking but certain platform" (Appendix 5). This seems apt: while Head's other heroes and heroines show that they have long ceased to believe in the reality of an actual utopia informed by a Christian philosophy, Makhaya still hovers on the brink. And to embody Makhaya's beliefs, Head creates an embryonic, new society, one in which natural instincts become synonymous with Christian humanism in a world ahead of profane social systems.

In the expectation that this society will flourish it portrays not "the mature mind's sophisticated and cautious adaptations of the child's or the dreamer's desires" but "the original and innocent form of those desires, with all their reckless disregard of the lessons of experience" (Frye 1975, 58). This is clearly one explanation of escapist literature. But what seems most problematic about this novel is that while it portrays a utopian and pastoral retreat in the making, and one which is insulated from the political and social trauma of a harsher world, its main actor bears the multilayered consciousness of this external world. The narrative contains within it the seeds of its own uncertainty, the proof of its own lack of faith.

Head partially resolves the problem for Makhaya by emphasizing the importance of present concerns, that the "Good God" would "entangle this stupid young man with marriage and babies and children" (187). But what cannot be guaranteed is a safeguard against the encroachment of a world of experience that would literally and systematically invalidate the consciousness of the exile, the primitive, or the child.

Nevertheless, as Frye argues, it is the literary vision of what should be that conveys the "real driving power of civilization and prophecy" (1975, 58). To argue such a point, its contender must believe in a body of innate values and conditions that are integral and essential to human community but which can be destroyed in the social process. Head believed this, and in the writing of *When Rain Clouds Gather,* in order to recreate the origin of the utopian dream, she operates, to quote Frye, "a reckless disregard of the lessons of experience" (1975, 58) in order to create a society in which presocial, human instincts are the driving force of this small community. It is in *When Rain Clouds Gather* where the archetypes that endure throughout the whole of Head's writing, stereotypes that invoke the mutuality of essential human instincts with the natural world, are portrayed as the qualities needed to produce an ideal society. It is Head's first evocation of Botswana, the sanctuary that Makhaya discovers after he has fled from South Africa. The narrative ends with optimism. The vision it evokes may have little bearing on reality, but the needs of its protagonist make its claims more compelling. The author looks inward when she discovers that the potential for the innocent vision resides only within; but the validation of this inner vision becomes the artistic endeavor of her next two novels.

4

Maru

MARU, THE EPONYMOUS HERO OF THE NOVEL *MARU*, IS THE PARA-mount-chief-elect in Dilepe. However, superstitions circulating within Dilepe suggest that Maru's position of political authority is not wholly attributed to his royal birth:

> A terror slowly built up around the name of Maru. . . . In their con-versations at night they discussed the impossible, that he was the reincarnation of Tladi, a monstrous ancestral African witch-doctor who had been a performer of horrific magic. (*M*, 36)

Faced with the suspicion that their paramount-chief-elect has the power to bewitch his victims, the inhabitants of Dilepe find numerous examples in their folklore of individuals invested with the power to cast fantastic charms over lesser mortals. For the modern reader, not so inclined to accept the effectiveness of su-pernatural intervention, Maru's aura of mystical authority will be less admissible.

Maru is too unreal. Inspired by "the voices of the gods in his heart" (8), he feels alienated from the ordinary people more at-tuned to "petty human hatreds and petty human social codes and values" (67). With the help of his three spies, Maru con-spires to effect his marriage with Margaret, the victimized and racially maligned Masarwa schoolteacher. In their new home, thousands of miles away from Dilepe, Maru, now alone with "the sun of his love" (5), can "communicate freely with all the magic and beauty inside him" (7). Margaret, most of the time, feels "quite drunk . . . with happiness" (8). Moreover, her people, the downtrodden Masarwa, upon hearing of Margaret's marriage to the most important man in Dilepe, breathe in deeply "the wind of freedom" (126). Thus, *Maru* can be interpreted as a fairy tale, a romantic love story, or even the story of a political liberation—the empowerment of the downtrodden Masarwa of Botswana.

To reconcile these seemingly disparate elements becomes a

problem for the reader. The suspension of disbelief, which the reader willingly engages when faced with a conventional fairy tale, is not a literary response appropriate to the evaluation of the portrayal of political protest. As one critic writing on *Maru* observes, "there is the sense of an enduring problem resolved through fantasy only" (Peek 1985, 129). So Craig Mackenzie's contention that the "link between personal drama and social resonance is not satisfactorily demonstrated" (1989a, 26) represents what becomes the problem for most readers, that the fairy-tale happy ending is unconvincing as a solution to social conflict. For while the fairy story celebrates the asocial ideal world, the political fable demands an analysis of cause and effect that is fixed solidly within the bounds of reality.

Nevertheless, Head believed that with *Maru* she had shown the "hideousness of racial prejudice" and had at the same time created something "so beautiful and so magical" (*AWA,* 68). The moral imperative of a fairy tale depends on the recognition that "good" as an absolute force will triumph over evil. The good in *Maru* rests upon the hero's ability to interrupt the vicious cycle of prejudice that defines the relationship between tribe and race. Daniel Gover defines "the force for good" as "the fairy tale aspect of love" that "as a mysterious power" can "rescue victims of evil" (1990, 116). Clearly, Maru, by falling in love with Margaret and rescuing her does, if nothing else, disturb the local inhabitants' complacent belief in the naturalness of their prejudice.

Head is not concerned merely to portray the oppression of the black races by their colonizers, In a letter, she laments the racism she witnesses in Botswana: "I saw black people here as being no different from the Boer. They are blind in their racialism and they are no different from the white man" (Appendix 20) So, in *Maru* she explores this profound maladjustment in human relationships, a pathological neurosis that has been socially determined, and is characteristic of all societies:

> How universal was the language of oppression! . . . The stronger man caught hold of the weaker man and made a circus animal out of him, reducing him to the state of misery and subjection and non-humanity. The combinations were the same, first conquest, then abhorrence at the looks of the conquered and, from then onwards, all forms of horror and evil practices. (109)

The fairy-tale element, which Gover identifies as "mysterious power," can be seen to mean an asocial alternative to the socially endorsed parameters of power and opportunism that define other relationships within the novel. For Maru's "dreams and visions" are a reminder of "an atmosphere where not only he but all humanity could evolve" (110). The success of the author's endeavor lies with her discovery of an essence within the human psyche that is not only asocial but also presocial. Paradoxically, within the social context within which Head writes, her antidote must also be antisocial if it is to resist what appears to be the inevitability of social contingency. Thus the fairytale quality of *Maru* is Head's imaginative response to a specific social reality— what Jung would define as the artist's need to restore "the psychic equilibrium of the epoch" (1934, 197).

THE COMPENSATIONS OF ROMANCE

Within the romance genre, writers can resist the socially determined limits of reality. Thus the critic Paul Rich contends that romance is an understandable response to an impoverished social situation, arguing that it is "the strong element of the irrational in psychologies of racist thought" that accounts for the appearance of the romance mode in South Africa. While literary realism "looks outward towards a stable set of social norms," romances are "more inward-looking" and "tend to imply wish-fulfilment and childhood fantasies" (1984a, 122).

There is an explicit element of fantasy in *Maru*. The way in which the hero rids Dilepe of three of its most prominent villains, Seth, Morafi, and Pete, may be psychologically plausible, but there is nevertheless a strong suspicion that Maru, like all superheroes, is possessed of secret powers. Northrop Frye identifies the significance of such heroes as a literary convention:

> The essential difference between novel and romance lies in the conception of characterization. The romancer does not attempt to create "real people," so much as stylized figures which expand into psychological archetypes. (1990, 304)

This explains the way heroes are often thinly disguised caricatures of masculine power and authority, qualities that determine their role within a literary genre. The superiority of the hero over other male characters guarantees his attraction for the heroine, and the heroine who has the good fortune to win the love of the hero is especially fulfilled.

However, for feminists, the insistence of the romance upon the power of the hero, the privileging of masculine characteristics, the way in which archetypal resonance suggests natural or eternal qualities, are all means by which sexist ideology maintains the power of the male over the female. Feminists argue that it is in this way that woman is manmade, that her gender is a socially constructed concept that sanctions her subordinate role within a patriarchal society. Because the romance by its very nature perpetuates this false myth, feminists feel that it can only hinder the feminist cause that seeks to correct the sexism inherent in all spheres of private and public life, and by extension the false premise upon which all human relationships are built.

Thus, the absolute power that Maru wields over Margaret may well cause the reader to question the novel's commitment to human freedom. As M. J. Daymond points out, "Margaret's marriage to Maru is virtually an abduction and so denies her the very freedom of choice which the creation of new worlds seeks to provide" (1988, 248). There is much in *Maru* that bears out Simone de Beauvoir's contention in *The Second Sex* that romantic love keeps women weak, passive, and humanly crippled. Margaret's happiness seems to depend entirely upon Maru's avowals of love:

> Most often she felt quite drunk and mad with happiness and it was not unusual for her to walk around for the whole day with an ecstatic smile on her face, because the days of malice and unhappiness were few and far over-balanced by the days of torrential expressions of love. (8)

This is why some feminists are antagonistic to the romance genre, because (as Paul Rich indicates) in demanding "the subordination of the female to the male idea of the romantic, the bland and passive submission to masculine concepts of the desirable and beautiful," the romantic ideal can "have no place for the autonomy of the feminine mind" (1984a, 124).

Head, too, was conscious that her creation of grand men could be read as evidence of her nonparticipation in the "big feminist movement in the world today" (Adler et al. 1989, 16). But there can be no doubt that her heroes, in spite of their dominant roles, or indeed even because of their roles as leaders, are intended to lead the way towards the creation of relationships based on love and respect rather than self-gratification. In this way, Head's heroes have an important part to play in her self-acknowledged didacticism. They counteract the evil that exists in society because, Head writes, "There were really only two kinds of men in the society. The one kind created such misery and chaos that he could broadly be damned as evil. . . . [T]hat kind of man was in the majority" (*CT,* 91). This condemnation is pervasive in *Maru*: "Three quarters of the people on this continent are like Morafi, Seth and Pete—greedy, grasping, back-stabbing, a betrayal of all the good in mankind" (68). Hence, the need for heroes to redress the balance. So in spite of the fact that the happiness of the heroine seems to depend heavily on romantic fulfillment, Head's heroes are not the romanticized embodiments of traditional sexism they may at first seem. Instead, as liberated men they can be seen as questioning sexist ideology. Indeed, Maru's manipulative behavior is justified by the reasons that compel it:

> he intended coming out on top, as the winner. It was different if his motivation was entirely selfish, self-centred, but the motivation came from the gods who spoke to him in his heart. They had said: Take that road. Then they had said: Take that companion. He believed his heart and the things in it. They were his only criteria for goodness. (73)

Some feminists recognize the positive element in such portrayals. In Alison Light's view, "Romance imagines peace, security and ease, precisely because there is dissension, insecurity and difficulty" and that romances are "'symptomatic' rather than simply reflective." They function "as a protest against, as well as a restatement of, oppression" (1990, 143). So if the male assumes a position of authority—Johnny over Mouse, Makhaya over Paulina—it is simply to ensure that the female is guaranteed protection and immunity from the overwhelming menace of society. Also, even though happiness for these women can only be achieved through a successful marriage, the same also holds true for the men. Maru's vision of a new world always includes a footpath of yellow daisies, for these flowers symbolize "the face of his wife and the sun of his love" (5). For Head, love becomes a political endeavor, the most fundamental means by which wrongs can be righted. Head shares the views of Cixous, one of the most radical feminists, who writes that "everything we will be calls us to the unflagging, intoxicating, unappeasable search for love. In one another we will never be lacking" (1976, 893).

THE NATURAL

It is important to understand exactly what Cixous means by love, to see how it connects with Gover's idea of the "mysterious power" that can rescue the heroine, to see how in its elemental and eternal quality it belongs to Frye's archetypes and by inference to Head's heroes. It is only by examining the implications of love that it is possible to understand how the love that Maru professes for Margaret is perhaps the only way pathological relationships will be avoided, even allowing for the explicit domination that Maru exercises over Margaret. Mackenzie's view, that the relationship between Margaret and Maru portrays "the communication between souls on a psychic level" (1989a, 28), is one interpretation that recognizes the need to ignore normal or conventional evaluations of the relationship that develops between the hero and heroine. For Maru's transpersonal role, his function as an archetypal hero, depends on the presence of a heroine to complement him. In his transpersonal role, Maru exists as a psychological phenomenon stripped of all personality factors that will detract from his single function.

For what Head does in her creation of Maru, is to portray an alternative development of the human psyche irrespective of social, historical, or cultural conditioning. In Mackenzie's view, Head shows "the inexorable forces operating beneath the events of the workaday world" (1989a, 28). Head suggests the presence of innate human instincts in the human psyche. But, unlike Freud, Head sees these qualities as harmed rather than improved by socialization. Indeed, it is interesting that the only concession that Maru will make to his society is that he stands for every thing that it is not. From Head's perspective, to fulfill her political endeavor it is vital that the essential qualities for which Maru stands are seen to be a valid expression of the potential humanity in each human being; she explores what Mackenzie refers to as "the realm of the soul" (1989a, 27). Head argues that "man's intuitive sense is at one" (Appendix 17). It is for this reason that Head must resist the theories of feminists, who in order to negate the patriarchal claim that gender is essential or God-given privilege the theory that meaning is a social construct.

The portrayal of Maru as a romantic hero is certainly not consistent with the claims that Catherine Belsey makes in an article called "Metaphysics of Romance":

love, desire, the body are all meanings. As meanings, they are the condition of our experience; and at the same time, as meanings, they are culturally produced and historically limited. It follows that they are not inevitable, necessary or eternal. (1992, 191)

The view that meaning is a social construct is pivotal to the feminist theory that gender is also not given but is socially, historically, and culturally defined. Thus, there need be nothing intrinsically natural about heterosexual bonding, and "essential" female qualities are a patriarchal invention to safeguard the status quo. So anxious are the Anglo-American feminists to defend their belief in nurture rather than nature as the determiner of meaning that they condemn the French feminists" celebration of specific and essential female qualities embodied in *jouissance* or *l'écriture feminine*. It is when an examination is made of what exactly the French feminists mean by "essentialism" that its relevance for Head can be appreciated.

The French feminists are no less anxious than Anglo-American theorists to insist that to perceive gender roles as natural rather than constructed does cause the sexism inherent within society. In *The Newly Born Woman*, Cixous writes, "One can no more speak of 'woman' than of 'man' without being trapped within an ideological theater" (1986, 83). As Toril Moi explains, Cixous argues that "terms like 'masculine' and 'feminine' themselves imprison us within a binary logic, within the 'classical vision of sexual opposition between men and women'" (1990, 231). Thus, it is important to recognize that the essentialism of which the French feminists speak is presymbolic, before language can play its part in creating meaning—it is neither masculine nor feminine. As French feminists argue, if this essentialism is interpreted as feminine, it is so simply by the resistance it presents to a world defined by a hierarchy where the feminine is always seen as the negative, powerless instance in the face of the positive, powerful masculine. It is only this presocial realm that can ultimately subvert the power of the social. As Sandra Gilbert writes, Cixous's "notion of *écriture feminine* is thus a fundamentally political strategy, designed to redress the wrongs of culture through a revalidation of the rights of nature" (1986, xv). Thus, a refusal to accept the socially determined limits of Belsey's claims is fundamental to Cixous's design to see beyond what can only be socially prescribed, to discover some quality that is not only natural but is also eternal, the "mysterious power" of which Gover speaks. This is what Head strives to achieve. The challenge to the cultural context in which she lives must come from within. For Head then, resistance to the social is, as it is for the French feminists, a dependence on the presocial, the presymbolic realm, nature before nurture.

Head's privileging of the natural as an affirmative quality within her protagonists begins in *The Cardinals*, where Johnny and Mouse, albeit in different ways, resist the socialization process that impairs the personal development of other, minor characters. An extreme example of this impoverishment is apparent in Head's portrayal of the villain Pete in *Maru*. He is bereft of any natural, good inclinations:

> There might have been a time in his life when he had smiled naturally—say, when he was two years old. But he had a degree and a diploma and with it went an electric light smile. He switched it on and off. (38–39)

In *When Rain Clouds Gather,* the peace of mind that Makhaya discovers in Golema Mmidi becomes fused with the natural world around him. This natural world stands in stark contrast to the world of profane and alienating social intercourse. In *Maru*, this idea is developed even further. The "magical" qualities owned by Maru account for the way that he remains in touch with his innermost and essential instincts:

> There had never been a time in his life when he had not thought a thought and felt it immediately bound to the deep centre of the earth, then bound back to his heart again—with a reply. (7)

It is in this way that he guards against the corruption of the "glitter and impact" of his "earthly position" (68).

THE HERO MYTH

An asocial quality is a major characteristic of Northrop Frye's archetypal hero. He writes that in contrast to novels that deal with characters who wear "personae or social masks," the romance deals with "individuality, with characters *in vacuo* idealized by revery" and that "something nihilistic and untameable is likely to keep breaking out of [the] pages" (1990, 305). Frye argues that archetypes as a literary convention operate to unify and integrate literary experiences, but they are purely literary devices. Nevertheless, it was from Jung that Frye borrowed the term "archetype," and for Jung an archetype, or primordial image, was a structuring element within the human psyche, a manifestation of the functioning of the collective unconscious. Jung believed that the unconscious possessed a compensatory potential within the psyche, the appearance of an archetypal image representing that which is lacking in the cultural dominants in currency. Erich Neumann developed Jung's work on the role of archetypes within myth, and it is his observations on the form and function of these images that will be used here to demonstrate how closely Maru resembles the archetypal hero.

One of the most striking features of the hero is how he stands in relation to the patriarchal law of the father, and how this attitude is different from that shared by his peers. The normal procedures by which paternal laws are passed from father to son are interrupted by the hero figure, who, like all mythical heroes, will also possess a transpersonal father, a "god." There is a conflict, Neumann argues, because "the 'inner voice,' the command of the transpersonal father, or father archetype, who wants the world to change, collides with the personal father who speaks for the old law" (1973, 174).

Maru recognizes that "life had presented him with too many destinies but he knew that he would accept them all and fulfil them" (5). In order to do so, he must abdicate from the position of chief that he is due to inherit from his father. He declares his intentions to Dikeledi: "'I was not born to rule this mess. If I have a place it is to pull down the old structures and create the new'" (68). For the "inner voices" invoke instead "the gods who spoke of tomorrow," gods who were "opening doors on all sides, for every living thing on earth, that there would be a day when everyone would be free and no one the slave of another" (68–69).

That there is no limit to the trickery or deception that Maru will employ in order to achieve his purpose is clearly indicated:

> It was the kind of tangle and confusion of events Maru revelled in. Half truths, outright lies, impossible rumours and sudden, explosive events were his stock in trade. He used them as a cover up for achieving his goals. People would thwart him otherwise and he never liked to be side-tracked. He never cared about the means towards the end and who got hurt. (86)

Nowhere is this made clearer than in Maru's manipulative and imperious treatment of Margaret. There is no declaration of love or any of the conventional trappings of courtship. Even his response to news of her illness is coldly calculated: "let her suffer a bit," he says to Ranko, "it will teach her to appreciate other things" (120). Maru simply conspires to prevent any relationship developing between Moleka and Margaret and, with Moleka committed to Dikeledi, takes Margaret far away from Dilepe. The author makes no concession to the normal exposition of romantic involvement. It is the end that is important, not the means taken to ensure it. It is sufficient for Maru that the unconscious link between him and Margaret, made manifest in her paintings, emphasizes that they share the same values, so he is assured she "would love [him] in the end" (124).

Maru even has the help of supernatural agents to assist him with his trickery. Ranko his chief spy, is Maru's "second sight," and to all intents and purposes can make himself invisible to his victims. Moseka and Semana, Maru's lesser spies, can bewitch Maru's enemies. These three characters fulfil the same function as Perseus's winged sandals or the helmet of invisibility in ancient mythology, providing the hero with superior powers. Or, from a legend closer to home, Ranko possesses the same magical power as Chaka's Ndlebe, his ability to catch the faintest whisper from miles around. It seems that Maru is assured success, but only because, as Neumann contends, "the hero myth is never concerned with the private history of an individual, but always with some prototypal and transpersonal event of collective significance" (1973, 197). Indeed, this is how Maru justifies his ruthless behavior:

> In the end, nothing was personal to him. In the end, the subjection of his whole life to his inner gods was an intellectual process. Very little feeling was involved. His methods were cold, calculating and ruthless. (73)

Maru uses his power to oppose rather than deploy the privileges to which he is heir. Within this narrative Head juxtaposes the characteristics of Maru with Moleka to explicate more specifically the nature of the power she is describing. Moleka is, after Maru, the second most important man in Dilepe. He and Maru are inseparable, and it is with Moleka that Maru shares "all the secrets of his heart, because Moleka was a king with his own kingdom" (37). The close kinship of these two has its paradigm in mythology—the twin brothers, the one immortal, the other mortal, "both begotten in the same night by different fathers" (Neumann 1973, 181).

The significance of this within the novel is that Moleka, the "mortal" twin, will inherit Maru's "earthly position" (68), leaving Maru with the "freedom to dream the true dreams, untainted by the clamour of the world" (70). Moleka becomes the preserver of the paternalistic society. His suitability for this role rests upon his eminently masculine qualities. It is Moleka who fulfils the normal male role, the one who reaps the benefit of his masculine privileges in a sexist society. The moon/sun imagery that Head uses to draw a contrast between the personalities of Maru and Moleka defines Moleka as the more arrogant and dominant character. Moleka is "a sun around which spun a billion satellites. All the sun had to do was radiate force, energy, light" (58). Maru, on the other hand, prefers "to be the moon," with "an eternal and gentle interplay of shadows and light and peace" (58). His display of power is functional: "Arrogance was a show with him, to frighten people. He was very humble" (110). Maru concedes that Moleka is "greater than [he] in power" (58), but he recognizes the implications of this power, the extent of its strengths and weaknesses: "Did the sun have compassion and good sense? It had only the ego of the brightest light in the heavens" (58).

The difference in their personalities is reflected in the way they separately conduct their relationships with women. Moleka is "arrogant and violent," his "permanently boiling bloodstream" is irresistible to women, but at the end of each affair, Moleka is "the only one to emerge, on each occasion, unhurt, smiling" (35). Head's portrayal of Moleka's preoccupation with the physical aspect of his relationships emphasizes the more spiritual idealism of Maru. There is quest behind all Maru's affairs, a search for "mystery and hidden dreams" (35). With the failure of his hopes, "a deep sorrow would fill his eyes" (35) and Maru would succumb to some unknown illness. Of the two characters it is Moleka who embodies the masculine qualities, the "instinctual and destructive" characteristics of Neumann's mortal hero. It is Moleka who walks "blindly through life" (37), who continues to exact his privileges within a patriarchal society: "In reality, he had lived many kinds of married lives. They consisted of giving orders: Do this! Don't do that!" (77).

In contrast, Maru struggles in all his relationships to prove "that goodness between friend and friend was mutual, and goodness between lover and lover also" (69). With Margaret he knows that he has found someone who is "more than his equal" (64). Unlike the women with whom Maru has had affairs, Margaret does possess "an inner kingdom." Moreover, although Margaret's surrogate mother had believed totally in the doctrine "environment everything; heredity nothing" (15), and that it was only through nurturing that Margaret could rise above her lowly Masarwa status, the author emphasizes that Margaret's inner kingdom has "nothing to do with the little bit of education she had acquired from a missionary" (64). Here again Head is stressing the importance of some essential presocial quality. It is Margaret's "great vigour and vitality"—which has survived in the face of all the humiliation that she has encountered—that empowers her to look down on Maru "indifferently from a great height" (64). The relationship that Maru wishes to establish with Margaret is to be founded on equality and compatibility.

Within the mythical, transpersonal level of the novel, Margaret is the heroine, the captive, rescued by the hero. And there are many elements to support this. There is an interesting parallel between Neumann's description of the mother of the hero/heroine figure and Head's description of Margaret's natural mother. The elder Margaret Cadmore had made a drawing of the dead Masarwa woman who had given birth immediately before her death. On completion of the sketch she had added the words, "She looks like a Goddess" (15). The artist noted the expression of the dead woman, "It was a mixture of peace and astonishment . . . but so abrupt that she still had her faint eyebrows raised in query" (14). Neumann records that this astonishment at having given birth arose out of primitive woman's belief that birth was a miracle which they ascribed to "the *numinosum*, to the wind or ancestral spirits" (1973, 134). It was a supreme moment as Neumann indicates: "the creative energy of woman comes alive in the miracle of birth, by virtue of which she becomes the 'Great Mother' and 'Earth Goddess'" (135). This is the aspect of the Masarwa woman that Margaret Cadmore records—this, in spite of the thin stick legs, the callused feet, and the soiled shift dress. Thus Margaret is the daughter of a Goddess, a mythical heroine, who, having suffered emotional and physical collapse within the course of the narrative is rescued by the hero from "joyless depression" (Neumann 1973, 201).

THE DRAGON FIGHT

To see Margaret as "rescued" is the way that Maru justifies his prevention of her union with Moleka: "Moleka would never

have lived down the ridicule and malice and would in the end
have destroyed her from embarrassment" (9). However, as a
transpersonal figure, Margaret's major significance is the contribution she makes towards the fulfillment of Maru's destiny:

> the conditions which surrounded him at the time forced him to think
> of her as a symbol of her tribe and through her he sought to gain
> an understanding of the eventual liberation of an oppressed people.
> (108)

She is a passive participator in Maru's schemes, her role defined
by Maru's needs. Marriage to Margaret would ensure that he is
"never tempted to make a public spectacle" of himself, or that
they would "never make the right, conventional gestures" (70).

However, the union of Margaret with Maru has a greater significance, one that is related to the development of the wholeness of Maru's psyche. The winning of the heroine is, within
myth, symbolized as the "dragon fight," and the idea of a "battle"
is dramatized within Maru. For although Maru plays a transpersonal role within the novel, all his actions ruthlessly calculated;
he knows that there are sacrifices he has to make in order to
maintain his integrity. The fact that Maru accepts responsibility
for his conduct, that he is prepared to question society's codes,
sets him apart from his peers, who are content to accept the inevitability of human failings. "That is the world, they said, as
though all the evils in human nature were there by divine order
and man need make no effort to become a god" (36). So there is
loneliness that Maru experiences, loneliness that he must endure in order that he is not driven "to the busy highway, where
he would meet his doom" (64). Moreover, discipline is required
to ensure that all "the visions and vivid imagery" to which he
is subjected direct his "footsteps along a straight road—that of
eternal, deathless, gentle goodness" (37).

There is a temptation, when denigrating the influence of nurture, to seize upon nature as the affirmative value to oppose it.
The danger herein is to confuse the natural only with the instinctual, with that which lacks thought, to interpret Maru's "visions and vivid imagery" as the unmediated response of the
unconscious. For as Maru observes, "true purpose and direction
are creative. Creative imagination he had in over-abundance,"
while "Moleka had none of that ferment, only an over-abundance
of power" (58). Jung provides a useful interpretation of creative
imagination that suggests that the optimum power of the psyche

is achieved with a synthesis of the conscious and unconscious processes, that which occurs when the artist "seizes this image, and in the work of raising it from deepest unconsciousness and bringing it nearer to consciousness, he transforms its shape" (Neumann 1973, 376). Head portrays within the novel how the unconscious can hold the potential for both positive and negative qualities of the psyche. Its dual role is portrayed in Margaret's ferment of activity as she allows herself to give artistic form to that "part of her mind that had saturated itself with things of such startling beauty" (101). Nevertheless, productive though it may have been, "the images and forms . . . imposed themselves with such demanding ruthlessness" (100) that with a complete absence of "discipline and control," Margaret is brought to the verge of "total collapse and breakdown" (101). In contrast, Maru's dreams and visions are the creative assimilation of his unconscious:

> Who else had been born with such clear, sharp eyes that cut through all pretence and sham? Who else was a born leader of men, yet at the same time acted out his own, strange inner perceptions, independent of the praise or blame of men? (5–6)

The paintings that emerge from the "images and forms" that "imposed themselves with such demanding ruthlessness" upon Margaret make it clear to Maru that they dream the same dreams. Margaret is aware that she has drawn her inspiration from the depths of her unconscious, from "something inside her" that "was more powerful than her body could endure." She also understands that in the future such impulses will need to "be brought under control, put on a leash and then be allowed to live in a manageable form" (102). But here and now, within the context of this narrative, Margaret is merely the passive participator in Maru's destiny. This aspect of the heroine is accounted for within myth as the "sisterly side of woman, standing shoulder to shoulder with the hero as his beloved, helpmate, and companion, or as the Eternal Feminine who leads him to redemption" (Neumann 1973, 201). In the novel, it is with Margaret by his side that Maru can follow the dictates of his "gods": "'Take that path,' his heart said. 'You have no other choice.' Each time he hesitated. It was too lonely. No other companion trod that road" (64).

Jung interprets the female archetype within myth in psychological terms as the anima of the masculine psyche, a contrasexual component within the masculine psyche to compensate his ego-consciousness. Thus, the captive, the hero's prize within the myth, symbolizes that part of a man's personality he needs to discover in order to achieve psychic wholeness. The anima element is lacking within the masculine psyche when the hero engages in relationships that are not built upon equality and mutuality. Thus, Maru endures the destructiveness of relationships with women who fail to live up to his idealism: "No wound had healed. He had only to touch the scars for them to bleed all over again" (69). The dissatisfaction and self-destructiveness of these relationships is paralleled by the violence of their endings. Like the mythical hero, Maru "kills . . . the terrible side of the female" (Neumann 1973, 199).

> "I hated her because she thought too much of herself. I hated her because she was only flesh. No flowers grew out of the love, and when I said: All right, this is over, she still thought the flesh had captivated me forever, until I had to kill her. I killed them all because of their greed." (69)

It is a rite of passage: the hero needs to free himself from the seductive power of the unconscious, the "devouring" or "castrating" "Terrible Mother" before he can submit to relationships built on mutuality and equality. Margaret with her "inner kingdom" stands closer to Maru. As his anima, she represents the heroine, that "picture of woman that is closer to [the hero's] ego and more friendly to his consciousness than the sexual side" (Neumann 1973, 201). The anima has also a wider significance, "the symbolic marriage of ego-hero and anima . . . offers a firm foundation on which the personality can stand and fight the dragon, whether this be the dragon of the world or of the unconscious" (Neumann 1973, 213). It is a denial of the anima component in the personality that condones hierarchies of power. Laurens Van der Post recognized this when he wrote that "the deep rejection of woman in our man's world proceeds directly from the failure of man to honour the woman in himself" (1985, 30). Moleka's extreme masculinity is determined by the fact that he "is only half a statement of his kingdom" (58). All the qualities required by Maru to fulfil his destiny as a reformer are due to his possession of what Head describes as "feminine reasoning with a few masculine stop gaps" (Vigne 1991, 157).

The notion of a contrasexual component within the individual psyche, one that is also natural, is fundamental to the beliefs of the French feminists; their idea of a presymbolic, essential femi-

nism implies a resistance to the rationale that demands a prescribed masculine or feminine gender. To escape from the
conception of gender identity as oppositional masculine or feminine constructs, these feminists define sexuality as "a contin-
uum which allows for degrees of difference" (Weedon 1993, 127).
The reservations that Head expressed about feminism were
based on her assumption that to embrace feminism meant denying the value of masculinity per se. Her sensitivity to the differ-
ences between masculine and patriarchal qualities becomes
clear. In *Maru*, she argues that it is only the masculine hero,
sustained by his feminine anima, who can destroy the patriarchal structure of society and thereby erect new freedoms for all.
She wrote, "I have needed a masculine vehicle just because there
was nothing else that would suit it" (Adler et al. 1989, 12).

Paradoxically, it is in the creation of Maru, who appears to be
the most sexist of her "grand" men, that Head approaches a reconciliation of the masculine and feminine. In the union of Margaret and Maru, Head celebrates the complementary and
egalitarian aspects of male/female relationships rather than a
union of opposites. What Gover calls the "mysterious power,"
"the force for good" that rescues the "victim of evil" has transpersonal and universal significance. For the role of the hero in freeing the captive, is not simply to secure the satisfaction of his own
personal needs, but "to free, through her, the living relation to
the 'you,' to the world at large" (Neumann 1973, 202). Then and
only then will the hierarchical structures upon which racist and
oppressive ideologies are founded be subverted.

THE BEGINNING AND NOT THE END

Thus far, the story is moving towards a satisfactory conclusion. Married to Margaret, Maru feels that he has "inherited the
universe" (124); for Margaret, Maru is "some kind of strange,
sweet music you could hear over and over again" (124). Nevertheless, the fairy tale quality of *Maru* lies in the promise it can
offer rather than the actuality it presents. It is, as the author
suggests, "not the end. . . . but a beginning" (126). And this new
beginning is fraught with apprehension and misgiving: "black
storm clouds clung in thick folds of brooding darkness . . . prison-
ers pushed back, in trapped coils of boiling cloud" (5). They reflect, for Maru, "the storm in his heart" (8).

Maru's brooding melancholy is caused by the knowledge of

Margaret's dream. This recurring dream is about Moleka, who appears "trailing a broken leg with blood streaming from a wound in his mouth and his heart" (8–9). The imagery of Margaret's two rooms, one of which contains Margaret's dream about Moleka, suggests different levels of consciousness. In one room, Maru's wife "totally loved him; in another, she totally loved Moleka. . . . [S]he had no mental impression of her dreams, except those of the room in which she loved Maru" (8–9). The ambivalence of Margaret's feelings cannot sustain the ideal that Maru envisages: "there had to be perfection. It had to be almost ready-made, for use" (69).

Premonitions of disaster are hinted at within the text. In Dilepe, Margaret had "recorded the hour of peace" (115), the time in which she had lived serenely in the knowledge of Moleka's love. But it is only a prelude before "finding herself tossed about this way and that on permanently restless seas" (115). Also, back in Dilepe, during the trancelike state in which she had produced her paintings, she had imagined, again and again, the image of an "embracing couple" who "did not want anyone near them" (103). For Margaret, the exclusiveness of this couple's love symbolized the idea of "a secret which ought not to be disclosed" (103). It was only by committing this image to paper that Margaret was able to rid herself of its obsessive claim on her subconscious. But, nonetheless, she still dwells almost exclusively within Maru's power.

The problem lies with Margaret's role within the novel. As the passive participator in Maru's schemes, she does not decide her fate. She exists merely as a pawn in Maru's destiny. But she is still enthralled by the attraction she feels for Moleka's charismatic masculinity. For although Maru is confident that his love is superior to Moleka's, Margaret knows nothing of this. Part of her being still dwells in the memory and the hope that Moleka "belonged to her in a way that triumphed over all barriers" (99). Maru feels that, given the opportunity, his love "could grow and grow beyond the skies or the universe" (110). But there can be no true union between the divine and the human. Like Olive Schreiner's Lyndall, Margaret can "see the good and beautiful" but has "no strength to live it" (Schreiner 1983, 213).

There is an interesting distinction inscribed within the novel. The creative power of Head as an artist imagines Maru, the hero with the strength to transcend universal ills. However, Head, in later years, expressed her reservations about the heroic stature of her hero—"the dubious Maru, painted up as a God" (Appendix

5), and as such he symbolizes the obsessive focus of the author's unfulfilled personal needs. Perhaps he is, in the best tradition of the romance, what Alison Light calls "a 'triumph' over the unconscious" (1990, 142). Or, as the cause of that "something inside her . . . more powerful than her body [can] endure" (102), it is perhaps, only Margaret's unconscious desire for Maru's rival, Moleka, that protects her and her creator from total dependency on an obsessive relationship. The strange dichotomy within the novel, the way that it is a fairy tale without a happy ending arises because Margaret is not yet ready to fulfil the role of the fairy-tale princess. Rather more than most romances *Maru* portrays the "ideal of the pursuit of the unobtainable" (Rich 1984a, 124). While there can be no doubting the strength and vitality of Head's artistic vision, it takes her own experience of mental breakdown, anticipated by Margaret's dilemma, to dismantle her faith in such heroes, and to raise up in their stead a more human potential for optimism.

5

A Question of Power

SHORTLY AFTER FINISHING *MARU*, EARLY ONE MORNING BESSIE HEAD rode into Serowe on her bicycle and pinned up a notice outside the post office, accusing the president of Botswana, Sir Seretse Khama, of incest with his daughter. Diagnosed as mad, Head was hospitalized in a mental institution. Returning home "cured," a few months later, she wrote *A Question of Power*, an account of her two-year battle with progressive mental illness. Her reasons for writing were twofold. As therapy, it was to be "an examination of inner hells" that "was meant to end all hells forever" (12). It was also an opportunity to explain her irrational allegations against Seretse Khama:

> I could only record what I loathed and how it broke me. I had to do that because I really did put that notice up at the post office. . . . What else could I do but explain my side? (Appendix 7)

The novel, written in the third person, records Elizabeth's mental disintegration. The first indication of this is the telepathic communication that Elizabeth has with a godlike figure vaguely resembling a man called Sello, who is an important person in Motabeng. Elizabeth's "absent-minded life" (25), her feeling that to the local people she is "an out-and-out outsider and would never be in on their things" (26), corresponds with her curiosity about the living Sello. It is not long before the godlike figure becomes a physical presence in her hut, a figure wearing the "soft, white, flowing robes of a monk" (22). Elizabeth engages in long, "absorbing conversations" with the white-robed monk, whom she addresses as Sello, and soon "her slowly unfolding internal drama" is "far more absorbing and demanding than any drama she could encounter in Motabeng village" (29). Their "pursuit after the things of the soul" (11), cannot preclude an examination of Sello's "inner life." Sello, indeed, has his "shadow,"

89

the evil Medusa, and his goodness is strangled "to death with evil" (100).

Elizabeth's internal drama becomes increasingly dominated by nightmarish hallucinations, and her mind disintegrates: "It was a state below animal, below living and so dark and forlorn, no loneliness and misery could be its equivalent" (14). Elizabeth becomes a "replica of the inner demons," her relationships with friends and acquaintances slowly deteriorate. To avoid confrontation she turns "to flight before her own hatred" and resolves never to "see so-and-so again" (136). Finally, however, she cannot escape from the "satanic image of Sello, his boyfriend, his little girl with her face upturned in death" and "her screaming, agonized nervous system snapped to pieces" (175). Following her libelous attack on Sello, "words" and "the jumbled sentences she utter[s]" throw "her straight into the loony bin." Her hospital notes are "the typical record of a lunatic" (179).

The reader will accept, as Arthur Ravenscroft does, that "the phantom world that comes to life whenever Elizabeth is alone in her hut" could only have been invented by a novelist who had "herself gone through similar experiences, so frighteningly and authentically does it all pass before one's eyes" (1976, 184). This recognition, however, does not assist the reader in unraveling this complex narrative. The problem lies in the long, incoherent description of dreams, the hallucinatory experiences combining highly condensed imagery with an elaborate procession of figures from myths, world religions, the Bible, and history. These figures jostle with one another for space in the text, physically merging into one another. Charles Sarvan and Jane Watts both feel that Head fails to achieve coherence because there is no separation, despite the fictionalized third-person perspective, "between the suffering individual and the creating artist" (Sarvan 1990, 12), no opportunity to "recollect" in "tranquillity" (Watts 1989, 141). R. Langen writes that "the text itself is 'mad'" (1989, 10).

Langen suggests that the very nature of the experience itself resists interpretation. It must be read with the understanding that "the barriers of the normal, conventional and sane" are "all broken down" (15). Craig Mackenzie writes that the nature and content of her breakdown was for Head a subject of confusion that she never resolved in her lifetime (1989a, 34). Head's letters to friends record this confusion. "I am in a weak position recounting it because I had to wait to gather enough clues to unravel the plot of the devil" (Appendix 7).

THE SOCIAL AND POLITICAL CONTEXT

Because of the sheer complexity and range of issues contained within *A Question of Power*, there is a tendency for critics to isolate individual themes in order to illustrate a particular theory they are explicating. Sometimes the inchoate is simply translated as metaphor. This is Holst Petersen's view, that the insanity of Elizabeth's experience is a portrayal of the extreme irrationality of the apartheid principle. (1991, 131). This kind of analysis assumes that Head's portrayal of mental disintegration is the product of her creative imagination rather than the source for it, and indeed there does come a point when it is difficult to separate these two conspiring elements—what Elizabeth controls and that which is forced upon her. Clearly, there is evidence within the text that Elizabeth herself draws a parallel between the "torture" of a racist society and the "torture" of her hallucinations, the "vehement vicious struggle between two sets of people with different looks; and, like Dan's brand of torture, it was something that could go on and on and on" (19). Thus, Dan's torture, the recurring hallucinations of "dominant, powerful persons" with their "flashes of lightning, bolts, [and] powers of the spirit" (62), symbolizes the meaning of colonization for its victims. For Roger Berger, this is evidence that Frantz Fanon's belief in the inevitable psychopathology of the colonized subject explains Elizabeth's breakdown, suggesting that racist oppression can cause "a collapse of the ego" if the "psychic structure" of the victim is weak (1990, 34). Nonetheless, there seems to be no justification from accounts of Elizabeth's everyday life to isolate racial oppression as the major cause of Elizabeth's breakdown, or to reach the conclusion that as "a colonized person," she "attempts to become white" (Berger 1990, 34). Acknowledging the prevalence of this myth Jaqueline Rose points out that

> Paranoia—voices in the head—is of course the perfect metaphor for colonisation—the takeover of body and mind. In this case, the use which Head makes of it in her writing also serves to undo one of the prevalent myths—African women do not go mad—of colonisation itself. (1994, 405)

The critic Katherine Frank reads Head's portrayal of Elizabeth's insanity as a valid response to patriarchy. Subscribing to Sandra Gilbert's and Susan Gubar's theories, Frank argues that

> If the madwoman in the attic is the spectre that haunts woman-au-
> thored nineteenth-century English fiction, it is the madwoman in
> the village who haunts the novels of Rebeka Njau and Bessie Head.
> (1984, 39)

Within this interpretation, Elizabeth is seen as a symbol representing the author's female feelings of fragmentation. However,
what is clear in *A Question of Power* is that Elizabeth does not
haunt, she is haunted, albeit (as Rose suggests) Elizabeth is as
much the "agent" as the "recipient" of her drama (1994, 415).
But she is not a feminist symbol, the "maddened double" that
functions as "an asocial surrogate" for a "docile" self, as the application of Gilbert's and Gubar's theories may imply (1979, ix).
For the resolution within *A Question of Power* rests not upon society accepting a hitherto repressed female element but upon
Elizabeth's ability, as an individual, to talk herself through her
drama, to discover peace of mind, and thus to reclaim her "docile
self." It is clear that Frank's feminist reading of this novel iso-
lates issues of gender from other concerns. In so doing, a feminist critique can be reductive, and this is a fear that Head often
voiced, one that made it impossible for her to subscribe wholeheartedly to its principles.

For other critics, the context and content of *A Question of
Power* invite a variety of psychological readings. These critics
point to particular aspects of Elizabeth's hallucinations to show
how they reflect the problems she faces in her every day life, and
thus the source and nature of Elizabeth's neurosis is explained.
This kind of interpretation of mental illness is widely accepted,
and one that assumes that dreams, hallucinations, and night-
mares are "metaphors in motion" (Hall 1977, 49), their imagery
reworking only the same problems that the victim confronts in
reality. Thus, Elizabeth Evasdaughter diagnoses Elizabeth as
suffering from paranoid schizophrenia, caused partly by "culture
shock and partly [by] hostility among the Batswana toward half-
breeds, members of other tribes, and women with education and
professional authority" (1989, 73–74).

For Margaret Tucker, too, it is Elizabeth's immediate circumstances that make her a most likely subject for psychotic disorder: "As stranger, exile, bastard, and woman, she is the Other,
the dispossessed" (1988, 170). As the illegitimate offspring of a
liaison between a white woman and a black man, fostered and
orphaned, with the added stigma of a "mad" mother, Elizabeth
is most certainly handicapped. And all these factors contribute

towards the "loosely-knit, shuffling ambiguous mass which was her personality" (62). But Elizabeth herself refuses to accept that these facts of her nurturing are the cause of her breakdown. Instead, just as the knowledge of her mother's assumed insanity is claimed "to add to [Elizabeth's] temperament and capacity to endure the excruciating" (15), so the blending of "the normal and the abnormal . . . in Elizabeth's mind . . . was manageable . . . because of Elizabeth's background and the freedom and flexibility with which she had brought herself up" (15). Thus, to a certain extent, Elizabeth is prepared to acknowledge the existence, the reality of extraworldly experiences. She tries to account for the mysterious origin of her hallucinations as fragments of "past lives . . . upheaving" (Appendix 18). Elizabeth had at one time lived among Asians in Cape Town, had become interested in Eastern religions, and had accepted the belief in reincarnation. Thus Sello, perhaps belonging to a past incarnation, has

> the air of one who was simply picking up the threads of a long friendship that had been briefly interrupted at some stage. It was if he was saying: "Do you recall this occasion when we met and worked together?" Because a spectacular array of personalities moved towards her, crowded with memories of the past. (24–25)

However, Elizabeth is duly forced to admit that the appearance of Rama, Krishna, and other Eastern deities can only account for a fraction of her vision. Elizabeth cannot recall anything from written history to equal what she has encountered: "none of mankind's God-like figureheads recorded seeing what she saw on this nightmare soul-journey" (35).

This attempt to find a cause for the onset of her hallucinations is a dimension within the text that Caroline Rooney refers to as "the will-to-interpret" (1991, 118). Elizabeth, the speaking subject, does reflect on the meaning of her hallucinations. At the simplest and most obvious level, she decides that the hostility to which she is subjected by her Medusa is a direct expression of "the surface reality of African society" with its "strong theme of power—worship running through it" (38). Another source of psychic power to which Elizabeth fears she may have fallen victim is witchcraft. The personality who holds her "life in a death grip must really be the master of the psychology behind witchcraft" (21). Tangible manifestations of witchcraft practices include a dead owl outside the door and a heap of charcoal dust in the middle of Elizabeth's hut. But even in the midst of her despair she tries to provide a logical reason for their occurrence—the owl may have "died of old age" (48), and the fire may have started because "she might have left a cigarette lit" (93). But she concedes that witchcraft as a weapon in "a real, living battle of jealousy, hate and greed was more easily understood and resolved under pressure than soaring, mystical flights of the soul" (66). In one of her letters, Head also suggests that a medical diagnosis of her experience of evil, "like paranoia or insanity," was preferable to the alternative explanation, that she had been "possessed by the devil"—that it was this that accounted for "things that took place over a long period with a seemingly logical pattern" (Appendix 4)

Another level of interpretation that occurs within the text is what Margaret Tucker defines as the mediation between the "namer" and the "watcher" (1988, 171). Although this authorial intrusion is very unobtrusive, and occurs when the author, with the authority of hindsight, comments on an incident that overwhelmed her persona, critics have suggested that the significance Head attaches to her breakdown is contrived. Carol Davison argues that Head's "didactic approach tends, at times, to stifle her art" (1990, 26). Elizabeth Evasdaughter interprets Elizabeth's newly conceived resolution about the meaning of God as "comic," or part of the "joke" element (1989, 82). Joanna Chase feels that Elizabeth's role as "a universal soul face to face with evil as an abstract force" is responsible for her "unsatisfactoriness as a character" (1982, 72).

The stylistic problems, the complexity of *A Question of Power* are a reflection of the nature of the experience Head is attempting to communicate. What has to be made coherent are the disordered, fragmented delusions of a mind out of control. There is an obvious difficulty in attempting to describe any dream experience, the "immense gap, the qualitative incommensurability between the vivid meaning of the dream and the dull, impoverished words which are all we can find to convey it" (Felman 1978, 339). Head writes of her own creative battle to find a "mouthpiece" for her thoughts: "I sometimes stand still for hours in the room struggling to find someone to say it with form" (Vigne 1991, 152). Here, the author is acknowledging the mediation of the "namer," the intervention of a writing subject. This creative act ensures that

the integration of diverse meanings in a literary work through its various symbols and metaphors, is of a qualitatively different nature from condensation in dream imagery—where there is little if any true integration of the component parts, and where meanings are derived from the dreamer's associations rather than from those of the listener. (Roland 1978, 259)

In *Maru*, Margaret recognizes that complete, conscious control has been lacking in her obsessive activity of painting. Head's narrative, in contrast, shows some evidence of the "ego's attempt to integrate aspects of the id, super-ego and outer reality into a workable synthesis" (Roland 1978, 255). However, although Head's choice of a third-person account may well have been a conscious attempt to achieve some coherence by creating a space between herself and the subject of her narrative, it does not mean that she is wholly successful. In a letter to Vigne, Head describes her experience of "remembering" what had occurred:

I can catch on to some lovely lines—"innate goodness makes a man seek tender and short-cut routes to heaven," then I don't quite know who is saying that because I have no strong control over my mouth-piece. (Vigne 1991, 152)

Perhaps, as Charles Sarvan suggests, a space between suffering individual and creative artist does not exist. Head herself comments on the artistry of *A Question of Power*: "Most of the soliloquies are done by Elizabeth. They are shouts of agony without any beauty—they just pour out" (Appendix 6). What is certain is that Head, as mediator, attempts to interpret only a fraction of her hallucinations. What is in question is the inseparability of that which the conscious minds perceives as happening to it and that which it initiates. Elizabeth herself acknowledges the sheer inexplicability of most of her experiences, which Caroline Rooney explains as "the impossibility of the attempt to transcribe it further" (1991, 118). As Elizabeth claims, "It couldn't be that simply put" (98). Head acknowledges herself the implications of this for the reader: "it needs a sort of gymnastic mental performance to make it coherent, a constant leap from reality to unreality and at times the two merge so totally that confusion can arise" (Appendix 6). The challenge to the reader is to accept that the most complex and elusive of these symbolic figurations are as valid as those with a more explicit and direct relationship to the author's circumstances. Lilian Feder's observation is a useful reminder of their significance:

Literary interpretations of madness both reflect and question medical, cultural, political, religious, and psychological assumptions of

their time . . . they explore the very processes of symbolic transformation of these influences and disclose their psychic consequences
in the minds of individual characters or personae. (1980, 4)

It is important to allow the text to speak for itself, to understand
that the creative act of the author is, perhaps, hardly distin-
guishable from the emerging consciousness/unconsciousness of
the subject of the narrative. Jacqueline Rose's contention, that
"It is not clear whether we are dealing with an outside in or inside out situation; the writing doesn't let you decide" (1994, 415),
suggests the inseparability of that which is imposed on Elizabeth and that which is imposed by the author. It is almost impossible to analyze the creative act, but in *A Question of Power* a
synthesis of unconscious imagery with the material reality of
Head's/Elizabeth's world becomes a telling critique of the problems of human society. As Elizabeth is shown, and as Head sets
out to show, responsibility for oppression and repression rests
ultimately upon a question of power.

JUNG AND THE UNCONSCIOUS

The reading of *A Question of Power* that most effectively accounts, psychologically, socially, morally, and even aesthetically
for the form and content of this novel, is a Jungian analysis. A
Jungian theory of the psyche proposes the idea of a many-lay-
ered consciousness. Jung described the unconscious as consist-
ing of two elements, the personal unconscious and the collective
unconscious. The personal unconscious, as in Freud's version,
contains all the repressed infantile impulses and wishes of the
individual. The collective unconscious, a deeper layer within the
psyche, is composed of the inherited tendencies of the human
race. These are

> a priori, inborn forms of "intuition" . . . of perception and
> apprehension. . . . Just as his instincts compel man to a specifically
> human mode of existence, so the archetypes force his ways of percep-
> tion and apprehension into specifically human patterns. (Jung 1967,
> 8, par. 270)

In the collective unconscious, archetypes or primordial images
are the form that these instincts assume; imagery derived from
the universal mythmaking that has engaged mankind from the

earliest time, in his attempt to comprehend the meaning of life and death, of creation and destruction, of being and nonbeing.

Much controversy has surrounded this area of Jung's work for many psychologists have expressed their misgivings at the unscientific foundation of Jung's theories. Nevertheless, even skeptics admit to the frequency with which disturbed patients describe dreams crowded with archetypal imagery. Freud, too, in his later work, acknowledged that aspect of the unconscious that contains "the archaic heritage of mankind . . . not only archaic dispositions but also ideational contents, memory traces of the experiences of former generations" (1939, 159).

Head's own experience of her hallucinations convinced her that "each individual is the total embodiment of human history and a vast accumulation of knowledge and experience . . . is stored in the subconscious" (Appendix 18). Indeed, Elizabeth is always struggling to make sense of the imagery with which she is confronted:

> There was a strange parallel in her observations to mankind's myths—they began to seem vividly true. Nearly every nation had that background of mythology looming, monstrous personalities they called "the Gods," personalities . . . who assumed powerful positions, presumably because they were in possession of thunderbolts, like the Medusa. (40)

Inevitably, the archetypal imagery becomes tangled and confused with elements from Elizabeth's own personal unconscious. Thus, Medusa also represents personal anxieties or desires:

> Then again the story was shaded down to a very personal level of how a man is overwhelmed by his own internal darkness; that when he finds himself in the embrace of Medusa she is really the direct and tangible form of his own evils, his power lusts, his greeds, his self-importance, and these dominate him totally and bring him to the death of the soul. (40)

In this way, dreams, as manifestations of actual life preoccupations become "the royal road to the unconscious" (Hall 1977, xxiv), the unconscious here meaning the Freudian site of repressed wishes and fears banished from conscious recognition. So Medusa becomes the insistent voice of Elizabeth's accuser, intimating that Elizabeth is flawed by her own latent racism: "'you hate Africans, you don't like the African hair. You don't like the African nose'" (48).

Jung offers an explanation for the reason why various levels of the unconscious merge, and also why mentally ill patients seem to be in touch with the most submerged elements of the collective unconscious. What is forced into action is what Jung labels the "libido," or psychic energy. A useful explanation of this process is given in Victor White's summary:

> The psychological law of compensation teaches us that the hypertrophy of one set of functions and attitudes, and the consequent atrophy of their opposites, call forth the compulsive domination of those opposites. Thwarted in its centrifugal flow into an external world, which it is unable to assimilate and integrate, the "libido" of necessity is forced to flow back, centripetally, to the interior world of the collective unconscious. (1964, 208)

Elizabeth herself recognized that "it was only when her life was assaulted like that that peeps into the boiling cauldron were allowed" (39–40). She also persistently refers to the physical nature of her mental conflict, "her whole form seemed to turn into channels through which raced powerful currents of energy" (36), forces that "rumbled beneath her consciousness like molten lava" (98).

Jung's theories also explain the way in which the collective unconscious compensates for the particular deficiencies of the individual. He describes how a patient who has experienced inadequate mothering will be suffering from a loss, and this loss represents an instinctive claim on the collective unconscious for fulfillment. A practicing psychologist, Clifford Allen, who expresses his unease at what he feels is Jung's unscientific approach to the analysis of the psyche, points out that in his experience of dealing with the "thinking of the insane," a delusion shared by many of his patients is their implicit belief in their role as creators. One patient insisted that she was "the mother of all living things" (1965, 109). Allen acknowledges that Jung's view of the collective unconscious, as one that surfaces at times of great personal stress, will account for the commonality of patients" delusions. So he concedes to Jung's view: that which "keeps alive an indefinite but painful longing" is "the collective image of the mother; not of this particular mother, but of the mother in her universal aspect" (1965, 198). Similarly, in *A Question of Power* Elizabeth speaks of the "peculiar sensation" she has "of sleeping with a whole lot of people in (her) arms like a great and eternal mother" (86). A Jungian analysis of this dream, taking into account the universal implications to be discovered in Elizabeth's breakdown, might suggest that Elizabeth, within the context of her interrogation of flawed human relationships, catches hold of an image powerful enough to redeem this impoverishment, and charges herself with the responsibility for embodying it. It is too, as Jung suggests, compensatory, for "Elizabeth had no experience of love, but she had powerful imaginings about it; its quality and beauty were like a deep, hidden symphony in her heart" (86).

It is significant that this loving and nurturing figure is not the only image of motherhood in A *Question of Power* for, inevitably, images from the collective and personal unconscious merge. On one occasion, Elizabeth is confronted by a "monstrous woman." She looks "hideous with teeth about six inches big," but "shining out of her eyes [is] the tender, blue glow of a great love" (33). The dream describes how a "slenderly-built woman" steps out of the monster and, placing a "glittering crown" on her head, points at Elizabeth's heart and says, "This is my earnings with you. . . . I made that heart of compassion," whereupon, she walks "into Elizabeth's person" (33). Speculation would only reveal infinite possibilities of interpretation. Elizabeth's challenge to the monster/slenderly built woman—"why did you do it?" (33)—might suggest unresolved anxieties concerning her separation from her mother, the portrayal of the monstrous woman as both monster and nurturing, might reflect the ambivalence of Elizabeth's feelings with which she has never come to terms.

As Jung pointed out, myth has always allowed for the "terrible and devouring" mother (Allen 1965, 194); for Jung, the mother can be the source of the libido, so that "every obstacle which obstructs his life, and threatens his ascent wears the shadowy features of the 'terrible mother'" (Allen 1965, 194). In one of her letters, Head provides a colorful description of the "fearful female principle" who

> combines the terror of destruction with the reassurance of motherly tenderness. She is the cosmic power, the totality of the Universe, the glorious harmony of the pair of opposites. . . . She is the Universal mother, the All Powerful. . . . She is the highest symbol of all the forces of nature, the synthesis of their opposites. (Appendix 17)

There is much of this idea in the relationship between Sello and Medusa, and as Medusa plays such an eclectic role in Elizabeth's fantasies, the universality of Sello's predicament is emphasized.

For Medusa is Sello's mystical madonna, she is Mahamaya, the Weaver of Illusions; she is responsible for shattering Sello, in his role as Osiris, into a thousand pieces, and she is the evil woman who completely dominates Sello. Jung's "terrible mother" "paralyses [man's] energy with the consuming poison of the stealthy, retrospective longing" (Allen 1965, 194). "[T]hroughout that long year . . . the hideous display of Medusa's power" paralyses Sello, who "sat in death, incapable of thought, feeling, movement" (100). For his salvation, Sello, like Maru in his destruction of the women with no "inner kingdom" (*M*, 64), must end his association with Medusa.

Jung believed that archetypal imagery reflected the anxieties of the patient, and that to understand this imagery is a means to self-knowledge—"perception by way of the unconscious" (White 1964, 210) So Jung made an exhaustive study of worldwide mythology in order to understand the delusionary experiences of his patients. Unlike Freud, Jung did not believe that psychotic disorder was simply a retrogressive illness; he believed that the patient had to become ill in order that he or she might become well. It is clear that the narrative form of *A Question of Power* assumes a process of learning and resolution. As Rooney comments, this narrative is "written from the place [it is] heading towards" (1991, 123). Elizabeth constantly remarks that she is "learning, internally" (133); there are so many "terrible lessons" (36) she must learn. For Elizabeth this process of learning becomes a quest, and the prize she has to earn is "a pale blue rosette" that is "symbolic of the brotherhood of man" (37). Very early within the narrative the author states clearly that the learner will become "totally free from his own personal poisons—pride and arrogance and egoism of the soul" (11). And in her personal letters, Head confesses to "an arrogance of soul that was submerged," that it takes "a long time to learn a humility" (Appendix 4). Within *A Question of Power*, Elizabeth must free herself of her obsessive love for Sello; Head states in her letters that she has to learn never to mention "so-and-so" again.

The superior claim of a "brotherhood of man" is seen, in *A Question of Power*, to depend upon Elizabeth's ability to rid herself of her obsessive love of Sello. As a powerful father figure he bears some affinity with the role of Johnny in *The Cardinals*, a further rendering of what Freud would identify as the female's natural and instinctive desire for her father. Most feminists reject the significance of this theory in the development of the female psyche, viewing it as just another example of male-orientated ideology. Feminists are also anxious to resist the theories that insist on universal patterns in the development of the female psyche in order to protect their belief that gender identity, like all forms of social meaning, is constructed through language. This resistance is a challenge to Claude Levi-Strauss's universal theory of human society that takes the oedipal triangle and the incest taboo as social norms underpinning psychoanalytical theory. As Weedon argues, the only psychoanalytical model acceptable to many feminists would be one that "does not make universal claims but is historically and socially specific" (1993, 50). Elizabeth's obsession is indeed socially engendered, her hallucinations can be read as compensatory, she is responding to *lack*, she is seeking to fulfil needs that have never been satisfied. But it is also a *lack* that is also most adequately explained by Freud's Electra complex, albeit a theory that is revised to see this complex as significant only for individuals with impoverished nurturing, but which nonetheless draws attention to the existence of innate drives and instincts—described by Jessica Benjamin as the universal need for the child to be met as a "sovereign equal" (1990, 12).

Head depicts Elizabeth as a character most clearly identified by her social and historic relationship with a hostile society, but nonetheless compensation for this is sought at a more personal level by her imagining of a relationship with a powerful leader. Her recourse, in order to combat the worse excesses of her society, is to find that meaning does exist outside the discursively produced limits of her subjectivity. This is the other level of experience, one that is not necessarily socially or historically produced, one that can only be "universal"—embedded as it is deep in the personal psyche. So she learns that the pathological nature of her obsession is a parody of the power and domination responsible for racist and oppressive ideology.

Whether the reader will see *A Question of Power* as not only a credible account of Elizabeth's psychic functioning but as an account of the psychic revelation of knowledge potentially available to all humankind depends on his/her prior convictions about the relativity and construction of meaning. For the Jungian psychotherapist this novel could be used to support Jung's hypotheses of a body of archetypal imagery common to all; that when nurture fails to humanize, there is nature that is human, instinctive, essential, and universal—a body of knowledge apart from the discursively acquired socialization of one's subjectivity. Jung's belief in some such body of knowledge led to his interest

in the metaphysical speculations of gnostic beliefs, that liberation lay not by "faith, love or deeds, but primarily, even solely,
by knowledge—knowledge of that kind of introverted intuition"
achieved through the unconscious (White 1964, 210).

For the Jungian psychologist, Head's description of Elizabeth's psychotic disturbance would affirm their own beliefs, and
a Jungian reading would start from the premise that Elizabeth
has made contact with the collective unconscious of mankind.
Taking into account Caroline Rooney's warning—that *A Question of Power* is a "sophisticated" critique in itself that "may
serve to interrogate that which would interrogate" it (1991,
121)—it may nonetheless prove fruitful to draw the reader's attention to the intertextual connection between *A Question of
Power* and one of the few surviving gnostic texts, *Pistis Sophia*,
in order to establish for oneself the persuasiveness of Jung's belief in universal paradigms of human behavior.

Pistis Sophia, which was known to Jung, dates, as far as scholars can tell, from the fourth century; it is claimed to be the work
of the gnostic sect of Valentinus. It is a rendering of the mythic
descent to the underworld, a universal quest for mankind's redemption. There is no doubt that the quasi-biblical language of
this text has little in common with the twentieth-century realism of Head's narrative form, but nonetheless the implied moral
imperative of the *Pistis Sophia*, the way in which the heroine is
shown the true nature of her obsession, bears an uncanny resemblance to Elizabeth's own fate in *A Question of Power*. For as
White states, the *Pistis Sophia* can be read in "Freudian terms
. . . as a transparent account of the formation of an Electra complex." Victor White's version, taken from Gilles Quispel's translation of Irenaeus's *Adversus Haereses,* is quoted here to show
the unmistakable resemblance between the origin of Elizabeth's
and Sophia's psychic journey, the enduring significance of the
Electra myth:

> Sophia-Acamoth [feminine Wisdom] suffers passion and desire
> apart from her consort. . . . she was led astray by disordered love,
> which was actually *hubris*, because she did not . . . comprehend the
> all-perfect Father. . . . Her passion was a desire to know the Father,
> for she craved to grasp His greatness. Unable to realise her hope,
> because she aimed at the impossible, she fell into extreme agonies
> because of the unfathomable depth of the Father's unsearchable na-
> ture and her love for Him. Always yearning for Him, she would have
> been annihilated in His sweetness and dissolved into His infinite

being, had she not been restricted by that power, *Horos* [the Limit, Finiteness], who exiled her from the Pleroma. (White 1964, 217)

Sophia-Acamoth's fate in the *Pleroma* is summarized for the reader by White: "she finds herself imprisoned, tortured and subjected to the tyranny of the other Aeons in the material chaos, which is . . . the product of her own disordered emotions." In White's understanding, Sophia-Acamoth's "impossible, forbidden passion for the 'Father'" is countermanded by "the *Horos* or Limit," which plays "the repressive function of the Freudian incest—prohibiting Censor" (217–18).

Sello, in Elizabeth's delusionary world, fulfils many functions. As "king of the Underworld," "Wonder There" and also "The Father" (30), he is one of Head's "grand" men, a godlike hero figure that appears as a central character in all her writing. Johnny, in *The Cardinals*, is the model for these masculine heroes, as well as the actual, biological father of the heroine who falls in love with him. It is a dilemma that is never satisfactorily resolved at the close of the novel. Thus, it is not too improbable to suggest that the theme of *A Question of Power* is another reworking of an intractable longing, that Elizabeth is still undergoing the trauma of an unfulfilled desire.

Sophia-Acamoth is condemned for her hubris, her yearning for an impossible love. In *A Question of Power*, even the very elusive connection between Elizabeth and the real Sello discloses enough to show that the local inhabitants are hostile to Elizabeth, accusing her of wishing to be "important." Although Elizabeth denies this charge, she is nevertheless dismissive of Sello's wife, describing her in terms that emphasize her physicality. "She looked as though she were just content to dress well and eat well and had a heavy, stuffed-up-with-food way of walking" (26). Her own relationship with Sello concentrates on the spiritual, and her own eminent suitability for this role; like Sello, she had the "capacity to submerge other preoccupations in a pursuit after the things of the soul" (11–12).

With the appearance of Medusa, Sello's godlike aura is dramatically transformed. "He fell back on a haggard pose, shrinking and shrinking in size until his monk's cloth began to flap on his person like a scarecrow's rags" (64). Subsequently, Elizabeth, like Sophia-Acamoth, is subjected to the torments of the "abyss." She is assaulted by instigators of torture who, like the Aeons in *Pistis Sophia*, attack her physically and mentally: "the torrent of hatred [Dan] felt for Elizabeth was hitting her daily such terrible blows, she was barely alive. It was done under cover of the parade of the nice-time girls" (168–69). One of the most difficult aspects of Elizabeth's internal drama is to understand the reason for Sello's fall from grace. It evades the normal expectations of romantic fantasizing. White's interpretation of *Pistis Sophia* shows how Sophia-Acamoth's fall into the abyss symbolizes the work of the instincts of the collective unconscious to effect an obstacle to the success of "disordered emotions," to prevent incest.

Like Sophia-Acamoth's "disordered emotions," Elizabeth's ambivalent feelings about her sexuality conjure up Medusa, Dan, and his "nice-time" girls, whose overt sexuality parodies and diminishes the true relationship that Elizabeth desires with her once-powerful, godlike hero. Dan's role, like Freud's moral censor, is to "smash the prophet image of Sello" (169). Early on in her hallucinations Elizabeth had been warned. "There is an evil in your relationship with Sello. He knows. He is controlling your life in the wrong way, and he does not want to give it up" (32). But Elizabeth, "her heart . . . crying for that beauty, that perfection" (99) has, like Sophia, to learn to "recognise the insolubility of her conflict and the impossibility of her yearning" (White 1964, 223). She must be thankful for the restraint of the *Horos*.

And this is what happens in *A Question of Power*. Dan's display of obsessive and repeated acts of physical and mental rape as well as the "suffering she had endured had sealed her Achilles" Heel, that of the brutal murderer for love" (202). She accepts that "love-relationships are like an eternal damnation . . . and the deeply drawn links of soul to soul have to be discarded" (99). It is with this interrogation of a revised meaning of love, which is implicit within the resolution of *A Question of Power*, that the author is able to depart from the preoccupations of the romance theme of *Maru*. The nature of the triumph of the Margaret/Maru relationship must be re-examined. Margaret's painting of the embracing lovers, which represents in *Maru* an unequivocal symbolism of ideal love, is recreated in *A Question of Power*, but with a different emphasis—one that draws attention to its obsessive exclusive nature:

There was a heaven there where the light had shaded down to a deep midnight blue. A man and a woman stood in it, wrapped in an eternal embrace. There were symbols of their love. There were two grape trees with the roots entwined; there was a broad wide river coming down in full flood, with a tremendous roar, supposedly symbolic of a powerful, blind all-consuming love. There was nothing else, no people, no sharing. It was shut-in and exclusive, a height of heights known only to the two eternal lovers. (108)

Freed from the domination of obsessive love, Elizabeth can now recognize the value of the human kindness offered by Mrs. Jones. "There was something on her face she had not seen for a long time; the normal, the human, the friendly soft kind glow about the eyes" (196). So Elizabeth is able to "treasure the encounter with Dan" (202). Symbolizing the *Horos*, he has endowed Elizabeth with the "freedom of heart" that allows her to "love each particle of earth . . . the everyday event of sun-rise . . . people and animals . . . and the whole universe" (11).

This is the significance that the *Pistis Sophia* shares with *A Question of Power*. For just as Sophia is granted deliverance from "the empty space devoid of insight" (White 1964, 218), so Elizabeth's internal drama is the means through which Elizabeth can come to terms with the void left by a private, personal love:

> They had perfected together the idea of sharing everything and then perfectly shared everything with all mankind. . . . It was the point at which all personal love had died in them. It was the point at which there were no private hungers to be kissed, loved, adored. . . . That was the essential nature of their love for each other. It had included all mankind, and so many things could be said about it, but the most important was that it equalized all things and all men. (202)

JUNG AND THE "COLLECTIVE" MAN

What begins as the fulfillment of a personal need is seen to have relevance for all mankind. It becomes "the message of the brotherhood of man" (201). White's appraisal of the *Pistis Sophia* acknowledges that the gnostics would have penetrated more deeply into the allegorical story of Sophia-Acamoth, and so, White comments, "we may . . . see the Freudian myth itself as a shadow of the more metaphysical yearnings of the finite for the infinite" (1964, 218).

It is not easy to understand why an allegorical account of the Electra myth should contain the possibilities for such far-reaching and profound conclusions that touch on questions of human connectedness for mankind. Lévi-Strauss argues that the taboo against incest is one of the most fundamental laws of human culture (Ellmann 1994, 15), and Freud believed that it was the universality of the incest wish that necessitated the taboo. Evaluated in this way, it is possible to see why the Oedipus/Electra complex is banished to the unconscious, as Freud would have it, or, in the Jungian equivalent, shaped by the instincts into some archetypal image of the collective unconscious. Thus, when the individual libido is frustrated in normal relationships, the unconscious compensates by introducing universal archetypes that include both the object of desire and the moral censor. The discursive battle that follows interrogates questions of power. It is as though the sum total of human knowledge, Elizabeth's "soul power," is inevitably turned towards the quest to discover the most fundamental law for the human in relationships, and this must mean the renunciation of Freud's primal urge that represents instead relationships based on power and obsession, ones that are shut-in and exclusive.

Thus, what begins as Elizabeth's irrational fantasy over a father/hero image becomes increasingly internalized, so that

> A darkness of immense dimensions had fallen upon her life. . . . People cried out so often in agony against racial hatreds and oppressions of all kinds. All their tears seemed to be piling up on her, and the source or roots from which they had sprung were being exposed with a vehement violence. (53)

The poem by D. H. Lawrence that Head uses as a foreword to *A Question of Power* invokes the risk attached to that seeking after insight:

> That awful and sickening endless, sinking
> sinking through the slow, corruptive
> levels of disintegrative knowledge . . .
> the awful katabolism into the abyss!

For Head, Lawrence represented the "Great Teacher," one who provided her with an interpretation of "the hidden darkness, the hells of the worlds within individuals" (Appendix 26). Thus, Elizabeth feels that, as the "queen of passive observation of hell" (148), she is becoming acquainted with

> mankind's universal knowing of the fall and the dark times when civilizations were swallowed up in holocausts; when powers of in-

creasing evil fought to the death over the small bones of their own self-importance and lusts and greed. (54)

Elizabeth's "journey into the soul" portrays the paradox that knowledge, which of necessity will include the relevance of evil, is disintegrative. It is, Elizabeth reflects, easy to accept the "delicately-buffered pillars of principles and platitudes," but these are the preserve only of "blank, shut-eye goodness" painlessly resolved by "disciplined meditation" (65) under bodhi trees. In contrast, "concerted evil" is so powerful it throws Elizabeth "flat on her back" (85). It is a "complexity so monumental that everything becomes a tangle of lies" (65). But this knowledge of the "abyss of utter darkness" (173), the recognition of the "roots of evil" operates as a "creative propelling force" (85), and "it was out of death itself that a great light had been found" (57). On one level Dan may have enacted the role of moral censor in the Electra myth; on another level he is, Elizabeth acknowledges, "one of the greatest teachers" that she has ever worked with, although he "taught by default":

> he taught iron and steel self-control through sheer, wild, abandoned debauchery; he taught the extremes of love and tenderness through the extremes of hate; he taught an alertness for falsehoods within. . . . And from the degradation and destruction of her life had arisen a still, lofty serenity of soul nothing could shake. (202)

It is interesting that the significance of Dan's physical materialization, the equation of phatic qualities with material forces, bears a close resemblance to the apocalyptic imagery that signals creation and destruction in the *Pistis Sophia*.

> One half of him seemed to come shooting in like a meteor from the furthest end of the universe, the other rose slowly from the depths of the earth in the shape of an atomic bomb of red fire; the fire was not a cohesive flame, but broken up into particles of fine red dust. (*QP* 104)

The origin and significance of fire in the *Pistis Sophia* is echoed in *A Question of Power*:

> earth rose from [Sophia's] *despair*; water from the agitation caused by her *sorrow*; air from the materialisation of her *fear*; while fire, causing death and destruction, was inherent in all these elements, as lack of insight [*agnosis*] lay concealed in the other three passions . . . (White 1964, 218)

Dan materializes from the earth and from the air; he does bring Elizabeth to despair. She is also deceived because she is "living in the glow of that meteor-ride to the end of the universe" (114). She is devoid of insight. As she reflects, "I could not grasp the darkness because at the same time I saw the light" (190). But from the destruction of fire, there arises the potential for re-creation, and it is significant that Head's explanation of the relevance of Lawrence's poem emphasizes the idea of rebirth. She writes, "there is that symbol he used, the phoenix rising from its own ashes. The key word is own, to find redemption in one's own power . . . not the mystical and absent" (Appendix 26).

The significance of "power" here is that which is secured after healing. The imagery of the phoenix rising from its own ashes explains metaphorically Jung's conception of psychosis as a process towards empowerment for the individual. But in a novel that persistently identifies power as responsible for the impoverished nature of relationships of race, gender, class, and nation, it is important to recognize the difference between Elizabeth's newly acquired sense of self, her individuation, as opposed to individualization, which can develop into the source of strife and oppression.

Significantly, within the text of *A Question of Power* Head identifies and dramatizes what Jung conceives to be a deadlock in the psychotic process: when the power of an ego, persuaded by its own inflation, succumbs "to the fascinating audience of the archetypes." Head acknowledges this inner, destructive potential of the individual:

> people, in their souls, were forces, energies, stars, planets, universes and all kinds of swirling magic and mystery; that at a time when this was openly perceived, the insight into their own powers had driven them mad, and they had robbed themselves of the natural grandeur of life. (35)

Thus, this excess of power advocates "assertion and dominance to the exclusion of other life" (35). It is like Elizabeth's "pride and arrogance and egoism of the soul" (11), the source of her early identification with Sello, and it is like Sophia's lack of insight that leads her to mistake "the light of the Aeons for the One True Light" (White 1964, 224). It is within this line of analysis that Elizabeth arrives at her conclusion about the meaning of God. For, as she has decided, "the title God, in its absolute all-powerful form, is a disaster to its holder, the all-seeing eye is the greatest temptation" (36–37).

It becomes clear why Head sees the subject of her novel as "a question of power," for she interrogates the source of power to its very depths. She finds that power, as a compensatory move, serves as a debased substitute for the failure to fulfill basic human instincts; the eternal return to relationships forged by variations of the Oedipus/Electra myth. For the dominant figure in this state of unequal relationships, power brings with it back into the real world a desire only to repeat the psychosis of an inflated ego. It leads to a state where men become "totally disassociated from each other, as though they faced each other with blank eyes, neither recognising the other for centuries and centuries" (53). As Elizabeth indicates the consequence of this has been the reoccurring history of human misery—Caligula, the Nazi holocaust, the Ku Klux Klan—and, for Elizabeth, the atrocities of the latter are proof that religion has also played its part in that history of oppression.

Head's debate on the potential for institutionalized religion to become an oppressive form of power, which she begins in *When Rain Clouds Gather*, is continued in *A Question of Power*. Here Head anticipates current trends in feminist theology in its criticism of monotheism for its tendency to "reinforce hierarchy, for it creates a chain of command" (Hampson 1990, 153). Makhaya is critical of the monotheistic Christian God of the missionaries because its followers, concerned for their relationship with a powerful God, share in his reflected glory only by virtue of the exclusion of others. Elizabeth articulates the lengths to which this exclusion can be taken. She reflects how the Ku Klux Klan "said they were worshippers of Jesus Christ and they lynched people; they committed so many atrocities" (92).

There is an antidote to all this, and the answer is worked out in the process of Elizabeth's healing. For Elizabeth does recover. With no treatment except for sedatives, Elizabeth is left all day long to stare "through a window at a hillside on which trees grew, and watched the movement of the sun from sunrise till it set behind the hill. The small boy always came walking down the dusty brown road at sunset, lost in his playtime thoughts" (182). She was left to ponder the meaning of her internal drama. However, there is one incident that occurs during her stay in the hospital that startles Elizabeth out of her passivity. This is her sudden realization that the European doctor assumes that she shares the same feelings of superiority towards the Africans as he does himself. "The shock of being thought of as a comrade racialist . . . abruptly restored a portion of her sanity" (184). For as

Elizabeth has so far discovered, this debased form of ego power is at the root of mankind's suffering.

It is belief in the potential for human equality to be recognized that is the resolution in *A Question of Power*. One of Elizabeth's final statements is to assert that "there is only one God and his name is Man. And Elizabeth is his prophet" (206). This is Elizabeth's endeavor to see religion not as it divides but as it draws man together, and with it the possibility for spirituality within and not without. In *When Rain Clouds Gather*, Makhaya had condemned the God of the missionaries for appropriating all spirituality for his own, and depriving the natural world and ordinary people of its wonder and divinity. So what must be rediscovered is the spirituality of man. At one stage in her breakdown, Elizabeth is tormented by the sound of an "unseen female choir" asserting the "absolute supremacy" of God with the words "Glory be to God on high." Elizabeth fears she is being subjected to this "shattering," "insistent record" because she has "committed some terrible form of blasphemy against the unknown God" (109). Head's letters register her constant struggle to define the meaning of "divinity," the need for "people to see and understand everything with their inner eyes awakened" (Appendix 2):

> One half of me feels that there ought to be something holy and infinite somewhere. The other half of me was pulled towards living things as though all the stirrings of wonder, the things that made the earth glow, the loves that moved and created history were to be found in living people. (Vigne 1991, 149)

But as Elizabeth comes to believe, "God is people. There's nothing up there. It's all down here" (109). Jung believed that the healing process involved a recognition of man's essential spirituality, "its mysterious relation to the inner man" (Fordham 1991, 74). And, more controversially, at least from an orthodox Christian point of view, it becomes as possible to say that "humanity is involved in the redemption of God as to say that God is engaged in the redemption of humanity" (Dourley 1990, 39).

Shortly after completing *A Question of Power*, Head, in a letter to a friend, confided her hopes:

> Perhaps I imagine a world where people see they are God and the greeting changes and people say to each other: "Good-morning God." You couldn't possibly kill God if it was you, could you? You couldn't

possibly exploit or do evil to God and God and God. That's more or less your "triumph of love." (Appendix 17)

It has taken three years of a disintegrative mental process to bring Head to this resolution, but it is as she says a "triumph of love." For, as Jung believed, the healed self recognizes "his brotherhood with all living things, even with inorganic matter and the cosmos itself" (Fordham 1991, 78).

For Elizabeth, "the awakening of her own powers corresponded to an awakening love of mankind" (35). Thus, the interdependence of the "I" of the individual and the "we" of society is realized and the significance of Jung's "collective man" established. That Head can offer the resolution that she does confirms Lloyd Brown's view that "the artist's reminder of the power of the inner self constitutes a splendid defiance of the wasteland" (1981, 169). In *A Question of Power*, Head retells her story of mental breakdown, and in so doing presents a powerful critique of the sickness within society and the measures that can be taken to heal it.

6
The Collector of Treasures

IN A SHORT ARTICLE ENTITLED "DREAMERS AND STORYTELLERS," Head defines her perception of the function of the storyteller. He is needed, she writes, because

> Each human society is a narrow world, trapped to death in paltry evils and jealousies, and for people to know that there are thoughts and generosities wider and freer than their own can only be an enrichment to their lives. (*TTP*, 141)

With the envisioning of Maru's ideal society, the storyteller's art is stretched to the limit, the "other" world only a "probable impossibility" of the artistic imagination (Frye 1975, 58). The utopian resolution at the heart of Head's writing rarely extends beyond the examination of fulfillment for its heroes and heroines and destruction for its villains. The relatively "real" world encountered in *The Collector of Treasures* is explored in stories that recount what Head refers to as the "calamities women experience in the village" (Mackenzie 1989a, 42). In these stories, the author focuses her attention on human beings who are neither too heroic nor too villainous. Head also seems willing, in *The Collector of Treasures*, to confront the inevitability of human failings as a normal and dynamic force in social intercourse. There is a marked acceptance that "nothing new could be said about human nature—it had all been said since time immemorial and it was all of the same pattern, repeating itself from generation unto generation." (62). Within the context of the *"kgotla,"** the "twitter of birds in the ancient shady trees" (61) symbolizes the unerring constancy with which human nature repeats its same mistakes.

---

*"Kgotla": a traditional meeting place in the center of a traditional village where local disputes were heard and discussed and settled by elders and chief of the village.

Because of the more detached relationship that exists between the author and the characters she creates, Head is able to dispense with her total dependence on archetypal imagery and transcendental themes as the only resolution for the plight of her protagonists. The human predicaments that beset these characters, usually women, are shown to be the consequence of an intolerant and rigid cultural milieu. Sometimes, in individual stories, the storyteller exists as a participator in the drama, presenting the opportunity for "wider and freer . . . generosities," to alleviate the plight of her victims. The author's role, like the storyteller's, is in this volume the more conventional one of arbiter in the judgment of human folly. This is dramatized in the portrayal of Thato—for she, with "the unerring heart of a good story-teller" (108–9), will not only find the power "to sift and sort out all the calamities of everyday life" (108), but she will use her art to seek and to find "gold amidst the ash" (91).

COMMUNAL AND TRADITIONAL VALUES

It is because of the priority Head gives to the need for the broadest human perspective that it is difficult to view her stories as a continuation of an oral tradition. Nonetheless, this is a view much favored by critics, and one that seems to be supported by the author's addition of the subtitle "other Botswanan village tales." Craig MacKenzie interprets this as an indication that the stories included within this anthology "follow, bear, or purport to bear, some relation to a village oral tradition" (1988, 237). It is a claim that seems to confirm Head's move away from the subjectivity and interiority of *A Question of Power* to a closer identification with Botswanan society. The psychic and emotional trauma explored in Head's third novel is finally overcome when Elizabeth "placed one soft hand over her land. It was a gesture of belonging" (*QP,* 206). Cherry Clayton interprets this as the way in which Head claims her "writer's territory" (1988, 56) and, subsequently, what follows, in the form of *The Collector of Treasures*, critics see as a writer establishing new found links with a hitherto hostile environment by celebrating the traditionalism and communalism embodied in the orality of a bygone era.

That the indigenous writer will find much to celebrate in a portrayal of traditional Africa has always been an assumption made by critics and reviewers. From this perspective the African writer will bear witness to a communal, cohesive society that is threatened by a materialistic colonizer more inclined towards a philosophy of individualism and Cartesian dualism. Traditional oral literature will still reflect the collective needs of its people in a way that is not possible for the cultural representations of an alienated and fragmented Western society. Mazisi Kunene describes how the oral short story is the repository of the tribal culture in that it transmits

> a serious system of ethics which it enforces . . . a nexus that produces a logic, not only between past and present generations, but also in the whole cosmic phenomenon. . . . [O]ral literature is not specialized in the sense that literature is for western intellectuals. Every man, woman, or child is expected to be steeped in the literature of the country. (1976, 28)

The African writer, responsible for the transmission of this culture, will invariably choose to use oral techniques, for (as Chinweizu argues) it is traditional oral narrative that serves "as the ultimate foundation, guide post, and point of departure for a modern liberated African literature" (1983, 2). Another critic, Mbulelo Mzamane, argues that for African writers the retrieval of oral techniques is natural, for "the African writer who has been Westernised to the extent that he has been cut off completely from his roots does not exist in reality" (1984, 147). However, because the oral tradition depended for its survival on a monolithic and unchallenged culture, the infiltration of alternative belief systems immediately undermined its authority. As Jane Watts writes, "the oral tradition is fragile in that the social system in which it operates has broken down" (1989, 24), and so, as she argues, "it is no longer enough to be the conformist celebrant of convention that the oral poet was in the tribal village, strengthening conservative values by creating praise poems for heroes, and castigating deviations from the accepted code of behaviour" (21). Increasingly, cultural diversity disturbs the certainty of monolithic tribal traditions. Jack Goody and Ian Watt define this as a dilemma for the literate individual who has "so large a field of personal selection from the total cultural repertoire that the odds are strongly against his experiencing the cultural tradition as any sort of patterned whole" (1963, 58).

Makhaya's voluntary exile in Botswana is not only an escape from the politics of South Africa but also represents his desire to free himself from the restrictive ties of tribal customs. In her personal letters Head expressed her misgivings for ancestral laws and traditions: "Botswana is a tribal, tribal land. if you care to touch that side of it" (Appendix 20). So, as Kenneth Harrow suggests, the focus of Head's work is on "boundaries"—"the forces that maintain and perpetuate them, and the forces that dissolve them" (1995, 195). Thus, in a sequence of stories Head portrays the narrow-minded and repressive nature of traditional society's mores and customs, and shows that it is only the widening of sympathies that can mitigate their authority. Although it is a portrayal of the victimization of which Botswanan society in particular is guilty, it is also, by extension, an exposé of the intolerance in which society, in general, participates. Thus, it becomes difficult to see *The Collector of Treasures* as evidence of the author's new-found solidarity with Botswanan society, or a continuation of an oral tradition that served to consolidate and explain a society's laws and traditions to itself.

Instead, Head offers the "counsel" (1970, 86) that Walter Benjamin says the storyteller has for his readers. It is the primacy of this counsel, informed as it is by the "lore of faraway places" (1970, 85) that offers the most effective challenge to repressive and intolerant codes and practices. Head herself was not enthusiastic about the label "Botswanan writer" often used to describe her writing. For, as she argued, writing "as a nationalistic activity" will only reflect "the subdued communication a writer holds with his own society" (*TTP*, 141–42). It might, like Kunene's description of oral literature, project "the examples of socially desirable actions, making heroes of those who uphold the highest communal values and villains of those who violate them" (1976, 32), but this is not Head's imperative. Writing for, and from, one's community is seen by Head as a limiting of horizons— almost a literary handicap.

Even when Head does seem to be drawing directly upon the legacy of oral literature, as in "Heaven is not Closed," she does so with the understanding that the reader holds a very different relationship with the dramatized storyteller than the one experienced by the storyteller's immediate audience. In this story, Head uses the convention of a traditional storyteller with an eager fireside audience to narrate how the saintly Galethebege is expelled from the Christian church because she marries a non-Christian, to whom, as the missionary tells Galethebege, "Heaven is closed." MacKenzie writes that "what is of particular interest" in this story "is the interpolation of traces of an oral culture in the written form" (1988, 241), and that these stories are "the kind of stories that the villagers tell each other" (1989a,

39). Head in this story does, as Mackenzie suggests, recreate the aura of intimacy between the storyteller and his audience, and she does use for her material the gossip with which a village would abound. However, whether this kind of anecdote would be included within the original repertoire of an oral performer is very doubtful indeed, for evidence points to stories of a rather different nature; creation myths, trickster tales, epics, and animal fables.

Nevertheless, what is made possible by the interpolation of oral techniques into the written form is the addition of a further dimension of meaning. Thus, the exploration of the hopes and aspirations of individual characters in "Heaven is not Closed," which would not concern the oral performer, are extended by the inclusion of an additional narrative voice in the shape of the storyteller. The author conspires with this storyteller to point out the tensions that a present day and more culturally diverse perspective will bring to the reading. The collective representation of myth and epic has been replaced by an examination of the individual and the ambiguous relationship the individual holds with his society.

For all Head's "real" characters, freedom from die-hard traditional customs is necessary for their fulfillment. To highlight the qualities necessary to enlarge the sympathies of entrenched, conservative customs, Head takes as her subject the *kgotla,* and portrays how this traditional seat of wisdom and judgment within the tribe needs to adapt to change in order to function adequately. It is significant that in an earlier portrayal of the duties of the *kgotla,* in *When Rain Clouds Gather*, Head allows a far more romanticized version of the *kgotla* to emerge, when it functions as the dispenser of compassionate justice to a victim of superstition and malice. In this instance, it allows one of Head's "good" characters to display his ideal qualities, as, in order to save the life of a helpless, victimized old woman, he becomes both judge and jury. Similarly, in the later narrative in *The Collector of Treasures*, the story also opens with a scene evoking peace and calm as two ancient old men "shuffled their way" to the "wide, semi-circular wooden enclosure of the kgotla" (61). However, the confident authority with which the chief acts in *When Rain Clouds Gather* is not repeated in the short story. Even the fact that the dispute is settled is greeted with surprise by the two onlookers. As one observes to the other, "You know very well that we can never settle cases at kgotla and this case looked impossible from the start" (68). That it rises to the occasion in this instance calls forth the grudging approval and admiration of the old man. "I have seen a wonder today, Thatayarona," he says (68).

In the first incident the settling of the dispute is, fundamentally, a clear choice between good and evil. The right choice that the chief makes is an indication of his status as one of Head's "grand" men, and this justifies the idealized portrayal of the *kgotla,* and is part of Head's design to portray the potential humanity of which an ideal community might be capable. What becomes more important in the second incident is the portrayal of the intractability of human nature. To accommodate this, Head does not portray the kgotla as an avatar of age-old wisdom, but shows that it cannot function wisely if it harbors intolerance or resists change. She also prevents the story from being interpreted as an example of a glorious traditional past by making the solution to the dispute one that can only be operated in a significantly freer present. The young wife, an injured party in the dispute, will become a wage earner in order to pay off her husband's debts. The wife is also an outsider, the significance of which is not overlooked by the two observers when they comment "the forefathers were right when they said that the finest things often come from far-off places " (68). Here, Head is echoing the view of Walter Benjamin, that the storyteller needs to have at his disposal "the lore of faraway places" (1970, 85) in order to broaden the sympathies of the listener.

Head seems capable of deploying a more objective stance in the writing of her short stories. Certainly, central to the creation of *The Collector of Treasures* is the outsider view, and this is Head's role as storyteller as she carefully undermines the affirmation of a cohesive society, the creation of which is important for Head's more romantic endeavor in *When Rain Clouds Gather*. Many of the stories in *The Collector of Treasures* highlight the inability of society to fulfill the aspirations of its citizens, even when these hopes only amount to a desire to be left alone, to live decently and simply, or to survive economically, as in "Witchcraft" and "The Special One." Although as Head herself shows in "The Special One," women are complicit in their own victimization, she also acknowledges that most of the calamities happen to women. And, because for Head, the whole question of the impoverishment in human relations is caused by the abuse of power, it is women who, as the most vulnerable members of a patriarchal society, are the most likely victims.

In the story of "Life," it is such an abuse of power that is responsible for Life's murder. Because of the difficulties Life encounters in adapting to the life in a rural village, after her experiences as an independent single woman in Johannesburg, her murder "might," Head intimates, be the inevitable outcome of "That's What Happens When Two Worlds Collide" (46), a Jim Reeves song that is popular with the beer-drinking women amongst whom Life finds cronies. On her arrival in the village, before her marriage, Life has found plenty of men only too willing and eager to pay her for sex. But on her marriage to Lesogo, he announces his "authority and dominance" over her by commenting "indifferently and quietly," as though he never expected "to encounter any challenge," " 'if you go with those men again, I'll kill you' "(43). Life is unable to analyze the effect that Lesogo's threat has on her, but "something seemed to strike her a terrible blow behind the head" (43). As soon as the opportunity presents itself, Life, unable to stand the boredom of being a village wife, returns to her old ways and Lesogo murders her. However, within the context of the story, there is nothing to suggest that Life's behavior is so outrageous, for, the reader is told that the villagers' "attitude to sex was broad and generous" (39). It was expected that Life's behavior would provoke the "usual husband-and-wife scene" (45), and Lesogo's friend cannot understand why Lesogo didn't just "walk away" (46). Life, however, had intuitively recognized and internalized the threat of Lesogo's power and domination and she "rapidly began to fall apart" (43). This internalized threat, like Elizabeth's assault in *A Question of Power*, is given the characteristics of an actual physical onslaught—"a terrible blow behind the head" (43). But here the perpetrator is also named, and so Life's murder is inevitable, not because of the clash of two worlds, but because of Lesogo's absolute certainty that he has the right of possession over another human being. It is an abuse of power equally destructive in whichever of the "two worlds" it may exist.

LITERACY

One of the ways in which Head extends the range of sympathies aroused by her stories is her recognition of their literary potential, the presence of a reading subject, who shares the same distance from the area of study as the author herself. In *A Bewitched Crossroad*, Head celebrates the importance of literacy, not only for the opportunity it presents as a recorder of events but also the access it offers to knowledge, to new ideas, to the extension of dialogue that she describes in her last book. In a letter she states that "the written word is the highest form of human expression" (Appendix 8).

The first story in *The Collector of Treasures*, "The Deep River," recounts how the quiet flow of communal life, when the people are "like one face" (2), is disrupted when these same people are suddenly faced with the necessity of having to make individual choices. They have to decide whether to remain loyal to entrenched traditional mores or to support their new chief in his decision to leave the tribe rather than forsake the woman that he loves. What seems to be happening in the telling of this story is that Head is dramatizing the shift from communal acquiescence to individual choice in such a way that the change is also rendered stylistically as a shift from an oral to a literary frame of reference.

Head dramatizes the time in which "the people lived without faces, except for their chief, whose face was the face of all the people" (1), so that their story is as formulaic and repetitive as the incremental pattern of a rhyme. The form underpins the activity it describes; the unquestioning obedience of the people to the rules and regulations of their chief, laws that control to the last detail the way their lives are shaped. Sonorous, measured tones chronicle the ritual and rhythm of their day to day living. It is a pageantry that highlights collective and communal aspiration.

Significantly, the style of the narrative changes when the narrator informs the reader that "the people awoke and showed their individual faces" (2). With the introduction of "now," the pace of the story changes as the narrator describes the events that "ruffled" the "deep river." Formal stylistic patterning disappears as individual feelings are forced to the surface, relationships within the society become more problematic as the needs of personal fulfillment are measured against communal responsibility.

Walter Ong, in his discussion on the development from orality to literacy, suggests not only reasons for the specific form of oral literature but also the implications for conceptual thought that such forms dictate. Because it was necessary to create material that could be more readily committed to memory, a form developed relying upon rhyme and repetition and epithets, a form ideally suited to portraying a highly polarized and agonistic world of good and evil, virtue and vice, villains and heroes. Although

Ruth Finnegan refutes any claims that the thought processes of preliterate man are any less sophisticated than those of his literate heirs, the consensus view is that the growth of literacy has been concomitant with the possibility for abstract conceptual thinking denied preliterate man. As Lévi-Strauss has claimed, "the savage mind totalises" (Ong 1982, 39). Ong, in developing this theory, explains how writing "makes possible increasingly articulate introspectivity, opening the psyche as never before not only to the external objective world quite distinct from itself but also to the interior self against whom the objective world is set" (1982, 105).

The possibility for the examination of interiority, its precedence over the claims of the external world, characterizes Head's literary treatment of Sebembele, the hero of the first story in *The Collector of Treasures*. No longer just a figurehead, his dilemma presents him as an individual, neither villain nor hero. He becomes "a man with a weakness" (6), but the wider perspective made possible by a literary exploration views this "weakness" with delicate ambivalence; his weakness is also his strength. Examined in this way, it becomes clear that in "The Deep River" Head dissolves the rigidity of communal laws, "the tyranny of the present" (Goody and Watt 1963, 53) that informs the oral consciousness, replacing it with the potential for a more compassionate vision and resolution. The old men, who, at the end of the story, still claim that "women have always caused a lot of trouble in the world" (6), represent the prejudices, the deadlock of the preliterate world.

In the story "The Special One," Head uses the first person narrative voice. Thus, not only does she become a character in the story—who, as a newcomer to the village, demonstrates an ironic stance to the village customs—but as writer of the story, communicates with the reader in a way that is not possible between herself as character and the other protagonists within the story. A shifting perspective is communicated by the literary relationship she holds with the reader.

The story relates how a philandering husband is granted a divorce from his wife on the grounds that she "pestered him day and night for the blankets, and even wanted him to do it during the time she was having her monthly bleeding" (84). The villagers accept the husband's version with voyeuristic delight, and his wife Gaenametse is faced with ridicule and ostracism. The authorial voice presents a different perspective, suggesting to the reader that the husband would have "anticipated this social reaction to his wife and deliberately invoked the old tribal taboo to boost his image" (85). However, this interpretation is for the reader alone; for, when the narrator, as character, is informed of Gaenametse's "crime," she carefully adapts her response to a point of view that Gaenametse's accusers will more readily understand. So she explains to her interlocutors that it is acceptable that she should talk to Gaenametse because, where she came from, "the men usually slept with the women when they were menstruating" (85). The narrator confesses to the reader that she really knows very little about such taboos, but her reply to the other villagers, intending to mitigate the harshness of the community's condemnation, is all she can offer under the circumstances.

Thus, the appeal to "wider generosities" is, in this story, for the reader alone, and throughout the remainder of the story the author engages with the reader's sympathies, following Gaenametse's progress until she finally finds a partner for whom she can become "the special one." The literary mode can accommodate the communication with an outside audience in a way denied its oral antecedent.

ROMANCE AND REALISM

One of the most interesting features of Head's short stories is that they include two distinct types of characterization. One type, the noble hero or heroine, is characteristic of all Head's work when she is intent on creating her vision of an ideal world. The heroic characters in Head's short stories are more "romantic" because, like Maru, their claim to reality depends upon their adherence to the "immaterial reality of the inner world of the self in its relation to eternal rather than temporal reality" (May 1984, 329). The other type is the "real" character inhabiting a "real" world, and, denied the protection of Head's other ideal world, their progress is marked by trial and tribulation.

So, the short stories "Looking for a Rain God," "Witchcraft," "The Special One," and "Life" are more concerned with exploring the dilemma of the protagonists, their problematic relationship with the society and the environment in which they live and their struggle for emotional or even physical survival. Within these stories there are no grand men to provide an alternative vision, no real villain to blame for the protagonist's plight, and no allegorical resolution to form the reader's response. Instead

there is the protagonist's interaction with his society in a particular place, at a particular historical moment. Furthermore, the
Botswanan landscape that has served so often as a symbolic
guarantee of rebirth and regeneration in Head's writing becomes, in "Rain God," a harbinger of death and destruction when
the reality of relentless drought is foregrounded. In "Life" as in
"Rain God," the odds against survival are set too high; these stories show the arbitrariness of survival, the inevitability of
human tragedy. In "Witchcraft," Head resists the temptation to
romanticize Mma-Mabele's survival, to show it either as the consequence of any supreme personal quality that she possesses, or
as the result of divine intervention. Instead the fact that she
lives rather than dies is seen by Mma-Mabele as a matter of
sheer necessity, by the reader as merely fortuitous.

The way in which these characters interact with their environment means, as Mackenzie points out, that the village is always "felt" (1989b, 143). Head's heroes, on the contrary, are
usually outsiders. They can never react satisfactorily with their
environment unless Head also creates that environment. Jacob
must live at the "sun-rise" end of the village, and Maru must
have a path of sunflowers to his door. The realism that structures her romantic stories is seen most clearly in *Maru* as a subjective act, when the writer/protagonist projects subjective
meaning onto the external world and then responds to this "reality" as though, in fact, it is real.

The "real" characters" relationship with external reality is
less tenuously realized. They represent the indigenous population, their conflict arising from their struggle with the demands
of a specific social reality. Charles May argues that the short
story, because of its length, is ideally suited to establishing "the
primacy of an 'experience' directly and emotionally created and
encountered" (1984, 328). What is relevant for this process is the
exploration of the true relationship of the human subject and the
objective world, a world that is given a temporal and a spatial
context. The human subject in the real world will be a typical
character. However, "type" here does not mean a character representing good or bad qualities but is, as David Forgacs explains,
"the character or situation in the literary work which brings together the general movement of history and a number of unique,
individual traits into a distinctive particularity" (1992, 173). It
is the interweaving of such features into the human dilemma defining the Mokgobja family in "Rain God" that makes them infinitely more comprehensible than Head's heroes, upon whom she

expends a great deal of description. As Forgacs explains, "the "type" gives the work the "three-dimensionality" which is the essence of realism" (1992, 173).

It is a real world in which the susceptibility of the protagonists to respond to different pressures acknowledges the validity of a world that is more random, less controlled, than the one that Head usually chooses to create. This particular characteristic of her real stories Kathleen McLuskie and Lynn Innes interpret as an indication of the "intractability of Botswana experience to the orderly constraints of narrative closure" (1988, 7). This does not mean that Head's rather bleak portrayal in these stories is evidence of Bernard Bergonzi's claim that the form of the short story "tends to filter down experience to the prime elements of defeat and alienation," or that it is limited in "its capacity to deepen our understanding of the world, or of one another" (1970, 215–16). As Charles May argues, Bergonzi's view is based on "unstated assumptions about *how* one understands the world and *what* one takes to be the reality of that world" (1984, 330). In contrast to the romanticism with which Head normally engages, the "realism" in her short stories is marked. But, nonetheless, an examination of reality means for Head the imperative to subvert rather than merely echo the norms of society. When this society is invariably found wanting, when, as Frank O'Connor suggests, the short story presents a sense of "outlawed figures wandering about the fringes of society" (1963, 19), there is another dimension of meaning—the reader's response, carefully shaped as the story develops. And it is this that ensures that the resolution reached is not marked by "defeat" and "alienation."

The mediation of the author into the predicaments of her protagonists produces what Georg Lukács in *Writer and Critic* refers to as "a more profound and comprehensive reflection of objective reality than is given in appearance" (Eagleton 1992, 50). Thus, as Terry Eagleton points out, "objective reality," the "apprehension of the external world," for Lukács, implies more than merely a "reflection" of the external world in "human consciousness." As Eagleton explains, it requires the intervention of the human consciousness of the artist rather than mere "sense-impression" to transform a mimetic reproduction of objective reality into a form invested with greater significance. Thus, it is not a crude, mimetic portrayal of Gaenametse's plight in "The Special One," or Mma-Mabele's dilemma in "Witchcraft" that gives these stories their power and significance, but how the consciousness of the author, understanding the categories of meaning that underlie the external appearance, makes this meaningful configuration a part of the narrative.

It is in this way that "Rain God," a story that depicts child murder, becomes transfigured into one more concerned to evoke human compassion: compassion that embraces equally the children and their murderers, for they are all victims. The narrator portrays the innocence of the children without resorting to sentimentality, the plight of the Mokgobja family without bathos. The unfathomable and arbitrary nature of life is also posed in "The Wind and a Boy." This story narrates the life of a boy and the close bond that exists between him and his grandmother. Tragedy strikes; the boy is killed when a car collides with his bicycle; the grandmother, when told of the boy's death, collapses and dies within days. That the boy dies as the result of a car accident is not intended as a critique of Western intrusion into traditional society, for here the car serves only as the harbinger of sudden death from which man, in whatever age, has never been immune. The story shows the love and devotion that can exist between people, human interdependency that controls every aspect of the protagonists" lives. The awful fear with which the villagers observe the process of the grandmother's mental and physical decline reflects the universal incomprehension that accompanies the seemingly arbitrariness of fate, its wanton cruelty.

The death of Isaac in *When Rain Clouds Gather* is given artistic significance hinted at by the carvings that he leaves, and Paulina has Makhaya to protect her. Head's last words on Friedman are "The boy's pretty face was a smear all along the road and he only had a torso left" (74). The single effect of "The Wind and the Boy" becomes the tragedy of the deaths. O"Connor writes that the short story is approached in a different mood: "The eternal silence of these infinite spaces is frightening" (19). Friedman's grandmother, until she died, "sang and laughed and talked to herself all the time" (75). It is a sight that her neighbors cannot bear to witness and so they keep away from the hospital. One old women voices the fear they all share when she says, "It would kill my heart" (75). Friedman's death is an accident, arbitrary, but it is the response to it that informs this story, one that rescues it from being merely a record of a tragic accident. It is in this way that the realism of Head's short stories accords with Lukács's view; that it sees absurdity in all its undisguised and unadorned nakedness, and the exorcising power of this view, without fear or hope, gives it the consecration of form; meaninglessness as meaninglessness becomes form; it becomes eternal because it is affirmed, transcended and redeemed by form. (1971, 51–52)

All Head's "real" short stories are tightly controlled vignettes, the author's detachment allowing a more objective perspective. Although her real characters are a product of their environment, it is one that is different from Head's own. It is this cognitive difference that makes it possible for her to adopt a more ironic stance towards these characters, allowing them the space to respond to beliefs and values that might be different from her own but are nevertheless valid and fundamental to their way of life. Head never treats either her heroes or her villains with the same kind of skepticism; they exist unequivocally to be loved or hated. Their philosophies, ideals, and aspirations are inseparable from her own and are charged with a universal significance uninformed by time or place. Hence, the subsequent projection of intense subjectivity onto either character or environment enables the author to re-create or to invent; the degree to which the end result reflects reality will depend on the author's concern to undermine her perception of that reality. For Head, the romantic creation of her "grand" men testifies to her need to look beyond the reality represented within the boundaries of social and historical limitations in order to achieve the moral and aesthetic order she craved. Paul Thebolo, in the story "The Collector of Treasures," is one of Head's heroes created to redeem the existence of men, who "could be broadly damned as evil" (91). He is introduced into the narrative with a description of his physical appearance:

> He was so peaceful as a person that the sunlight and shadow played all kinds of tricks with his eyes, making it difficult to determine their exact colour. When he stood still and looked reflective, the sunlight liked to creep into his eyes and nestle there; so sometimes his eyes were the colour of shade, and sometimes light brown. (93)

Although this description is filtered through the consciousness of Dikeledi, another "good" character, she is echoing the narrative voice and point of view. The effort expended in conflating physical and mental qualities into a persona radiating uncompromised goodness is the measure of Head's commitment to provide alternative visions.

In contrast to the vivid imagery of Thebolo's introduction, the personalities of her "real" characters are revealed as the story unfolds. The descriptions of the physical features of these characters are never detailed. What it is necessary to know becomes interwoven into the fabric of the narrative; they become part of the action that defines them. The hair-cutting episode in "Witchcraft" is treated with the same sense of awe and fear that Mma-Mabele experiences. The recognition that witchcraft may have no basis in fact does not detract from the reality of the power it can wield over its victims. On one occasion when Lekena, a witch doctor, is attempting to persuade Mma-Mabele to buy his potions, she stands firm, refusing to be persuaded, explaining that nothing could dispel "the thing" that haunts her nights. Lekena is so excited by this revelation that he draws in "his breath with a gasp of surprise: 'You mean you have seen a new thing, Mma-Mabele? I must say I didn't know it. We can never tell what will happen these days, now that we have independence'" (55). The author shows that, forever the opportunist, Lekena is already thinking of how to turn independence to his advantage.

The skepticism of the narrative voice is a sophisticated device in the sense that the significance of the meanings communicated by the characters to one another is enlarged for the reader. The particular irony with which Head treats Lekena reflects not only her own rejection of witchcraft but also her recognition of the role that Lekena plays in exploiting fears and prejudices for his own financial gain. Again it is the abuse of power that Head wishes to reveal. The resolution of this story is reflected in Mma-Mabele's final retort, her denial of the possibility of either witchcraft to harm her or Christianity to protect her. It is a resolution that liberates both the protagonist and reader from the constraints of custom, convention, and traditional belief responsible for the growth of ignorance and prejudice.

Walter Benjamin writes that it is "half the art of storytelling to keep a story free from explanation as one reproduces it" (1970, 89). And the ironic detachment in Head's "real" stories functions to show rather than to explain and thus dispenses with the explicit telling and description that define her romantic works. The creation of ideal characters demands a great deal more explicit authorial intervention than that required for real or typical characters. The minimizing of detail is also considered by John Berger to be a significant feature of the short story. In "Stories Walk Like Men," he describes how the "spaces" in storytelling convey meaning. He defines a good story as one in which "its essential tension" lies

> not so much in the mystery of its destination as in the spaces between its steps towards that destination. . . . Each step is over a space of something not said. And it is those spaces—sometimes even the spaces between single words—which contain the profound shared experience of reader and writer. . . . The thrill of recognition, the impatience to discover more, the confirmation of one's own previous experience, all derive from the common unspoken assumptions made by the story. (1976, 409)

Structuring the spaces within the story both anticipates and controls readers' response. It occurs most frequently in Head's stories when she can afford a more detached relationship with the situation she is describing. An example of this occurs in "Rain God," when the narrator moves from the scene that dramatizes the two little girls playing with their dolls to the next scene in which all the horror of what has occurred is contained in the single phrase "After it was all over" (59). At this point in the story the author can use this stylistic device not only because she can rely on the reader to make the right connections, but because the chilling silence is an effective and evocative communicator of the horror of the situation. It is a complicit understanding between author and reader that cannot be taken for granted in a less realistic work. The random nature of the real, denied the "narrative closure" (McLuskie and Innes 1988, 7) of the romance is communicated by the new skepticism of the narrative voice, the form that she imposes on her story.

So, in her short stories, Head engages more directly with specific life events in a way that she has hitherto ignored in her concern to reject the reality of the profane social world and to erect in its stead her utopian vision. Nevertheless, her desire to portray through her art, the qualities needed for the creation of a more humane society, is never absent in her writing. Critics indicate that one of the peculiar features of the short story is its tendency to encourage a certain concentration of effect; revelation as opposed to evolution, Joyce's "epiphanies," and the isolation of a single meaning often charged with intuition and emotion rather than reason. Charles May even identifies a specific relationship between the modern short story and its oral antecedent that distinguishes them from the novel in the nature of the kind of "knowledge" they each purvey. He argues that while it is "a concept of the systematic pattern of social functioning" that informs the development of the novel, the short story is created upon a different premise. Thus, it can accommodate what May describes as "primitive man's feeling of a solidarity of life," and it was a feeling that "came to him in the midst of episodic encounters with the sacred, set apart from the profane reality of the everyday flow of life by his own individual emotional response to the experiences" (1984, 327). It was, May argues, these incidents in which "nature and the self were united in what for him was true reality" (327) that became the substance of the short story form.

The predominance of archetypal imagery in Head's earlier novels strives constantly after this effect, while the need simply to survive is uppermost in the minds of her "real" protagonists. In "Hunting," the last story in *The Collector of Treasures*, Head carefully intertwines the features of romance and realism. The narrator evokes the affirmative beauty of the natural world and makes it part of the "whole rhythm and happiness" of the lives of Tholo, who "cared about everything" (107), and his wife Thato. Against this background are the people for whom everything is a "muddle": newlyweds who cannot sort out their problems; Rapula, who has "taken up with a shebeen queen" (109). They represent the inevitability that the world will always be a "painful muddle" (109). In spite of this pain and turmoil, the possibility for harmony lies in the compassionate understanding manifested by Tholo and Thato. Here Head combines, in Walter Benjamin's words, "the multicolored fabric of a worldly view," her profane outlook, with an "eschatological orientation," one that emphasizes "the golden fabric of a religious view of the course of things" (1970, 96).

Head's persistent creation of a more ideal society nurtured by its organic affinity with the processes of nature is a yearning for the unifying function of myth, that in Yeats's words "marries" man "to rock and hill." It is this quest, which Benjamin interprets as the way in which the storyteller keeps faith with "the harmony of nature" (1970, 97), that marks her affinity with the first storytellers. It is also fundamental to her resolve to create "a view of a grander world, of a world that's much grander than the one we've had already" (Nichols 1981, 55–56).

And this is the storyteller's role in "Hunting." She, Thato, sifts and sorts. She creates order, and she embodies the potential humanity of human society. Thato cannot solve the problems she sees around her, but can, by the width and breadth of the understanding that she imparts to others, extend the capacity of her listeners to see along with her that "the crux of it all" is that "people don't know how to treat each other nicely" (109). It is left to the storyteller to remedy this, invested as she is with the power to "formulate a common language of human love for all people" (*TTP,* 143). And even within the profane world of Head's short stories, where new worlds are not always possible for the protagonists, Dikeledi, Head's most celebrated collector of treasures, from within her prison cell discovers "gold amidst the ash, deep loves that had joined her heart to the hearts of others" (91).

7
Serowe: Village of the Rain Wind

SEROWE: VILLAGE OF THE RAIN WIND IS A PORTRAYAL OF SEROWE, the village in Botswana that had been Head's home for many years. At the suggestion of her agent, Head patterned this book on Ronald Blythe's *Akenfield*. She divides it into various sections that recount the history of Serowe seen as a definite line of continuity from the era of the reforming Khama the Great to his son Tshekedi Khama, and so to the present educational reforms of a white South African, Patrick van Rensburg. Firsthand reportage pays witness to the influence of these three personalities and expands upon Head's preoccupation with education as a means of personal self-advancement and of promoting the well-being of the community as a whole.

When comparison is drawn with Head's earlier work, especially *A Question of Power*, reviewers and critics respond to what Paddy Kitchen, using Head's own words from within the text of *Serowe*, describes as its "sense of wovenness, and a wholeness" (1981, 23). Craig MacKenzie explains this as a new direction for the author, her "surmounting of the problems of isolation and alienation that characterised her earlier phase and a new commitment to Botswana, and particularly, the people of Serowe" (1989a, 48). Thus, Serowe, as a real village community, had been the inspiration for Golema Mmidi in *When Rain Clouds Gather*, the potential community of Maru's dream, and even a location for the "brotherhood" that will heal the disintegrated personality in *A Question of Power*.

However, Head's projection of a utopian dream as a solution to the alienation of her protagonists never depends on its supposed affinity with reality. As has been shown, Head's resolution, her apocalyptic vision, is but "a pre-vision of the failure of [the] process of humanization" (Hartman 1975, 132). It is its alienation from reality that, for the artist, makes its claims more compelling. For, as Sara Chetin writes, "the myth is like the deep river whose only existence is in the power of our imagination, but it is the only direction we can travel in if we don't want to remain in exile" (1989, 116). Thus, it is within the imagination that the realization of true community is held.

The tendency for critics to equate the depiction of reality with a quantitative increase in coherence—to conclude, in Mackenzie's words, that *Serowe* provides a "symmetry and balance absent in the novels" (1989a, 48)—shows a failure to comprehend the totality of Head's artistic vision. Jane Grant's comment that due to the nonfictional nature of this work, Head has imposed a severe discipline on her normal style underestimates the mediation and control of Head's other work. Grant's contention that "the words take on the cadence of a song" (1981, 55) does describe Head's distinctively euphoric portrayal of Serowe. But the way that Grant accounts for this euphoria, that it is a manifestation of the intensity of Head's feelings for Serowe, fails to comprehend that Head is portraying how she would *like* it to be rather than how it is.

There seems, on the surface, much to be celebrated in *Serowe*. There is the author's euphoric response to the old men, to the "haunting magic" that surrounds them (66). They reflect the glory of a past age, "the grandeur and charm" of an "old world on which the sun is setting" (127). It is this past age that "has created its present" (77), and Head emphasizes a natural line of progression from the work undertaken by the "age regiments" of a previous era and the "work brigades" of the present. As she explains, "It is the underlying achievement of community service which I have attempted to re-invoke from some Serowans' testimony" (77). And, as in all Head's work, there is her celebration of the pastoral. Here, it introduces the reader to Serowe:

Where is the hour of the beautiful dancing of birds in the sun-wind?

All time stands still here and in the long silences the dancing of birds fills the deep blue, Serowe sky. (ix)

As is usual in Head's writing, the Botswanan landscape provides the "stage props," the "backcloth" for her creativity. It is the evocation of a numinous, mythopoeic, physical world that introduces and concludes this otherwise sociological study. It has "the cadence of a song," but a song that is sung by the author alone, and one that is often sharply at odds with the mood or testimony of her witnesses.

The contribution of the villagers is seen by Mackenzie to provide "subject matter which is an alternative subject of scrutiny" (1989a, 46). Head herself acknowledges that the people she interviewed developed "other themes . . . themselves during the year" that she "moved in and out of their homes" (xv). Consequently, Head is never wholly in control as she is in her fictional work, and this, inevitably, makes it more difficult to maintain coherence. Head's major contribution, the "stage props" that provide the background to all her writing, provide what Head herself calls only an "unfactual and intangible" relationship to reality (Adler et al. 1989, 21). But while they function as motifs that are integral to the romanticism of her fiction, they become incongruous within a sociological study largely comprised of the more prosaic comments of local inhabitants. Her romanticism is often compromised by a harsher reality. So, although within the introduction Head enthuses that people are "strange and beautiful . . . just living" (x), and that "women just go on having babies" (xi), later in the text, local women faced with the problem of rearing children on their own present a different perspective, and agree unequivocally that "it is not a good life" (65).

Head's romanticism infuses the world inhabited by her heroes and heroines with meaning and resonance, it speaks of other realities, other possibilities, an otherworldliness that is not the subject of sociological study. This is the problem with the *Serowe* book, for while these "stage props" can be fused with the "unreal" world of her heroes" imaginations, they have little or no relevance whatsoever to the testimony of the indigenous interviewees. There is no coherence; her archetypal imagery of the Botswanan landscape cannot be "assimilated to a larger unifying category" (Frye 1975, 68). There are no heroes within *Serowe*. "Work" is important primarily for its material gains; communal work is unpopular because it is not necessarily conducive to personal profit; ultimately, spirituality is reduced to the aspirations of self-appointed priests. The testimony of Mr. Quiet bears no relationship to the meaning of religion as it pervades the lives of Head's heroes. It betrays, instead, its collusion with the external trappings of institutionalized religion and the priest's position within this hierarchy: "All the decisions for my church come to me in my dreams at night. I dream about the uniform for my church. I dream about the correct treatment for ailments. A voice talks to me all the time. I believe it is God"

(36). Consequently, Head's attempts to endow *Serowe* with the qualities that define her imagined world serve only to increase the sense of the prosaic material existence of the larger part of the community she describes.

In order to project a certain image of community, Head, despite the fact that she named her book *Serowe*, confines her attention to only a fraction of the village population. An early report written by one of Head's literary agents queried the invisibility of the majority of the inhabitants. Out of Head's estimate of a population of thirty-five thousand, approximately only one hundred are interviewed; of this number, many represent those involved in the developments in education and the job-creation schemes at Swaneng School. It is for this reason that the agent's report challenges the authenticity of *Serowe*'s claim to present "any picture at all of what modern Serowe is really like," with no attempt made to explain the current political situation and its impact on the village ("Report A," n.d.).

Indeed, in *Serowe* the modern era is only defined as the growth of van Rensburg's Swaneng Secondary School, the work brigades that he initiated to solve the problem of unemployment for school leavers, and the Boitekos, the cooperative craft groups that, like the brigades, combined training and production. The Swaneng community is made up of outsiders of diverse nationalities. And, it is here, as in all her writing, that Head's community presents a curious paradox, constituting a disparate group of individuals united in their freedom from the prescriptive codes of another society. But whereas in her other works these outsiders present the most effective challenge to the oppressions of tribal, traditional law, in *Serowe* it seems to be Head's implicit design to portray Swaneng as a community very close in spirit to a "traditional" community. And "traditional" in this instance guarantees the existence of a continuing body of values and beliefs lost to the modern world.

In *Serowe*, when Head needs to emphasis the importance of Khama's reforms she affords "tradition" her usual interpretation, and thus writes of its "narrow outlook" (xiii). However, this is a contradiction to the normal usage in *Serowe*. For here Head is more anxious to emphasize only its exotic and romantic elements, thus authorizing her eulogy of "the times and seasons for everything; the season of ploughing, the season for weddings, the season for repairing huts and courtyards" (xi). It is a golden, preindustrial age in which its inhabitants have "intimate knowledge of construction" as they build Serowe with "their bare hands and little tools—a hoe, an axe and mud" (xii), creating mud huts that have "contributed much to the serenity and order of village life" (49). Here, Head is depicting the affirmative value of work, as it imposes a human face on nature. And again, while this is a common feature of her romantic writing, it is always intrinsically linked to the aspirations of her heroes and heroines.

The inhabitants of Serowe have different priorities from Head's heroes and heroines; for them, mud huts are not necessarily an attractive proposition. Their preference for "factory-made articles" rather than "slightly rough" locally produced goods (173) is witness to the greater appeal of novelty and their eagerness for change. It is, on the other hand, the novelty of the locally produced goods that makes them so attractive to the expatriate community: "Always lingering in the finished article is the faint smell of the goat and that might be a fascination in itself, to own something "real" in this age of plastics and chemicals" (161). The international community involved in the projects was, as Head was always anxious to point out, not made up of the "die-hard white settler" but the volunteers who, like her heroes and heroines, are "some other dream of finding out about people's humanity and working *together* with them" (Appendix 11). Tom, the basis for a character in *A Question of Power* and one of the international volunteers in Serowe, wrote later of the nostalgia he felt for Serowe: "how sensuous it was. How pale and dull the UK and USA! I daydream fondly of a Serowe crowd . . . and the colours, the smells, the sensuality. Sometimes . . . I am transported back to that Elysium" (Holzinger 1974). This euphoric response holds within it the assumption that contact has been made with a "traditional" way of life, associated with living closer to the earth, an aura, or spirit, the evocation of the sensual, the smells and colors of Africa, their "nearness to living nature" (53). It becomes inseparable from an ancient way of life that in *Serowe* is persistently romanticized.

The problem in *Serowe* is that the word "traditional" is never qualified. The particular difficulty with this arises because of what Marilyn Butler sees as the supposition that there is "something readily knowable called "tradition" to which we can attribute explanatory power" (1985, 37). Furthermore, as Butler explains, "though the invented tradition may invoke an actual historical past, may indeed unearth genuine evidence about parts of the past, the claim to continuity with that past is spurious" (38). Nevertheless, the desire to reinvoke traditions is one way of "selecting and ordering the past, in order to validate ac-

tivities and people, in the present" (37). In other words, it becomes a way of maintaining one's legitimacy, a ploy of
threatened minorities. And for this small group of volunteers,
their time in Serowe is often only a pleasurable interlude. They
can engage wholeheartedly with their perception of traditional
African life without any complex analysis of the impossibility of
arresting the oncoming future. A few years after the publication
of *Serowe*, Head stated in a letter that the Swaneng project had
"collapsed completely. . . . There's nothing left of it" (Appendix
24).

In order to persist in her assumption that she is witness to a
continuing "traditional" way of life, there are many preoccupations and hopes of the indigenous population that Head simply
overlooks. Thus, she never comments on the single most commonly expressed wish of these trainees, which is to achieve the
technical skills required to survive in a rapidly changing society.
For, as Ndoro Sekwati says, speaking on behalf of her society
"any education or new skill that can be taught is sacred to us"
(162). Even when she comments on the expectations of particular groups, Head is invariably at cross-purposes with them.
About the Boiteko workers she writes:

> The wonder of it is how eager and prepared very poor people are to
> share everything with each other—some work groups like the pot-
> tery house and the stone masons have higher earnings than the oth-
> ers and often tend to carry everyone else on their backs. (172)

One Boiteko weaver offers her point of view:

> I do everything; card the wool, spin it, dye it and weave it—but I
> don't get rich . . . But what I complain about is the way Boiteko is
> organised. We share the money equally among all the members
> while the group earnings are not equal. (178)

Head is also impressed by the way the organization of Boiteko
ensures that all trainees become familiar with each step in the
production of goods; in her words, "there is magic in seeing the
whole production line" (160). This practice rescues the Boteiko
project from any similarity it might bear to the concept of developed industry. Some workers themselves are less inclined than
Head to value this aspect of Boiteko, again more concerned with
efficiency and profit. As one worker explains, "in the near future
we may have an outside group of people to specialise in washing,
carding and spinning the wool, to save time" (163). The financial

reward of the work is always stressed by the workers and always takes priority over Head's more idealistic perspective. One interviewee expresses quite unequivocally the attitude towards communal work:

> Most of the trainees were not in favor of a co-operative because trainees knew that farming is very difficult here and they feared it would be a long time before they reaped financial rewards from this experiment. (150)

What is interesting is that Head in her fictional work does recognize the more human, less idealistic motives of her protagonists" behavior. In *A Question of Power*, she portrays a Boteiko meeting called to share out the profits. She depicts the indignation of some of the members towards those whom it was considered had shirked their share of the work. Nevertheless, she does not labor either the indignation of the protestors or the discomfiture of the accused, but portrays realistically the problems inherent in any scheme designed to meet the needs of a diverse group of people. And in a comment on Serowe in one of her letters, she makes no claims of an enduring tradition of African communalism as the impetus for the projects. Instead, she writes that "none of the dreams here get Africanised because all sorts of people work together" (Appendix 14). It is a balance that, in *Serowe*, the author never achieves.

Head's account of the period of history she describes also contributes to the celebration of the "traditional." Her determination to emphasize the humanity of this past era of South African history is also an understandable feature of history writing concerned with cultural retrieval. And so Head portrays the reign of Khama the Great, leader of the Bamangwato nation from 1875 to 1923, as one of unparalleled glory. He is without doubt one of her "grand" men. She wrote in a letter:

> I looked at the old man this way and that and fell violently in love with him. He is a classic, all by himself, the lofty God of Mount Olympus, the great Lincoln of Southern Africa. (Vigne 1991, 177)

Like the heroes in her fiction, Khama and his son Tshekedi make "great gestures"; "great gestures" that "have an oceanic effect on society—they flood a whole town" (xv). In the creation of the "grand" men in her fiction, Head consistently shows that their unique personalities are due to innate, essential qualities.

However, because in writing *Serowe* she is anxious to challenge what she perceives to be the judgment so often passed by the colonialists, that Khama's humanity was an exception to the general "savagery," "abominations," and "heathendom" (3) that otherwise flourished in his land, she must claim for all Khama's people his finer qualities. This she does by asserting that "overlooked is the fact that all men are products of their environment and that only a basically humane society could have produced Khama" (3). Thus Khama's grandeur is a reflection of his society and authenticates Head's view of the eminence of this past age.

Historians of this era, and the missionaries who worked closely with Khama, do agree that he was an enlightened ruler who could see that some traditional customs, from a Christian point of view, were inhumane, especially the *bogwera* or circumcision rites in which the death of one of the initiates was obligatory. Such customs Khama abolished; he also abolished *bogadi*, the bride price, and discouraged polygamy. So in her portrayal of the reign of Khama and Tshekedi, Head insists upon the existence of a cohesive, communal past that has left an indelible imprint upon the present age. She emphasizes how Khama's reforms have shaped Serowe, how "its past has created its present" (77). These reforms included schemes to develop education by using "age-regiments" to build schools, a policy continued by his son Tshekedi. And playing a significant role, Head believes, in the evolving, modern Serowe are the educational opportunities and self-help brigades initiated by Swaneng School.

Another tendency of history writing that has particular relevance for Head's scheme is what Marilyn Butler calls "linearity"—how historians are "taught to strive for an effect of coherence, and linearity or sequence contributes massively by its apparent explanatory function" (1985, 28). In this way Head can claim a definite line of progression from Khama to Tshekedi and so to van Rensburg. So the Swaneng project is not only directly linked to Khama's reforms, but can even be seen to be dependent upon them, thus appropriating the glory of a past age. It becomes possible to achieve this sense of continuity because of what Butler defines as a common error in history writing that supposes that when "event B follows event A, the reader infers that A caused B to happen." However, as Butler points out, "Post hoc has never officially meant propter hoc" (28). Nevertheless, reviews and critical writing on *Serowe* show their dependency on this misapprehension. For Mackenzie, the "subject of ultimate interest is, in the case of *Serowe*, the past and continuing history of a village in Botswana" (1989a, 46); Ronald Blythe, in his fore-word to *Serowe*, comments "rarely has the cadence and the intel-ligence of the four generations which lived through these years been caught so accurately or so movingly" (1981, v).

In spite of this, the firsthand reportage of the interviewees continues to contradict the mood or tone that Head is intent on establishing. There are, clearly, obvious benefits to be had from the demise of traditional practices in farming. As one trainee re-flects:

> It is easy now, once I have so much knowledge, to look back on our traditional way of rearing cattle and ploughing the land and be criti-cal of all the errors we made. At that time I was only aware that our suffering was great and the work very difficult. (152)

This is the way that Head has depicted traditional farming in *When Rain Clouds Gather* where the plight of Isaac, the young herder, is a direct consequence of a stubborn resistance to new ideas.

Many of the older contributors, invited to give their view on the work regiments that flourished under Tshekedi's rule, remi-nisce on the hardships involved. One firsthand account depicts the building work as arduous, unpaid, and compulsory. Mem-bers were expected to supply their own food. Lenyeletse Seretse recounts the suffering endured when rations ran out:

> Soon, we were all starving. Some members of the regiment had brought their horses. They died. We ate them. We ate wild rabbits or anything we could catch in the bush. So many men wanted to back out under such conditions but there wasn't any means to do so. Men who left a work regiment were put on trial and punished. (81)

There are witnesses, however, who praise Tshekedi's endeavor. One of the pioneer teachers at Moeng College defends Tshekedi against the charge sometimes made against him that he was "a cruel man, an exploiter of the people, and so on," because, as she claims, "no other man cared for us as much as he did" (85). Head is aware of the controversy surrounding Tshekedi's employment of the work regiments but concludes, nonetheless, that "it is one of the most glorious aspects of Serowe's history" (76).

Thus, in *Serowe* the reader is encouraged to assume an or-ganic connection between Tshekedi's work regiments and van Rensburg's training schemes for school leavers. Even if the reader is prepared to accept that Tshekedi's regiments functioned in a spirit of self-denial and communal pride, the fact that this labor was compulsory and often very arduous offers an immediate contrast with van Rensburg's scheme, which included payment whenever possible but, above all, provided training for future employment. The brigades flourished because of their emphasis on personal and not community achievement. As one trainee says, "If we do not find work after training, it is of no value" (161). From van Rensburg's own account, it is clear that he would not have agreed with Paddy Kitchen's conclusion that his brigades were "a natural progression from Tshekedi's work regiments" (1981, 23). Tshekedi's schemes grew internally, from the immediate needs of the community for buildings, for wells, for roads; van Rensburg's was an externally sanctioned idea to develop the resources of the people and the community. Also, it can be seen, from van Rensburg's account of his work in *The Serowe Brigades*, that he feared that should there be any suspicion that he was attempting to emulate Tshekedi's work regiments, his own schemes would be doomed from the start.

> The concept of voluntary communal work on projects is not easily accepted; people are very dubious that the work will be their own, subject to their control. They have no experience of it; traditional work of this kind before too often ended up for the personal benefit of a chief. There are suspicions of hidden motives of exploitation. (1978, 10)

Van Rensburg's analysis portrays the proprietary rights exercised by powerful chieftains in traditional society. It is an issue that Head condemns in her fictional writing.

In her earlier work, there is a different image of the "old man" that is more consistently invoked. He is the "man with no shoes" who portrays an amorphous mass of humanity, usually the victim of oppression, within hierarchical structures of society. In *Maru* he is the "primitive" Masarwa; in *A Question of Power* he represents the poor of Africa. Invariably his age symbolizes his familiarity with a world of experience, but nevertheless he maintains a core of natural but silenced humanity. When in Head's short stories her old men are given an individual voice, their views are seen to represent the closed minds of the "die-hard traditionalists" (*ABC*, 86) who stand in the way of enlightenment and progress. In *Serowe*, it is as the representatives of "old Africa" that they are venerated: "the lines of extreme quiet and humility on their faces" are evidence of their faith in a "whole body of holy customs and beliefs locked away in their subconscious minds" (67). The model for all the old men in *Serowe* is Khama the Great. Head writes in a letter, "First I had used my intuition about them. I didn't know Khama. I couldn't link it to anything, but now I see that they have his beautiful face" (Appendix 10). So "the older people all look like Khama. They move around quietly, Bible in hand" (58).

On some occasions her tone of approval is manifestly inappropriate for the scene she is describing. When she interviews Ramosamo Kebonang, a man who claims to be over one hundred years old, she writes "A number of servants moved quietly around the yard, busy with chores. They looked like Basarwa people" (69). The presence of these servants, she concludes, reflects Kebonang's importance: "he must have been a real V.I.P. in his heyday," she notes, adding that he is a "rather scornful old man" (69). She records what takes place, but in her summing up of the day's encounter she dwells on the impression she has of "stepping back into an ancient world when everything had been balanced and sane; a daily repetitive rhythm of work and kindly humorous chatter" (70). She quite overlooks the status of the Basarwa, the "slave" race of the Botswanan people, while at the same time emphasizing the importance of freedom for a dignified existence: "The white man hasn't trampled here on human dignity" (70).

This rewriting of her interview with Kebonang reflects Head's determination to celebrate this community. A day's interviewing that has gone well is later euphorically relived and recounted, and tribute is paid to the hospitality she has received. There is no doubting the sincerity of Head's appreciation of any welcome she is offered, an appreciation that is reflected in her determination to present each of her interviewees with a copy of the book when it was finally published. And Head was clearly gratified when those interviewed chose a copy of the book instead of a cash payment she was otherwise prepared to make (Appendix 24). Head's letters show that she had very few friends among the local people. She never learned Tswana, and so many of the interviews she conducted required the services of an interpreter. This fact alone would have increased Head's sense of her outsider status and perhaps made her feel more grateful for any welcome she received. Certainly, it is the friendship shown by these old men that Head responds to, and so issues that have been subjected to a complex analysis in her fictional work are ignored or dismissed in her summary of the day's proceedings.

In this way Head is able to preserve her euphoric image of Serowe as a cohesive, traditional community steeped in the glory of a past age.

At the end of *Serowe*, a "village" book that bears evidence of the personal contact Head has made with many people, she begins her epilogue with these lines from Rupert Brooke's poem, "The Great Lover":

> Oh, never a doubt, but somewhere, I shall wake,
> And give what's left of love again, and make
> New friends, now strangers . . .

It would appear that Head's contact with the people of Serowe has merely served to confirm her outside status, her aloneness. The poem she quotes shows that, for herself, fulfillment can be discovered only in another place and in another time. This is the literary resolution in all her fictional writing, and it is a coherent feature of the aspirations of her heroes and heroines as they face the alienating hostility of a disintegrated society. But here *Serowe* is supposed to be a sociological study of a community in which "each member is known to one another, the latest scandal, the latest love affair" (xii).

One of Head's letters expresses quite clearly her state of mind during the time in which *Serowe* was written. The book was, she claims, "really a temporary retreat from my own tortures" (Appendix 8). She was also aware of the kind of response that *Serowe* would receive, "the gushing tributes" and "the relief" that at last she was describing what was "really Botswana." But, as she adds, "they wouldn't know that for three quarter part of the time it is anguish to stay alive" (Appendix 8). The problem for Head is, that in spite of herself, she is often describing what is "really Botswana"; the comments of the indigenous population speak for themselves. Head's supposition that her romantic interludes and the aspirations of her interviews can be integrated is misjudged. For only a world defined entirely on her own terms can provide the coherence necessary to satisfy her own personal needs. The writing of *Serowe*, a sociological study, undermines Head's artistic endeavors, but in its contradictions, in its inconsistencies, it highlights Head's literary achievement in her other work.

8

A Bewitched Crossroad

I have always reserved a special category for myself, as a writer—
that of a pioneer blazing a new trail into the future. It would seem
as though Africa rises at a point in history when world trends are
more hopefully against exploitation, slavery and oppression—all of
which have been synonymous with the name, Africa. I have recorded
whatever hopeful trend was presented to me in an attempt to shape
the future, which I hope will be one of dignity and compassion. (*AWA*,
64)

A BEWITCHED CROSSROAD, WHICH HEAD CALLS AN "HISTORICAL
novel" and which her earliest biographers refer to as a "semi-
fictionalised history" (Gardner and Scott 1986, 7), achieves
Head's purpose—to record hopeful trends. From a historical perspective, Head burdens herself with the formidable task of re-
counting the history of the Bamangwato tribe from 1800–1895.
As Head explains in the foreword, the Bamangwato are "all the
refugees and diverse nations absorbed into the small Bangwato
clan during the era of nation building by chiefs Sekgoma I and
Khama III" (7). She also acknowledges in the foreword the origin
of her fictional hero Sebina and his son—that they are inspired
by an essay, "The History of the Makalaka" written by Peter Ma-
zebe Sebina.

In *A Bewitched Crossroad,* Sebina is a chief of one of the small
clans that seeks the protection of Khama III. As his life story
unfolds, it tells of a pattern of internal tribal disruption caused
by conflicts surrounding succession to leadership, the warmon-
gering between tribes, and wholesale slaughter by the Matabele.
Head builds on the idea of the constant migration caused by various conflicts, evoking a parallel between Sebina's clan and the
wandering tribes of Israel. It is Sebina who secures the destiny
of his people. As their patriarch, "greatly aged and completely
white-haired" (60), he delivers them safely to the promised land.
With Sebina, the reader witnesses the impact of Christianity

and the momentous success of Khama's negotiations to maintain Bechuanaland's continuation as a British protectorate, and thus to defend it from the designs of the British South Africa Company.

While this historical survey foregrounds the "hopeful trend[s]" of recorded political negotiations, Sebina's role within the unfolding of the drama is to personify all that is sublime and exalted. He is the guarantor of humanity in his lifetime, and his death is not an end but a meeting place of past and future in Head's metaphoric temporal crossroads. He dies in the knowledge that his heir, Mazebo, who "reflected the world of his grandfather where all life and thought floated with graceful ease on a broad, flowing, peaceful river" (82) will "see the sunrise" for him tomorrow (195). The qualities for which Sebina stands will endure as surely as the sun will rise. Head's endeavor is to narrate the implications of a past time for a present and a future existence. The title of this history speaks of a bewitched crossroad. It records a moment of significant merging, and one which, in that it is "bewitched," heralds the sublime potential of a future Utopia.

HISTORY AND THE SUBLIME

The merging of fact and fiction, upon which Head's vision depends, is seen by Mackenzie to be responsible for the creation of a novel that is "deeply flawed" (1989a, 47), failing both as "a piece of fiction" and as a "thoroughgoing historical work" (47). Its failure as history is due, Mackenzie argues, to the absence of the "dry unremittingly factual quality of the school text-book" (18). He quotes Barry Ronge's contention that what is frustrating about *A Bewitched Crossroad* is that

> A special effort is needed to perceive the different social and religious organisation of these people, and the names are tongue-twisting mind-benders. It is disheartening when you have painstakingly re-read several pages, sorted out the names of tribes and chiefs in your mind, only to have them perish forever on the very next page. (Ronge 1985, 27)

Most readers would agree that Ronge's comment is justified, especially if, anticipating a novel, they are not expecting to have to engage with the complexities of nineteenth-century tribal dispersal and integration. Indeed, *A Bewitched Crossroad* does, too often, read like a history textbook.

What seems to be more clearly at the heart of Mackenzie's criticism is that Head's willingness to use fiction, especially her acknowledged debt to fiction, makes her "vulnerable to the charge of masquerading as historical fact what is in reality little more than conjecture" (1989a, 18). Thus, Head is compromising any claim to authority by incorporating a fictional element within her historical overview. And even more tendentiously, this fictional element is deeply implicated with Head's endeavor to inscribe what Mackenzie calls her "highly partisan" interests (48). History is not being accorded the objective analysis to which it is accustomed. Here Mackenzie is conceding the widely held view of a distinct epistemological difference between fiction and history—"history" is true and objective, "fiction" is untrue and subjective. By confusing the two disparate conventions, Head's novel is a literary failure.

Most readers would also agree with Mackenzie that *A Bewitched Crossroad* is not a success, but this is not necessarily for the reasons that he suggests. For the problem seems to be not that Head fails to identify the two disparate conventions, but that the line between fact and fiction is too clearly demarcated. So, paradoxically, what is missing in *A Bewitched Crossroad* is the order and coherence of historical narrative—the "story" that postmodernists say has been imposed upon history since its scientific disciplining in the eighteenth and nineteenth centuries. What Head offers instead is an unmanageable mass of historical names, dates, and events (of which Ronge complains); but more significantly, the order which she then inscribes, clearly separated from the historical chronicle, is explicitly of her own making, engineered by the interpolation of the fictional hero into her narrative. So what is important is that in spite of the flaws that Mackenzie says are "commonly noted by critics" (1989a, 18), Head's version of history, for postmodern historiographers like Hayden White and Keith Jenkins, holds as much "truth" as any history can lay claim to. For as Jenkins argues, all history is "a narrative discourse, the content of which is as much imagined/ invented as found" (1995, 134).

Jenkins, using White's analysis in *The Content of the Form*, discusses how White deploys the postmodern theory of the textually of all writing in order to deconstruct the old certainties of orthodox historical narrative. White argues that all writers of history, of whatever ideological persuasion and in spite of their claim to objectivity, all read the past from a "present-centred-ness" deeply inscribed with their own ideological views. To justify their particular and often disguised ideology, they impose order on the past, thus "pushing out the rhetorical, the speculative, the incomprehensible and the sublime" (Jenkins 1995, 141). White's signaling of the narrativity of these histories is not born of the nihilism with which postmodernism is often charged. As Jenkins argues, White challenges their claim to "truth" convinced that the eradication of such qualities has created historical narratives that are "a general ideological instrument of anti-utopian closure" (Jenkins 1995, 143). And to deconstruct their certainties is to open up new possibilities for "visionary politics." As White explains:

> insofar as historical events and processes become understandable, as conservatives maintain, or explainable, as radicals believe them to be, they can never serve as a basis for a visionary politics more concerned to endow social life with meaning than with beauty. In my view, the theorists of the sublime had correctly divined that whatever dignity and freedom human beings could lay claim to could come only by way of what Freud called a "reaction-formation" to an apperception of history's meaninglessness. (1987, 72)

This is where White's theories have relevance for Head's view of the use of history. For all Head's writing shows her reliance upon the "sublime" to justify any meaningful optimism for the future. Her last novel, which uses the death of her hero to immortalize the humanity for which he stands, reorganizes the parameters of historical narrative to finalize her project. As Jenkins comments on White's endeavor, the presence of the sublime is a "useful fiction" on which to "'base' movements towards a more generous emancipation and empowerment than is currently in place in order to realise a radical, liberal—but not much detailed—utopia" (1995, 145).

Maud Ellmann explains how "the sublime" has become a confusing term. It referred in eighteenth-century aesthetics to "the quality of awesome grandeur, as distinguished from the merely beautiful," the feeling of grandeur "aroused by nature's incalculable power" (1994, 174). In this discussion, Ellmann quotes Kant's description of the sublime as that sense which can be aroused by "the mind's exultation in its own rational faculties, in its ability to think a totality that cannot be taken in through the senses." Thus, she argues, "the Sublime involves two contradictory emotions, one of awe, one of omnipotence: the mind, appalled by the experience of vastness, triumphs nonetheless in its ability to contemplate the magnitude of its beyond" (174). Much of Head's earlier writing has concerned itself with the interaction of these themes, Freud's "omnipotence of thought," man's objective wonder in the face of the natural world, but fused with this an extreme subjectivity that absorbs the power of the natural into his own being. It accounts, in Maru's case, for an overwhelming sense of his own omnipotence. It becomes the principle through which Head can create her apocalyptic vision.

TO AVENGE THE PEOPLE

There is no doubt that, as Mackenzie claims, Head does hold "highly partisan" views, views that she acknowledges in her writing, in interviews, and on the platform at international conferences. Feeling no obligation to disguise these views, Head is open in her condemnation of those she feels are guilty of exploiting the people of Bechuanaland. In an article she wrote in 1984, she states a major concern: "the situation of black people in South Africa, their anguish and their struggles made its deep impress on me" (*AWA*, 86). Mackenzie's criticism of this overt subjectivity in *A Bewitched Crossroad* is based on a widely held view that truthful history can only be produced by those writers possessed of a detached and objective relationship with the past. However, as has already been discussed, postmodern historiographers question the very notion of objectivity, finding it most clearly lacking in writers who assume that their own beliefs and values are not ideological, but natural and true. Moreover, it is subjectivity that can produce a historiography that is "charged with avenging the people" (Jenkins 1995, 143). And for Head, like Jenkins, this does not mean advocating revolution or prescriptive forms of government, nor is it achieved by a false reading of the past; indeed, it is because Head has committed herself to recording all the historical facts she has discovered from her meticulous research that *A Bewitched Crossroad* often makes for such tedious reading.

For Head has set herself a formidable task, and although there are no footnotes indicating the sources of particular data and no index, there is a bibliography listing the primary and secondary sources Head has used. The imperial expansion of the nineteenth century meant that South Africa was confronted with a great deal of political, social, and economic upheaval, and in an attempt to unravel the outcome of this for the Bamangwato, Head re-tracks into the past to explain an exhaustive catalogue of occur-rences—the settlement of the British and Dutch, the incursions of the Boer Trekkers into South Africa, the discovery of gold and diamonds, the acquisitive schemes of the British South Africa Company under Rhodes's direction, the conflict between Boer and British interests, and the political transactions involved in the creation of the Protectorate of Bechuanaland.

Nonetheless, in spite of Head's endeavors to provide a system-atic account of historical events, it is only by incorporating into this "a recovery of the historical sublime" (Jenkins 1995, 143), that an alternative future can be imagined. The writing of *A Be-witched Crossroad* shows that Head's design "to avenge the peo-ple" is achieved by the assimilation of her archetypal imagery into the re-creation of a past time in which the sublime event, the quest to save Bechuanaland from the clutches of the South Africa Company, augurs well for the future.

The importance of the hero is paramount in any such process. Jenkins believes (with Northrop Frye) that in the romance mode of emplotment the hero effects

> a heroic type of release from, or transcendence of, the situations in which individuals or groups or nation, etc., have found themselves. These will be emplotments which stress the triumph of, say, good over evil, of virtue over vice, of the struggle and (maybe) victory of the oppressed over their oppressor(s). (Jenkins 1995, 162)

The hero of this endeavor is Khama III, the humane, Christian leader who withstood the might of imperial expansion to negoti-ate for his people their protection from tribal aggressors, acquis-itive Boers, and British settlers. It was Head's admiration for Khama that inspired her to write a novel based on his life; Head's biographer, Gillian Eilersen, recounts how Head planned to call the novel "Mother Winter" (1995, 261), a title of great re-spect given to Khama by the Bamangwato in a praise poem. The choice of a different title reflects Head's concern to portray the enormous significance of his reign. She describes how "the image of Khama . . . fell upon the land of northern Bechuanaland like a magic bewitchment" (57). It is he alone who is responsible for the destiny of his people. Before his coming, to the aggressor or the adventurer, "the indigenous people did not really exist, they had no power, they were heathens" (56). With the installation of

Khama as chief of the Bamangwato, "the image of the perfect black man [was] found at last"; he "was to create a pause in the activities of Europeans" (56).

As a story that tells of the deliverance of a nation from the evil designs of an oppressor, Head's rewriting of this phase of history sometimes reads like a contest between good and evil. And it is in the plotting of the story that deals with Khama as the heroic savior of his people that the aggressor is portrayed as an archetypal villain. Cecil Rhodes is indubitably Head's arch-villain. As Frye argues, the degree of the enemy's villainy bears a quantitative relationship with the portrayal of the hero's greatness: "the more attributes of divinity" granted to the hero, "the more the enemy will take on demonic mythical qualities" (1990, 187). Head never disguises the contempt she feels for Rhodes and his "feverish planning" (185) motivated entirely by "voracious" greed (184). She quotes the most extreme of his statements to show to what lengths he was prepared to go in his exploitation of the black people: "I have taken everything from them but the air" (193), and "If the canting niggers won't work, horsewhip them" (184). Thus, Rhodes is "an evil genius who looked on the resources of southern Africa as his own personal possession" (185). Head's portrayal of Rhodes as wholly evil reflects the role of the villain in romance, in which, as Frye argues the "central form" is "dialectical." As he explains: "everything is focussed on a conflict between the hero and his enemy, and all the reader's values are bound up with the hero" (1990, 187). Writing to "avenge the people" justifies the categorization of characters as either good or evil. The hero's success is the substance of the romance, and so Bechuanaland "remained black man's country" (196). That it was also a "bewitched crossroad" (196) describes also the power of the archetypal hero to free the sublime as the basis for hope for the future.

A literal account of this phase of African history cannot ignore the endless saga of internal plunder and strife, and Head does not. She describes the way "brother poisoned brother in the fight for power" (91), how war was endemic. "War, and it seemed unending, became the order of the day" (22). Head invokes a world of conquest and victory, but in her portrayal this world is one in which glory and plunder are one and the same. Tribal kingdoms become a "wonderland":

> drawing men like moths to a flame; a wonderland of fearful gods and terrible justice, but withal a world of discipline and order where men lived out their lives with thought and sweet communication. (61–62)

Within this novel, there is much in the tone of Head's description of the intertribal wars that invokes Mofolo's portrayal of Chaka's power and stature, a portrayal that Ezekiel Mphahlele argues evokes a Faustian hero (1962, 207). The lust for power that drives these leaders is not treated with the same authorial disapproval meted out to Rhodes for his similar ambitions. Instead, Head's description of the "great Mambo" celebrates his omnipotence: "Mambo was the leader of all rituals and magic in the land. . . . He was dreaded and feared and only had to point a finger at an object if he desired its death" (13). And so, Head concludes, "life was a pleasant round of sweet and courteous exchanges between men" (13).

Head here is dealing with the more distant past, an age that belongs more readily to a world of legend and myth, and one that accommodates more comfortably great warriors and legendary leaders, infamous for their display of superhuman power. And there is, implicit within Head's portrayal, a feeling of awe and wonder at their majesty—"the delight . . . one might feel in contemplating 'the uncertain anarchy of the moral world'" (Jenkins 1995, 141). The ideological implications of this, for a postmodern historiographer, is that instead of regarding history as merely a documentation of "politically domesticated" facts, to the exclusion of the sublime, it becomes possible to meditate "on the confusion that the "spectacle" of history displayed." Thus, the recognition of this confusion could

> produce a sense of a specific type of human freedom which, insofar as it did so, made "world history" appear to him as a "sublime object," transforming the "pure daemon" in human kind into grounds for belief in a "dignity" unique to man. (Jenkins 1995, 141)

In Head's account, in her determination to show that the history of Botswana was not "the great arid wasteland the history books would have us believe" (*AWA,* 87), she provides a past world that resounds with the glories and triumphs of legendary heroes and heroines.

Head's portrayal of this wonderland of plunder and strife does not invalidate the importance she attaches to Khama's significance as a humane ruler. Inspired to reform the traditional laws of his ancestors, Khama faces the opposition of the "die-hard traditionalists" (86). Thus, he becomes the archetypal hero who, in Neumann's view, is charged with the task of changing the patriarchal—the "old law"—of his society (1973, 174). This law is represented in Khama's society by "old men with fierce, malevolent faces, intent on shutting out any thing foreign and unfamiliar" (86); Khama's divergence from accepted custom means, as Maruapula interprets it, that Khama "insults the ancestors" (171). To see ancestral law implicated with "malevolence" is the way that Head usually interprets it, and her heroes always present the most effective challenge to the obduracy of these traditions. And this is what Khama's reforms effect. But although, as the author shows, Khama is "completely at peace with himself, secure in power and reassured that all his actions were the right ones" (65), nonetheless, like the earlier heroes Maru and Makhaya, who travel "a lonely road," Khama's obligations leave him with "the lonely look of a man who has forsaken the gods of his forefathers" (98). For the sake of his tribe there are sacrifices that Khama has to make, but it is the acceptance of his responsibilities that define his heroic stature.

Khama's reforms reflect the humanity of Christianity and effectively eradicate the more brutal aspects of tribal custom. He abolishes the secret initiation ceremonies, human sacrifice, and any traditional ritual that threatens "the freedom of the people" (55). This idea of freedom and tolerance is implicit within Head's portrayal of the changes that Khama imposes, and it is juxtaposed against the fear and suspicion (171) that had compelled the people's obedience to their ancestral laws. The abolition of *bogadi,* the bride price, paves the way for equal rights for women. Head measures the potential significance of this move by stressing the opportunity it opens up for a more mutual exchange between the sexes: "a relationship of love stimulated by the beginnings of dialogue between a man and a woman" (166). In *A Bewitched Crossroad,* Head constantly uses the word "dialogue" to convey the sense of the free play and exchange of thoughts and ideas:

> This dialogue is like a wave that builds up towards a climax or peak and then crumbles or disperses itself, while a new dialogue or interest takes its place. But before that dispersal or crumbling, a man or men in the society suddenly express the total perfection of that dialogue. (123)

The hero's role is to express the "total perfection" of the age that he represents, and this description of "dialogue" is also a version of the Hegelian dialectic, the reconciliation of opposites to produce the most perfect synthesis. Anticipating, as it does, a movement towards greater freedom, it reflects a measure of trust that the passing of time will produce a more tolerant worldview. It promises a process of becoming, an essential feature of any utopian realization. It suggests, in this novel, the function of history for the author. And, as usual for Head, it is only her archetypal heroes, ahistorical and universal beings, who have this power to reform and regenerate.

Clearly, Khama is the historical hero of *A Bewitched Crossroad*. Nonetheless, the clearest indication of Head's dependency on the sublime, upon which she seeks to establish her own formulaic expression of utopian fulfillment, rests in her transformation of the facts of history to create an essentially fictional hero: Sebina, another of her "grand" men. This does not diminish the importance of Khama, and indeed, Sebina is credited with many of Khama's qualities. Sebina recognizes their mutual compatibility: "He liked that austere face, cold and bleak in its goodness. It matched an austerity and goodness within his own nature" (65). However, it is only in the creation of her fictional characters that Head can establish the unique individuality of her heroes.

In her research into the details of Khama's rule, it would have been evident to Head from her reading of a book she lists in her bibliography, Anthony Sillery's *Founding a Protectorate*, that Khama was "never in any case disposed to tolerate opposition"; he simply regarded his "discontented relatives as dangerous rebels . . . making their life intolerable in all the ways open for that purpose to a powerful tribal leader" (1965, 207). She admits in personal letters that her earlier portrayal of Khama was often "gushy," and that in fact Khama was "very tricky material indeed. Some of him was good and some of him was very tricky" (Eilersen 1995, 261). What she refers to as Khama's trickiness in personal letters is defined in *A Bewitched Crossroad* as "cleverness." However, Maruapula, the character who is anxious to provide Sebina with evidence of this aspect of Khama's personality, disapproves of the way in which Khama "has seized immense power to himself" (100). So "clever," here, means devious or manipulative. As Maruapula tells Sebina:

> "You will have an opportunity to observe his methods at first hand, uncle. We never win against him! If he wants to abolish bogadi, he will abolish bogadi and we will help him to do it!" (168)

Head vindicates the autocracy of her earlier hero, Maru, because the end justifies the means. Nevertheless, to guarantee the survival of his idealism it is necessary that he abdicate all claims to authority, imperative that he avoids all the responsibilities and contingencies of rule that might compromise his values. This kind of escape from reality is not possible for Khama. As a "great lawgiver" (171) he, like Maru, is not motivated by self-interest; but unlike Maru, as a historical figure, his sense of duty ties him to his tribe rather than to an otherworldly place.

Even Khama's commitment to Christianity can be interpreted as careful and deliberated diplomacy. Head would have been conversant with the view that conversion to Christianity became a ploy of tribal leaders anxious to have a missionary in their midst to act as an advisor and intermediary between the indigenous people and the growing number of Europeans interfering in their affairs. Sillery comments on the consequences of this: "We may therefore doubt that many conversions sprang from reasons of faith" (1954, 76). Although Khama was widely considered to be an exception to this rule—and Head emphasizes this in *A Bewitched Crossroad*, stressing his sincerity—his role as a leader would have made it difficult for him to deviate. It was above all the respect with which Khama was held by the London Missionary Society and their powerful lobby in Britain that made it possible for him to negotiate politically for his people. No matter what Khama's deepest convictions might have been, it was politically expedient for him to assert his Christian faith.

As a fictional character, Sebina is free from the historical accountability that confines Khama and the other warrior kings— nor is he bound by the parameters of reality that define the interviewees in *Serowe*. Thus, he becomes the embodiment of the particular qualities of humility, goodness, and tolerance essential to Head's project. It is in this relative freedom of thought enjoyed by Sebina, a freedom not possible for one with responsibilities such as Khama's, that Head can pursue and concentrate on her persistent preoccupation, of outlining the essential qualities necessary to break the vicious cycle of will-to-power. Although Head maintains that as a "great lawgiver," Khama gives back "weight by weight . . . all that he takes away" (171), his first priority is to maintain law and order. Sebina, on the other hand, can reflect on the possibility for "happy," "corrupt," and "human" (56) to share a harmonious coexistence. He misses the "hearty laughter" of the trader expelled by Khama for selling beer, and reflects, "People who engaged in illegal activities often had a great deal of charm" (143).

Sebina welcomes the coming of Christianity into Bamangwatoland. To him it represents not a dogmatic creed of spiritual beliefs but a "new learning" that, in its "compassion for all human life" (50) and interrogation of current moral values, counters the rigid and often inhumane tribal traditions. But Christianity also presents a body of new ideas with the potential to stimulate further dialogue. This is its attraction for Sebina, not as a closed system of beliefs to replace ancestral laws but one whose very existence implies the relativity of all truths. John Mackenzie, a resident missionary, wins the approval of the tribe because he accepts this relativity: his "sympathies were broad and generous, his Christianity flexible and adaptable to all situations" (48). Head does not condemn Christianity, but only those who demand an unquestionable acceptance of its dogma. There is the teacher who believes that it is the duty of his pupils not to "question the ways of God, but to accept them" (135); and the missionary, James Hepburn, is "driven by an obsessive belief in the righteousness of his own cause . . . a human personality who was impervious to dialogue and exchange of thought" (73). Sebina, in his confrontations with Hepburn, shows himself to be the wiser man as he "graciously" holds "open the door to future communication, to learning, to dialogue" (73). Indeed, it is Sebina and not Hepburn who can comprehend "the magnanimity of Christianity" (132). Sebina can reconcile the religious beliefs of his ancestors and the new teaching of Christianity and affirm that their difference is "only a question of names" (130).

The comparison that is drawn between the two heroes, Khama and Sebina, constantly emphasizes the relative freedom of thought enjoyed by Sebina. He can entertain contradictory ideas without feeling intimidated: "Why did this town of Shoshong cause so many unexpected and contradictory thoughts and emotions to rush through him? He felt so peaceful" (97). It is these contradictions and confusions that give him optimism and peace of mind: "All new life depended on tomorrow, so that it was with vague, confused dreams and a sense of hope that he awoke at dawn to the continuous sound of bird-calls" (64).

It is clear that Sebina reflects the consciousness of his creator. Portrayed as one who recognizes the significance of historical landmarks that bode well for the future, he is "dazzled and blinded" by his participation in the signing of the Protectorate agreement. As Joyce Johnson observes, Head here is searching for "meaningful patterns" within history (1990, 129). Sebina reflects on the significance of events: "His final journey at such a great age was like an atonement for the past sufferings his people had endured" (64). Thus, the wanderings of Sebina's people are given symbolic resonance: "As they turned their gaze toward those mysterious dreaming mountains and flat open plains, they did not know then that the spirit of Ulysses moved them as a people" (9). Head endeavors to portray the Bamangwato as a people with a destiny.

It is in this narrative, which connects Sebina's present with the past on the one hand and with his hopes for the future on the other, that Head continues her tenuous examination of what, in the end, becomes her summation of the ideal condition for human progress—the need to free one's mind of its "shackles." As Johnny, Head's first hero, claims, "To me the history of the world is the history of man's search for freedom" (*C*, 87). And in Head's final novel, Sebina is the ideal representative of Head's belief in the correlation between the illimitable bounds of knowledge and human freedom: "He was the glorious representative of the past and tradition and yet he hungered for the new and unknown" (63). Richard Rorty interprets the primacy afforded the idea of quest as the premise upon which utopias are created. He argues that "the realisation of utopias, and the envisaging of still further utopias" is "an endless process—an endless, proliferating realisation of freedom, rather than a convergence toward an already existing Truth" (1989, xvi).

It is as a visionary rather than as a historical character that Sebina fulfils this role. Within this narrative, the analogy that is drawn between the cyclical movement of nature and the movement of history foregrounds the restitutive and eternal promise of sunrise. And Sebina is the hero in this solar myth. Head's motifs and archetypes here, as in all her writing, establish the hero's inseparability from the natural world, with its continuity, with its potential for rebirth:

> The old man had lived with birds all his life and their song was unchanging. They sang low notes, high notes and long slow notes but the song was always the same. They sang, "Happy, happy, happy!" all the time. . . . It had not mattered where the old man had migrated with his people, he had always looked out over an unchanging view of flat open plains and dreaming hills. (163)

And as religion, for Sebina, is most adequately explained as "a spirit who dwells in all things" (130), the divinity of the natural world is also confirmed. It is a form of religion that needs to be distinguished from that which is used to "reinforce the social contract" and as Frye argues it is only "in the eternal and infinite context that is given it by religion" that an apocalypse is possible (1975, 58). Like the immortality with which Head endows the natural world, like the birds who forever sing the same song, it is this animate, liberating, daemon quality that must survive for the benefit of a future time. The description of Sebina's death, the merging of his consciousness with the sun's "blazing orb of light" (195), his grandson's promise "I'll see the sunrise for you tomorrow," is the way that Head focuses on the validity of the sublime that Sebina has symbolized throughout the novel.

WRITING HISTORY

A postmodern historiography, in its deconstruction of the certainties of history writing, accommodates the kind of historical reportage with which Head engages. It acknowledges the present-centered account of the past, when the ideological persuasions of the author will reorder history writing in order to retrieve the past for an oppressed people. The significance of past events is heightened when it becomes the subjective response of characters to such phenomena that is communicated to the readers. Head also dramatizes the recognition of history as event. Sebina's moment of wonder comes when he is invited to add his mark to the document of 1885 that defined the terms of the original Protectorate agreement:

> that day he knew that a new era had begun; the document he had touched had preserved the deliberations of the day forever, never to be lost or changed in the faulty memories of men. (120)

Not only is Sebina conscious that this document is a testament that spells out hopeful trends for the future, but it is also witness of Khama's stature as a leader of his people. It was indeed the existence of records such as this that enabled Head herself to write a history that could "avenge the people." And one of the positive effects of the arrival of Christianity into Khama's country was the development of literacy: Moffat's Tswana translation of the Bible was the first reading material available to the Bamangwato. Sebina reflects how literacy develops "the calm, thoughtful rule of the mind" (121), the power of the written word lying with its ability to make accessible a multiplicity of ideas and interests. In contrast to this, those whom Head condemns, the Matabele and Rhodes, are possessed of "an inhuman brute force, that was

almost a kind of dull illiteracy" (156). For the Bamangwato, learning to read the Bible led to the opportunity to extend one's education and ultimately to have recourse to "human thought, now so
preserved like the fresh greens of early summer" (79).

A *Bewitched Crossroad* is the only one of Head's novels in
which she writes of the death of the hero. It is also her final
novel. Head endows Sebina's death with a sublime and exalted
significance, for she is not writing about death but about continuity. The inclusion of Sebina's story, the interpolation of the explicit fictive element within this history, indicates the author's
recognition and acceptance of her own ideological interests, that
she is in control of her own discourse and that she has achieved
"a higher level of self-consciousness than most of us currently
occupy" (Jenkins 1995, 177). It is interesting to read in one of
Head's letters that when she first decided to write history, she
anticipated that in contrast to her fiction, which often led to
"very strong mental attitudes, often not corresponding to real
life," nonfiction would make her "sound less insane" (Appendix
9). But clearly in her creation of A *Bewitched Crossroad,* Head
does not in fact depart from the priorities and concerns that inform all her writing. There is no doubt that she identifies closely
with Sebina. Maud Ellmann's argument that "in the struggle to
pre-empt the past," the "latecomer strives to anticipate his fore-
runner so as to invent himself anew, self-born and self-begotten"
(1994, 174), might explain Head's own subjective relationship
with this last novel. For this novel is the last, and the last of a
group of novels that have all marked "process." The point of
process that has been reached in this novel may pronounce on
the inevitability of death, but it is death only as it contributes to
the ever-turning cycle of renewal and rebirth.

Also in this narrative, Head celebrates the power of literacy to
preserve. And what she preserves, through her enduring archetypes, is the idea of an elusive desire for the concept of an eternal
and infinite oneness of man and nature. This kind of resolution,
this resort to an apocalyptic vision is seen by Hartman to signal
the failure of humanization (1975, 132). This describes Head's
apperception of the real world in which she lives and for which
her art compensates. But her vision, preserved as "human
thought," opens up "new worlds," which, as Sebina reflects, is
"the greatest, the highest duty of mankind" (132–33). Thus, A
Bewitched Crossroad, using a different convention from earlier
works, addresses itself to a future time. Head writes in expectation that "humanity . . . lives by memory of itself, that is history"
(Milosz 1990, 362).

Conclusion

Head always claimed that "every story or book starts with what I need" (Fradkin 1978, 430). This need gives shape to writing that touches on the personal, the local, the political, and the universal. These, indeed, are not separate issues, because Head's own personal circumstances were fashioned by the oppressive, racist regime into which she was born. Even more far-reaching than this, however, was Head's apperception of the fundamental cause of the oppression around her—the endemic nature of evil:

> I perceived the ease with which one could become evil and I associated evil in my mind with the acquisition of power.
> This terror of power and an examination of its stark horrors created a long period of anguish in my life and forced out of me some strange novels that I had not anticipated writing.
> It was almost as though the books wrote themselves, propelled into existence by the need to create a reverence for human life in an environment and historical circumstances that seem to me a howling inferno. (*AWA*, 77)

Thus, to write of oppression, both private and public, was a powerful imperative. In Head's first novel, *The Cardinals*, which she wrote while living in South Africa, the heroine, Mouse, is an emotionally disturbed, colored orphan who escapes the slum. Later in life, as a journalist she can write of the direct result of the dehumanizing apartheid laws that bring its victims daily to the courts. Johnny, a fellow journalist, sees far beyond local and national oppression, and consequently expresses his belief that the history of the world is the quest for human freedom, and this endeavor is bound up with the function of art, the purpose of writing. Head is defining connections between writing and the creation of other worlds, and significantly, at this early stage, it is the scribbling of a traumatized victim who will initiate this project. As Head's artists and writers create out of their needs, there is suggested an intrinsic connection between creativity and the impulses of the unconscious, that they become one in their desire to make "art" a repository for potential humanity, a quality of life not always evident in the political, social and personal lives of Head's protagonists.

The Cardinals mainly focuses on the personal development of the heroine and her relationship with the aggressive older reporter, Johnny. Here, Head deploys all the motifs of the popular romance to describe Mouse's role as the heroine, only to abort the possibilities of a happy-ever-after ending by making Johnny Mouse's biological father. This depiction of the biological nature of Johnny's and Mouse's relationship prevents closure, and the reader may well wonder why an author should present herself with such a problematic storyline. Alison Light, in her analysis of women as readers of romances, explains the attraction, even the addiction to this genre, as the way in which "romance offers instead of closure a postponement of fulfillment" (1990,143). She suggests that avid readers of the Mills and Boon romances value these stories as "ritual and repetition" and that "this compulsive reading makes visible an insistent search on the part of readers for more than what is on offer" (143). In this way, romance reading is compensatory, readers needing to relive that point of romantic encounter in order to assuage what Light describes as their "deep dissatisfaction with heterosexual options" (142).

When Head wrote *The Cardinals*, she was newly married, a marriage that brought little fulfillment. Creating romantic fiction in this situation can be seen as symptomatic of personal needs as Light suggests, but Head's idiosyncratic way of preventing closure in *The Cardinals* goes far beyond the literary norms of the popular romance. Head's admission that "it's almost as though the stories wrote themselves" may have some bearing on the curious elements woven into her narrative. It is clear that Head's own personal experience left her emotionally flawed and disturbed, that a psychological prognosis might have predicted that the maintenance of affective relationships could be problematic for one such as she; indeed, much of Head's personal correspondence reveals the volatile nature of the relationships she conducted with others. A Freudian analysis would be more specific and predict that the development of male/female relationships would re-enact positions of dominance and subordination, the basis of sado-masochistic relationships, the female seeking a powerful dominant male in order to find credence in her own existence. In a short piece written after *The Cardinals*, Head describes her ideal mate—"tender, violent, cruel, revengeful man, over-stuffed with vanity and self importance" (*C,* 140). Certainly, in Mouse's case, the heroine is seeking recognition from another who is powerful enough to bestow it, in Head's case she insists on the biological father, unconsciously resurrecting the most potent of masculine archetypes.

This need in Head's writing—the female's dependence on a powerful male protector—does, beginning with *The Cardinals,* move from a general need to one with more universal significance. This change is seen through the way in which the hero archetype also becomes the guarantor of a more just society. Here Head is intimating what Christopher Heywood explains as how "the world of the dream and the myth (the interchangeable faces of private and social regeneration) is integral to the work of art" (1991, 28). By the time of her fourth and most complex novel, *A Question of Power,* Head produces a unique and compelling portrayal of the way in which the examination of Elizabeth's personal psychosis reveals that healing brings with it a turning to collective responsibilities, the possibility of discovering a "reverence for human life." Indeed, as Jacqueline Rose notes, "That movement from the personal, to the historical, to the universal is . . . central to Bessie Head's writing" (1994, 411)

However, in Head's first novel set in Botswana, *When Rain Clouds Gather,* Makhaya's hopes are more straightforward; he wishes to find a rural idyll after South Africa, and this seems within the bounds of possibility. As an exile and a lone mother, Head's own priority was to establish a home. Hence, comparison can be justly made between Head's own aspirations and those of Makhaya, for as Head admits, "The male character . . . obligingly serves the author. . . . He is forced to choose beautifully: 'I shall choose the road of peace of mind. I shall choose a quiet backwater and work together with people'" (*AWA,* 78). Head did become involved in cooperative farming projects on her arrival as a refugee in Botswana, but plans for improving farming were initiated by outsiders; as in *When Rain Clouds Gather,* her imagined human community was composed of new and temporary residents of Botswana. On one level Head is using a rural Botswanan village to provide a community, but on another level she is creating a "universal brotherhood." The "stage props" are Botswanan, but the vision is utopian, a romantic vision bound by neither time nor place. Finding only loneliness and poverty in her early days in Botswana, Head settled for a literary resolution. As she wrote in 1965 to Randolph Vigne, "When life is a dreadful pain and bleak you sort of counter this with an opposite feeling" (Vigne 1991, 18).

Many years later, when Head decided to write a book on her adopted village of Serowe, the same impulse colors her writing. For, although she had made friends among the expatriates working in the Swaneng School, a sense of belonging was still not in her power to enjoy. Thus, in her ostensibly sociological study of Serowe, her inability to create an objective portrayal is so marked that *Serowe: Village of the Rain Wind* remains only as a testament to Head's romanticism, a romanticism that is seen to be wholly imaginary when compared with the more prosaic and often conflicting testimony of her witnesses. Their own apperception of their workaday lives invited and collected by Head herself is seemingly ignored so that Head is not forced to compromise the euphoric portrait of Serowe she desires to portray. As usual, Head's literary output echoes her current preoccupations and her reshaping of sociological reportage vindicates her own desires: "I had to create my own fire to keep me warm" (Vigne 1991, 60).

Nonetheless, in spite of Head's need to create other realities, the archetypes she uses to shape her romantic vision are literary, motifs that recur to validate the belief in the possibility of humanity to survive. It is a literary tradition, one adopted by writers after George Henry Lewes—writers like George Eliot, Olive Schreiner, D.H. Lawrence, and Thomas Hardy. Thus, Head peoples her stories with heroes and heroines who find rewarding work as they attempt to create homes close to the Botswana soil. This landscape is numinous, it accommodates a world in which "the eyes and soul of man" become "the wild, beautiful sunset flamingo bird flying free in the limitless space of the sky" ("Earth Love," *C*, 164). In this way, Head is employing stylistic devices, metaphors, symbols, and archetypes to describe a symbolic interpretation that re-enacts the source of regeneration in the individual and society. But, as Paul Rich points out, this tradition of romantic rewriting is a valid response to the particular horror of the apartheid society forged in South Africa (1984a). Northrop Frye also describes the hero figure needed to deliver the oppressed (1990), and throughout literature there surfaces writing that explores the restorative role of the Faustian hero, his descent into the underworld and his return empowered to regenerate and serve his society. In a similar way to the "stage props" that Head imaginatively creates to give credence to the "human" in nature, these hero figures are literary archetypes, archetypes in the sense that they are recognizable symbols to which writers have recourse in order to inform a particular literary mode.

This partially explains Maru's literary function. His role as an archetypal hero is manifested in the way in which he overcomes the law of the father in his tribe in order to effect an event of transpersonal significance. As with all Head's heroes, it is Maru who will fight oppression. Hence, he is responsible for beginning the process by which the liberation of the oppressed Bushman tribe will occur; by marrying Margaret, a symbol of her oppressed tribe, he is defying prejudice. As a transpersonal god, his role is never compromised, for he dreams of a "world apart" where "the human soul roamed free in all its splendour and glory" (67).

However, in spite of the literary precedents to whom Maru's creation is doubtless indebted, there is another dimension in his provenance. Indeed, Maru is so unreal that readers of this novel are uncertain as to which genre Head is subscribing. Early editors decided that it must have been written for younger audiences, so powerful are the elements of "fairy-tale" and "magic" inscribed within it. However, within the narrative itself, Head offers us a clue as to the origin of her protagonist. In her portrayal of Margaret's feverish painting, Head dramatizes how the creative act can control the creator. Margaret's trancelike activity produces paintings drawn deep from her subconscious; they are paintings that speak of her deepest yearnings in the depiction of the entwined lovers. In a short meditation "Where is the Hour of the Beautiful Dancing of Birds in the Sun-wind," written during her early days in Botswana, Head provides another rewriting of her persistent preoccupation:

> It is always there now, the voice of my private demon, insistent at asserting itself. I dare not heed it, as I am weakened by a bottomless and intense desire. It may leap out of control and spread the death-touch on love and freedom. After all, if all should end and I do not see my power-man again, I would have only pain to swallow and loneliness to watch over. . . . How can I be sure that this is my final stopping place? I cannot know myself too well, being only a minute dot in a vast and unpredictable complex. Still the unfathomable thing is why I need this, why I need that. I cannot pretend that the restless fevers are not there. They are very real and demanding. What I object to is their destructiveness . . . (C, 157)

Thus, it is an intensely personal impulse that brings into being Maru, her own "private demon," infused with life by the same process that gives birth to Margaret's paintings. It is an act that Frye refers to as one that "seems to be an activity whose only intention is to abolish intention, to eliminate final dependence on or relation to something else, to destroy the shadow that falls between itself and its conception" (1990, 89). This suggests that there were times when Head's personal needs were so compelling, so overpowering, that the writing that emerges, the archetypes she uses, are not only the archetypes of a creative literary imagination, but resemble more aptly those identified by Jung as part of the collective unconscious—archetypes resurrected by the unconscious mind to do battle with the pathological urges of the victim writing, as Head claimed of *Maru*, "right in hell" (Vigne 1991, 136). Margaret's paintings represent what Lillian Feder refers to as "*unlabelled* metaphors" (1980, 5). But within *Maru* itself, Head portrays how Margaret, while madly painting during "the torture of those days," from that "something inside her . . . more powerful than her body could endure" had "learned" (102). But it is later, in *A Question of Power*, that Head can explore the meaning of these metaphors when they are "filled out with the material of conscious experience" (Jung 1967, 79). It is the very exclusiveness of the love, "the death touch on love and freedom" described in Margaret's painting of the entwined lovers, that must be subverted in order to allow Elizabeth to focus on her concept of "brotherly love," a vital motif in any utopian reconstruction.

Thus, freeing herself from obsessive dependency becomes the purpose of Elizabeth's breakdown. In *A Question of Power*, Head describes her hallucinations, but she also describes Elizabeth's healing, the way in which Elizabeth confronts, assuages, and finally purges herself of her obsession. Sello is Elizabeth's personal god, another configuration of Maru; but like Maru, Sello has also a transpersonal role. This transpersonal role, the way in which Sello creates for Elizabeth "the Fall of Man" (Appendix 6), allows Head to propose a universal significance for her personal demon. Consequently, Elizabeth's pathological need for a powerful father figure is seen to symbolize the basis of all unequal relationships, all those abuses of power that makes themselves manifest in oppression, in wars, in racism, in sexism, and all hierarchical figurations that dehumanize humanity.

The creative act, the rewriting of the force and meaning of the archetypes, has much in common with the origin of Head's hallucinatory experiences, especially if the reader sees Elizabeth as the subject of as well as the victim of her nightmarish experiences. However, Head acknowledged that *A Question of Power* lacked the "sustained pitch of emotional intensity" (Appendix 6) that characterized the writing of *Maru*. This is accounted for in *A Question of Power* by the control of a mediating voice, a "shadow that lies between itself and its conception," not only as Elizabeth, the "watcher" on "the shore," attempts to interpret the origin and meaning of her hallucinations, but as Head the writer brings into being her conscious, creative control in order to give coherence to her vision. Elizabeth "lets go" of the exclusiveness of her drama and what begins as a private descent into a private inferno ends as a profound assertion of the power and function of the archetypes of the collective unconscious to keep alive the potential for "the warm embrace of the brotherhood of man" (*QP*, 206).

This acknowledgement did see a change in the writing that Head produced, especially in her ability to maintain a more explicit detachment between her protagonists and the writing subject. She was capable of writing carefully controlled vignettes describing the problems encountered due to issues of racism, sexism, and political oppression endured by her characters. She shows in the short stories in *A Collector of Treasures,* and *Tales of Tenderness and Power* that she can deploy irony with great effect to show readers the fundamental issues at stake. Nonetheless, in her dependence upon heroes and heroines, in her deployment of the story as the repository of art, Head never moves far away from her individualistic romantic optimism. Her "stage props" are never too distant, her villains always outwitted, and her heroes characteristically blessed by their mystical unity with cyclical regeneration. But, above all, their role as heroes guarantees their compassionate understanding of human folly as they muse over the constancy and consistency of human failings.

In two of her short stories, "Earth Love" (*C,* 164) and "Hunting" (*CT,* 104) Head describes the homecoming of two hunters, the ritual of their hearing from their wives the village gossip that recounts the "muddle" of people's daily lives. The hero's role here, rather like that of the storyteller's, is to disarm the significance of this muddle, to make it as immaterial as the behavior of the "foolish kudu." The wider generosities of the hero accommodates the banalities of mankind, rather like "the ache and pain and uncertainty of earth life" is "drowned in the peace and freedom of the sky" ("Earth Love," *C,* 164). Although Head wrote her short stories at different times, her final production of

The Collector of Treasures, the title she gives her collection, the deciphering of meaning dictated by the order of stories within, asserts her ultimate and final belief that the power of the artist, the role of the storyteller, and the presence of the hero are one—to keep alive the power to dream of other realities.

Thus, it is the storyteller, the writer, the artist who has visions of utopia, utopias that exist in some far-away place, some future indefinable time. Head's last novel adds to this process when she shows how there is a form of history writing implicated in a portrayal of past events whose prime objective is to release hope for the future. The title of Head's last novel, *A Bewitched Crossroad*, is a curious, albeit unwitting, testimony to Keith Jenkin's thesis that all writers of history interpret the past from a "present-centredness" that is deeply influenced by the writer's own ideological view point. Thus, just as Head's idiosyncratic portrayal of Botswana serves only as a "back-cloth" for her utopia, which, as Guthkelch remarks, can only exist in "a far-off new world" (1914, xxii), so her writing of history allows her vision of utopia to exist is some infinite, elusive, future time.

In accordance with a postmodern view, historical narratives set on "avenging" an oppressed people release the possibility for the "sublime event," and it is this sublime event that heralds hope for the future (Jenkins 1995). Avenging an oppressed people can take many forms. Head portrays the oppression that the black South African countries suffered under colonialism, and she vindicates their achievements by creating great heroes made mighty in their conquests and victories, and villains cast low in their cowardice and ignorance. The majesty of the tribal leaders and the anarchy of their rule is a rewriting of sublime enactment, as the mind triumphs in "its ability to contemplate the magnitude of its beyond" (Ellmann 1994, 174). Sebina is the embodiment of this principle as he leads his people who, possessed by "the spirit of Ulysses" (9), seek the promised land. Thus, the Bamangwato trek is symbolic of mankind's timeless search for its Eden, and Head's writing of history becomes atemporal, the past and future fused and inseparable. This is necessary for the author, for in order to create her belief in a grandeur of life markedly absent in her own, her hero must, in response to the present-centred circumstances of his creator, believe in a future dawning, the possibility of "an endless, proliferating realization of freedom" (Jenkins 1995, 118). Head's title *A Bewitched Crossroad* is portentous in its symbolism. "Bewitched" announces the debt Head owes to her dependency on an antithetical creation to her apprehension of reality, and "crossroad" to a temporal place that is any time, or no time, its relationship to measured time as elusive as any correspondence Botswana may have with Head's utopia.

This is the process that Head has reached by the time of her last book. Makhaya's rural haven cannot be created either by the introduction of new farming techniques or the revival of the spurious collectivism of a tribal past. Maru's dream of a "new world" can only be achieved by sacrificing the claims of a real world. And Elizabeth, freed from the clutches of her nightmarish hallucinations, may see herself as "saved" but this salvation is proposed only on the basis of a potential, rather than an actual, notion of humanity. But to hold fast to this belief is the function of all her artists, her storytellers, and her heroes and heroines. Arriving at this, the moment of her final contribution, Head pays obeisance to those who come after her. At the point of death, Sebina's grandson promises to greet the sunrise for him and Head's final novel offers the same optimism as Sebina's sunrise. Her writing may be proposing "probable impossibilities" (Frye 1975, 58) but, should the "present-centredness" of the writer's world demand such redress, then the need for the kind of art that Head produces is more essential than ever.

Appendix
A Selection of Head's Letters

AFTER HEAD'S DEATH IN APRIL 1986, HER CORRESPONDENCE WAS bought by the Khama III Memorial Museum in Serowe, Botswana, where it was catalogued, filed, and made available to researchers. This collection, of almost two thousand items, includes letters to friends, agents, and business associates. There are exchanges with other writers and students of her work, comments on books she has read, and vivid accounts of her trips to literary conventions around the world. Also found amongst Head's vast collection of papers were some essays and short stories, many, at that time, still unpublished. These became the substance of *Tales of Tenderness and Power* and *A Woman Alone,* published in 1989 and 1990 respectively.

The letters reproduced here are unchanged, except for the correction of minor typographical errors. Unless it is self-evident from letter headings, I have, wherever possible, indicated the identity of the addressee.

The original draft of a short piece, entitled "Reply to Index on Censorship," reproduced in *A Woman Alone* (61) from *Index on Censorship* (4.2) is included here (Appendix 12). This draft shows that this short piece was carefully edited prior to publication. The format of the original letter, with its uncontrolled hostility, suggests that perhaps Head was not anticipating its publication. The editing that ensues imparts a more detached and composed point of view, one more in line with Head's public voice.

There are also two minor, unpublished pieces on Camara Laye and D. H. Lawrence, which may be of some interest; a lively account of her eventful stay in Berlin; and an article, "Khama, The Great," which never seems to have been published. The only reference I can find to this article is in one of Head's letters to Giles Gordon in which she writes "don't worry too much about the Khama article, should it be sent back from Blackwoods. It can just rest somewhere" (Appendix 10).

Each separate article of correspondence bears a catalogue number. The letter referred to above is catalogued KMM63 BHP10. The letters KMM refer to the Khama Memorial Museum where the letters are held, BHP to the Bessie Head Papers, 63 to the file number, and 10 to the item number.

1. Letter to Jean Highland, editor at Simon & Schuster, September 7, 1968 (*KMM43 BHP2*)

P.O. Box 207,
Francistown,
Botswana.
7th September, 1968.

Dear Jean,

I am sending you the carbon of my letter because my typewriter ribbon is faint. I have been unable to find a substitute for sweetheart. Therefore I begin my letters in future as always: MY DEAR SWEETHEART. I hope you don't mind my lack of originality in this respect.

My darling, I quote the last part of your letter . . . "On page three you talk about the way the black man is going to die. But you end your essay with hope and expectation. Do both feelings grow equally strongly in your heart and mind? Is the one stronger than the other? Do you hope? . . ." You also say . . . perhaps . . . "I shouldn't ask because it's answerless?"

First let me thank you for sending back that piece because I wrote it not knowing that things were more decided and hopeful and certain than they are. At the time I thought that the bastards are going to still remain top dog and that he would pull the strings as silently as he has been doing. Who is he, you ask? He is God, like I've been telling Austin. The magazine I sent the article to also returned it. They said they could not forward it to Wole Soyinka because he is once more in jail. He was teaching for a time at a University in Nigeria and then he took a trip to Biafra. On his return Gowan had him locked up again. I know he will survive. Wole is going to be a truly great writer. I was telling Austin that he must not flinch before suffering. It is the only way of unfolding the power within. But I enclose the letter from the magazine.

The confusion in my letters to Austin, the confusion in my own feelings is that no matter what happens to me I still feel ordinary. As the days go by I become more ordinary still. I can't grasp all that has happened to me over the past four years and the last thing I sent you . . . PATTERNS . . . was an almost panic-stricken effort to piece together a very gigantic event. I did not put down half the pain and stress of my life because it is unbelievable. Another thing. The lovers and helpers of mankind are not born in a day. It has taken me thirty-one years to know who I am. It has taken my God 47 years. The two of us only finally knew each other in these past four or five weeks, though when he was born in Botswana a number of prophesies were made about him. I was included in them because the two of us have always been a team together. That is, when he was Jesus I was Paul. When he was Ramakrishna, I was Vivekananda. We are a compliment, each with his own function.

There are things I can tell you now because you will know me quite soon and him too. It is not for nothing that I love you and Austin. I am only amazed at the certainty with which you found me and the certainty with which our ideas coincide. That I was so funny as to pay great attention to my dreams used to embarrass me but it was only through them that I contacted my own people. Austin excited me beyond belief. Every letter to him was accompanied by an explosion while I have only dreamt of you once. In that dream you instantly recognised me. So did I. I want to leave it like that. You, of all people will know me completely as I know my God. We carry a chain. He creates disciples or helpers and so have I. You will know of your particular relationship to me because we are that close. So will Austin. So will Bob. But with you I don't have to talk much. It has always been that way, as though we are the same face, the same hands, the same heart, the same love. It makes me want to stand on my head.

Not all the keys are in my hands. I only have what I need to bring my own work in this world to fulfilment. My life and history has been that of the suffering of the common man and with me he comes into his own. With me too comes into fulfilment this new age of universal brotherly love. For while I am the symbol of the common man I am also the symbol of love. That's what I have always expressed and died for whether as the Buddha, David of the psalms or Moses fighting for the freedom of the human soul. Those dramas are mine.

We are almost at the end of confusion and are stepping into a new age where as Louis Armstrong has so correctly prophesied . . . in his song WONDERFUL WORLD . . . You'd think people are saying Hullo but instead they are saying to each other . . . I LOVE YOU.

The whole reeling horror of the last month, the Czech crisis, what happened in Chicago, the way senator McCarthy was undercut because he is clean and straight and the people want him not those swines, Nixon and Humphrey . . . the whole horror of Nigeria and every other place has behind it a network of dynamite. There are people ready to take over on the day after the judgement day. Also it is suddenly going to be a new earth because certain powers are going to make people live naturally with their spiritual vision awakened. This has been the cause of the hatred and turmoil. People could not see their souls, they do not know they are divine. Nor does the white man know that God has been living on this earth for 47 years as an African man. Would he not be ashamed to know this, that this very Jesus whom he went to pray to in segregated churches is a black man. Because he is. I was petrified. I thought he would remain silent. I thought that if they knew they would shout: KILL HIM. LYNCH HIM. KILL HIM. LYNCH HIM. I have been petrified for I have known for almost four years. I thought he would die silently. But he is coming out into the open. He is going to re-make this terrible hell into such a beautiful heaven. He's got even the devil on his side at last and he is so pretty and charming and sweet as a human being. I mean I have found this out from inner communication with him. Some people are going to be wiped out and killed, not by God but by the burden of their own evil destiny. They will be born again but by that time the innocent, who have always been their victims, will have taken a hold on the earth with a firm grip and we will force them into the harmonious and beautiful way of life. When they come back they will find a world where mankind bows gravely to each other. They say: How do you do but they mean: I LOVE YOU. Louis Armstrong will have the last word.

So my darling, I don't have to define imperialism any longer. The new world is a stone's throw away. The exact date I do not know. But it is coming. He, my God told me not to hate white people. With good reason. Most of the disciples I created are among them. They will know me. Also, he gave into my charge the protection of the innocent. Black people will be so hurt, that the day the door opens they will want to tear to pieces the innocent. This CANNOT happen. The new age begins without anymore bloodshed. Also they who kill with their spiritual vision opened, commit a greater crime than those who kill and know not what they kill . . . the GOD IN ALL MEN.

Much love. Much love. I shall also see you one day and Austin whom I love so intensely and Bob.

Bessie

2. EXTRACT FROM LETTER TO JEAN HIGHLAND, APRIL 8, 1970 (*KMM43 BHP72*)

. . . . It is not only my son who gets me down. My subconscious gets me down too, pulling strange tricks. One night I had a terrible dream. I found myself abruptly in a room filled with sixteen children. There was another woman in the room, ten times more beautiful than I could ever be and unknown to me. I said to her: "You must give Bakar and the children to me. I want Bakar." She replied that she was equally entitled to Bakar and the children and her eyes glittered with tears. At this I burst into loud sobs but the other woman continued to cry in a dignified manner. She walked up and down the room as though tortured and I kept following her with my eyes. Suddenly I awoke with the tears streaming from my eyes and my throat such a tight knot of pain it was agony to breathe. I thought: "What's this now? Who is Bakar? I must be mad." The dream so discomforted me because my sub-conscious is more determined than my conscious mind. As soon as there is a dispute about a gentleman I run away. Maybe I might put up a battle for a short period under unusual circumstances but I prefer to get the hell out, eventually. There is a horror somewhere in my mind Jean, a long story about a long string of gentlemen who always belonged to someone else, so my sub-conscious produces all kinds of people in advance whom I don't know. I shall one day write that drama of the genius of affection who woke up to find that all the men in the world belonged to other women—and how they terrorized me.

. . . . There is an aspect of godliness or soul greatness that is very akin to insanity. I have rarely seen the soul of gods without a vicious, dangerous side, as though total perfection, immediately acquired, would take the spice out of the game. So on the one hand there is an optimism about that new dawn, "with softly glowing colours" and on the other, a fear that all the balances of good and evil have not yet been worked out as though evil would always be there to test man's self control.

But balanced side by side with this was a slow awareness that the earth was being made safe enough for people to see and understand everything with their inner eyes awakened. Few nations had this, one was India which recorded all it could of goodness and at one time, I feel, the Jews. I think there was so much darkness all round because evil and selfish things really controlled the affairs of men, the government etc. and from my inner struggles, I have found that the balance of goodness is so precarious that the slightest error means a headlong fall . . . .

I thought that when that new day dawned, from that point onwards, I could retreat to a way of life that I loved very much, where as D.H. Lawrence said: 'in the new age, each man will sit alone with his own holy ghost.' It is possible because each man will have completed his cycle of evolution and as he turns his eyes inwards, he finds something pretty there to contemplate.

. . . . There were some other things I was curious about. You kept so silent about MARU, thinking perhaps that my stories follow my life. You know, MARU used to pursue me, telling every body he was either going to marry me or kill me. I said in the story it's better to marry me than end my life. He had an abrupt change of mind, saying that he was not as beautiful as I had figured out MARU. I was then left to choose another gentleman, not that I finally made up my mind. Do you think it's alright if I choose Ranko, the spy? I like his good heart. I was just thinking about the fact that I ought to marry someone but it means starting all over again and I don't know how one attracts the attention of such a good-hearted spy like Ranko. In other ways too, I am so ugly to look at that I don't think too much about these things.

3. EXTRACT FROM LETTER TO GILES GORDON, LITERARY AGENT, NOVEMBER 19, 1990 (*KMM24 BHP19*)

I am sorry that it has taken me more than three months to reply to your letter to David about whether I could write a non-fiction book, or have my letters strung together by Paddy Kitchen. I cancelled the letters as I told you, and also the reason. I am sending a copy of this letter to my agent, Hilary Rubenstein, because on November 10th he wrote to me saying that McCalls in America had made an offer for "MARU," with an advance, and if all goes well that advance might carry me through for some months so that I need not accept or that you should trouble to raise an advance for me for my third book. It also gives you and I breathing space to argue about the contents of the third book and that I can work at a reasonable pace and think things out carefully. I also want to be free to express myself as I like, and as you know from the work we did on 'MARU' I get slightly hysterical when we don't see, eye to eye, on eternity.

First of all, I don't lack material for my third book, but the issue at stake is whether Gollancz might find very off-beat ideas suited to the non-fiction bracket. For one thing, I could not produce a journalistic, well-informed non-fiction book on Africa, Southern Africa in particular, but I could produce a collection of essays, in free-wheeling, intuitive style on almost any of the sorrows which plague mankind and black people in particular, taking into account that I shoot anywhere and don't care much whom I kill especially if the victim is on the wrong side of truth.

A tentative title I had for the book was AFRICA & A NEW AGE. It sounds very dull and flat but the "new age" was absorbed from D.H. Lawrence, whom I read more than any other writer and it seemed to give me the kind of mental scope I need, a sort of springboard to use my intuition to interpret events, not the facts on the surface but the long term planning of the future and how it ought to be. That means I would mostly be concerned with the soul of man, the inner part and say that if that were not right and beautiful, then how could politics be? Or how could life be? And where do we go if we are just mindless guzzlers. And also, how akin to insanity and evil, is godliness, because, you know, God has to be "holier than thou" and I don't think of God at all like that but as a personality who ought to make straightforward statements like this; "Samuel, why the blasted hell, in this age and time, do you allow Delilah No.1 and Delilah No.2 to muck you around? The last time Delilah No.1 made you pull down the wall I told the committee that we had to re-organise you. You've got brawn but no brains. We gave you brains so that you'd not be the victim of sensuous women. Here we see you in a mess again. What gives? Haul yourself out, brother. Didn't I say, women ought not to get a man down? I'm not the kind of fellow who repeats myself." What I mean is that mankind ought to trust a God with a new image who makes plain matter-of-fact statements about situations, like we know what evil is and ought to avoid it, because it brings about death, suffering and oppression and poverty and often the real name of evil is greed—I want more than I have.

Now, on to the material I have, cluttered around for my third book. I send you a sample entitled—SOME HAPHAZARD THOUGHTS ON REVOLUTIONS—I have many such "Haphazard Thoughts" on everything in the universe and I feel they are better off than the letters because they are sort of pushed away from the immediate sorrows of my life and therefore have a wider perspective. So very little of my writing has been published but I have often, through publication acquired very stimulating correspondents who are so-to-speak very amenable company. They send me problems and I send to them, enclosed with letters: "Haphazard Replies." You will notice from the sample that the material is gay, carelessly written, in haste, but I could gather this material together and unfold it, into pretty grand prose, that is, if you like the base of what I have enclosed, because it gives a pretty good idea of how I think out life, peppered with swear words and sanity. I don't like the insane because it is vicious and cruel and always dog-eat-dog.

4. LETTER TO JEAN HIGHLAND, JULY 13, 1971 (*KMM43 BHP9*)

> P.O. Box 15,
> *SEROWE,*
> Botswana. Africa.
> 13th July, 1971.

Dear Jean,

I write to you again because an inner pain makes me long to communicate with someone and because I have sent you some things that belonged to a private world. I also wanted this letter to cancel everything I wrote to you and Austin. Nothing I ever said to you and Austin was accurate because what is truth unfolds slowly, bit by bit, with jolts and turns and shocks.

The first thing I have always done is to act on wild impulse and my temperament was unequal to what I lived through for three years or more. I seem to have taken a strange journey into hell and darkness. It was the darkness I did not grasp because at the same time I saw the light. There seemed to be a heaven in many human souls with a stillness and perfection complete within itself. I felt, at odd occasions the same completeness within myself. It was this which captured and riveted my attention. I thought that an inner heaven could make a heaven on earth. But it wasn't really what I was doing. I kept on trying to write of good things when in reality the inner world was a raging torment. It helped me if I kept silent while terrible things unfolded in wave after wave. The danger to me in all this was that my own personality was swept under. I had no time to examine myself. I merely lived in each thing before my eyes, mostly attacked and on the defensive.

I once, or many times said this and that about the Ku Klux Klan and other things. Those are real living evils with a shame about them and someone once told me those kinds of people don't seem to know what they are doing. In my inner world I found another kind of evil, consistent, unashamed, with a capacity to plan in advance the suffering of the future. I was linked to this kind of mind and suffered day and night. When I tried to explain a little to some sympathetic person she said: "Yes people can be possessed by the devil." If only there were a simple explanation like paranoia or insanity for things that took place over a long period with a seemingly logical pattern. There was too much good intermingled with too much evil. What helped me to survive was that the evil seemed constantly to be exploding itself. It was like a massive cleaning up was going on and bloody murder was taking place, not of the body but a huge soul body of evil. The language of demons I saw is rather one track: "There's no place for you. Die." There was a greed and a grabbing and an arrogance monstrously out of proportion to normal human feelings. Everything had this out of proportion feeling to it, especially love and human passion. It was my world for some time and when I look back now I must have already been insane with suffering by the end of 1969. There was always a flare up over small things and a war waged secretly, in silent endurance, began to emerge and get confused with everyday living and people because the internal dramas clothed themselves with the faces of real people. Just after Christmas I snapped, half following an internal thread to which I clung with desperate intensity half hitting out at people who were quite innocent. What was I doing except completely destroying my life? For too long it had been a world of no compassion, humanity or anything normal. I have made a terrible mess of everything and it is so awful the things I said and did that it seems no repairs are possible.

When I wrote that letter to Tom Carvlin in the loony bin, I was still sure I ought not to be there so much had I lost track with reality. I am not even sure of the details of how I got home again because not even the doctor in charge made any effort to convince me that so-and-so was not dead. . . .

It just goes to show what hell is like. When I thought it all out right to the end with all the contradictions I began to see why so many civilisations had disappeared from this earth. There's too much dog-eat-dog in heaven, or in the human soul and I seem to have seen, felt and lived through the whole horror. The thing is while I really felt pure hell there was a goodness protecting me all the time, like a God I had not seen was there. I was sure of this and unafraid. He just took a walk out for a breath of fresh air and left me alone because I lost that sense of the certainty of goodness surrounding me. After so many years I really have myself to me at last without hell in between and what I was blind to, my own set of errors, spread themselves before me now. It seems to take a long time to learn a humility. Half of me reels towards death, half of me reels towards life. I am so uncertain, except that the clamour is over. Sometimes one emerges from a darkness, bombed full of holes and very broken down.

There was something else that happened. It was the people I had to say sorry to. An old lady I gave a slight knock to forgave me so quickly and her old man too. I stared at their faces in disbelief. There was something there I had not seen for a long time, the normal, the human, the friendly with a soft, kind glow about the eyes. Some other woman who had taken in the verbal hell I let loose also had this same soft glow in the eyes. After so much turmoil, ordinary human kindness like that is something I cannot seem to absorb. I value it but my head and heart are stunned as though they are not there anymore. I keep on saying: "Is this the real world where people forgive so kindly? Is this what real people are like?" It had not been my experience for a long time, that is, internally.

Jean, I think people feel a consistent pattern of goodness within that helps them conduct their affairs rightly. It has not been like that for me. There has been a jumble of wild impulses, error and error and an arrogance of soul that was submerged. You might not like me at all if you knew me, but many things I said in my letters show this up only too well, especially the wild letters I wrote to Austin. I wish them destroyed as my former personality has been destroyed and something quieter, sorrowful and more thoughtful takes its place.

There is something else troubling me. I doubt very much if Botswana is a normal country. There's just bush here and a scattering of mud huts but within all this desolation and solitude a whole heaven and hell exploded in my face. There was too much effort made, a sense of back-breaking labour of the soul, too much direction and purpose for goodness. It was always never what I wanted but something else continually unfolding bit by bit.

Hell is like a can of trash you have to throw away so often at breakneck speed. It is nothing worth dwelling on, except to say that it ends human life and civilisations too. I thought that now that the worst is over, I could keep a little hope that the heaven I saw all along in the human soul would change life naturally.

Yours sincerely,
Bessie

5. LETTER TO GILES GORDON, LITERARY AGENT, JANUARY 22, 1972 (*KMM24 BHP34*)

P.O. Box 15,
SEROWE.
Botswana. Africa.
22nd Jan. 1972.

Dear Giles,

Thank you very much for the reviews. It is interesting to compare against the American ones. I am certainly closely tabbed in England and I should say really known as a person. It is a wonderful help. The accent in America was on the impact of the two black men in Maru. I found things like *black* people in *black* Africa, in all the reviews and wild claims that I was relieving people there of fruitless racial arguments. As for Maru he was swallowed whole, only one reviewer pointing out that he is really a combination of good and evil. Something tortures me slightly. I am dependent on an audience, seemingly hungry to comprehend "the real Africa" and over-eager to take a writer as the epitome of everything African. How much I am the displaced outsider, I alone know. I am just looking at the blurb on the cover of one of Miriam Makeba's L.Ps. It says: "Miriam Makeba, she *is* Africa." When the same is flung at me, my hair rises on my scalp. I am looking on at everything and as you know from my correspondence some time ago, I can reel considerably. To a great extent, I am the taught, in a strange, internal way. To a great extent my preoccupations are all within. I feel as though all writers are first Russian, British, French, American and only after that, universal humanity. My position is different. The basic suffering and learning turned me inwards and what I really say is that my soul is like a jig-saw puzzle; one more piece is being put into place but my teachers this time have not been Jesus and Buddha but the ordinary man and woman in Africa. People who are on a road of strenuous learning are dependent on their societies for their soul evolution and each society has something to teach, so very often by default. What startled me, to a great extent was that there was no default in what was happening to me. It might have only been one lesson I was learning: "Look here, the kingdom of heaven in Africa is really the man with no shoes, but *you* have to learn it and this is how we go about it and it's damn important for the future." I caught on to this eagerly, almost right from the start as soon as I sensed it but what I never anticipated was the hair splitting truthfulness that went hand in hand with the choice. I think I was unprepared to be that unimportant, that levelled down but at the end of it I am through sheer terror of its opposite, the V.I.P., the pride and arrogance and egoism of the soul.

Therefore, I have my development. It was first the dithering Makhaya. The dubious Maru, painted up as a God and from there a more or less shaking but certain platform—I don't like the company of Satan at all. These are my concerns. I am discomforted by the title, "genuine African writer", because I approach my concerns with a *knowing* that I am the learner and that this time, about the essentials for me, I am not directly pushing against the social grain. People here, inwardly have a complete statement about how man ought to conduct his affairs towards his fellowman. There are so many side agonies that I tend to make sharp outlines of good and evil in separate personalities. I am that much richer by having lived for a while in a death-grip of darkness and having been cursed and mocked by a vehement version of Satan. I know it took Jesus only 40 days to have a conversation with Lucifer. I hadn't expected my conversation to go on for three or four years and he was luckier than I. He did not seem to be scared at the end of it. I am.

So in many ways I have been enjoying a new lease on life, reflecting, "pottering" as Paddy likes to say, but now I am going to put on my sweat shirt, really type till 2 a.m. and set a tentative deadline of July for . . . . a typescript which has had many changes of title and none liked up till now.

Yours sincerely,
Bessie

6. LETTER TO GILES GORDON, APRIL 1, 1972
(*KMM24 BHP 35*)

P. O. Box 15,
SEROWE,
Botswana. Africa.
1st April, 1972.

Dear Giles,

I completed my typescript much sooner than the date I had mentioned in my last letter to you. I'd asked Hilary what I ought to do with the typescripts and carbons I have as McCalls wrote to me saying they were deeply interested in my writing and was I working on another book. I wrote back to Susan Stanwood saying yes, and the material was a mixture of many things, but mostly suffering. But I haven't really had a mental sort of continuity working relationship with anyone at McCalls the way I have had with you. Since I had everything ready and still had to wait another two weeks to hear from Hilary who seems to be on holiday, I thought I'd send the top copy of—A QUESTION OF POWER, to you and one carbon to Hilary.

In my last letter to you I mentioned my extreme anxiety about the book—it is either printable or totally unprintable. It is almost autobiographical but not in the usual way. The narrator or central character of the story, Elizabeth, lives more in contact with her soul than living reality.

At first I simply wanted you to read the typescript and see what you think of it. Afterwards I thought that the story itself creates difficulties for the reader of which I think I ought to make you aware. It needs a sort of gymnastic mental performance to make it coherent, a constant leap from reality to unreality and at times the two merge so totally that confusion can arise. The action is tightly packed around the life of Elizabeth; she is actually a walking household of internal drama. Half the reading problems are solved if one is able to put ones-self into the weird, flexible dream-like qualities of Elizabeth's mind. She is Alice In Wonderland who takes a tumble down a rabbit hole and falls and falls. Her white rabbit who invites her and attracts her into a horrific nightmare, is Sello.

Sello is the Makhaya-type man of my other two books. He is far worse off than the elusive, sensitive Makhaya who was at least alive and the complicated Maru. He is the peak development of these two men but so complex and yet I feel possibly, my top achievement so far. The Sello in the book is not flesh and blood, yet he is; there are indications that he is alive—they are almost incidental. The full concentration is on the soul.

Here is the crux of it. It is an allegorical novel. It is about God and Dante's inferno. Sello is the traditional image of God as Old Father Time, yet in no way does he give to Elizabeth a traditional explanation of God. He is doing several things at once—he is divesting himself of his vesture garments, he is partially creating for Elizabeth, the Fall Of Man, he is slaying Lucifer or the killer dog power theme that has caused so much anguish in human history. He goes about these activities in his own original way. Lucifer is Dan. He hears prophecies about Sello which occurred at the time of Sello's birth. He is Sello's friend. He despises him. He thinks, as the original Lucifer did, that he ought to be God, by himself, as his power impresses him. He makes every effort to convince Elizabeth that he is God by himself. He cannot be God by himself unless he totally destroys both Elizabeth and Sello as they oppose power. His main target is Elizabeth. He completely destroys her but she rises at the end to a brilliance of soul as extreme as the degradation he inflicts on her.

Except for the opening lines, which are a meeting point for the still, lofty beauty of the closing lines, it is not a beautiful book. Three quarter part of it is a descent into hell and deals with obscenities of all kinds. Just near the end of part one you think you have heard the worst, but a torrent of deep horror is unleashed by Dan.

The woman Elizabeth is broken towards the end because of an innate innocence, she fails to comprehend the ferocious, wild passions of the two men, especially Dan. But she is on Sello's wave-length. There are parts when he appears like Satan yet he is the real thread of coherent goodness in the story. He starts off as a majestic Christ-like figure and slowly does a spiritual strip-tease act before Elizabeth's eyes, in deference to African trends and the future.

This future is proposed as the brotherhood of man. Evils, the roots of Belsen, South Africa are tracked down to what goes on behind the scenes in the soul. There are four major characters— Sello, Elizabeth, Dan, Medusa but they are extended arguments for good and evil. Relentless, assertive, powerful, is evil. Precarious, tentative, soft, free and flexible is goodness. It is easily destroyed. The process of this destruction is carried to its logical end in Elizabeth's final mental breakdown—she has several along the journey.

There is almost despair in me. I tell an impossible story, like the ancient mariner to the wedding guest. Then your book THE UMBRELLA MAN arrived when I was half way through. It says on the dust jacket: "What is admirable about Mr Gordon is the impatience with accepted modes of telling a story" I wanted to dedicate the book, if accepted to Paddy Kitchen and two other people.

You once asked me to write about my garden work because you so liked the letters I wrote to Paddy about vegetables. The agricultural chapters are isolated from the fierce soul storm until the end where turmoil reigns. You see each agricultural chapter at the very beginning and it is retained as a whole, it sharply focuses reality, poverty (my usual theme) and I have a study of a Peace Corps Volunteer, who is also a philosopher.

I suppose writing a book is like getting a baby. One feels it's terribly important at the time the glow is still there. I spent hours reading MARU over and over. The style projected tremendous physical vitality. A QUESTION OF POWER lacks that sustained pitch of emotional intensity. There are only two of those vast, flowing Botswana landscape scenes I love so much, one for the sky and one for the surroundings of my home. The deep, slow paced soliloquies of Maru are missing. Most of the soliloquies are done by Elizabeth. They are shouts of agony without any beauty—they just pour out. It is only at the end of the book that I can give some indication of what is coming next. I project my best thoughts into very still vessels. That's why the Makhaya-type man was my favourite mouthpiece, as Paddy likes to say—still, passive. Dominantly independent, yet undominating.

I shall be reading UMBRELLA MAN, not Premchand. Then I'll write you a long letter again. I suppose it would be too much to ask for a copy of your poetry as well?

Yours sincerely,
Bessie

7. EXTRACT FROM LETTER TO GILES GORDON, NOVEMBER 19, 1972 (*KMM44 BHP 152*)

. . . . . All this might seem as though I am making a tremendous fuss about A QUESTION OF POWER. I do accept the contract from James and would even be grateful for a very limited edition of the book simply because there are things I do not care to die with. Deliberate malice and viciousness are not a part of my plans, nor do I support complicated filth and horror. People here readily dismissed my actions as one who is insane. They asked me if I suffered from amnesia, hoping to dismiss the horrible story. I remembered every detail and indeed, clung to the inner logic of the story, very much dependent on separating the two men. It was the clue to breaking the vice-like grip the soul of evil or "Dan" had on me. I am in a weak position re-counting it because I had to wait to gather enough clues to unravel the plot of the devil. I told you he is not nice company to have dealings with. It isn't as though "Sello" isn't a massive horror of silence too but within the reasoning of my argument, that story, in relation to "Sello" is dead straight and truthful. After that I don't care very much else what happens. I might follow up some private speculations later about so-called spiritual powers, the hoax they are. Have you read somewhere about everything basically being atomic energy? The bloody hoaxers of the past found a route to this energy, levitated, performed miracles and all sorts of messes, but machines and cranes do it more efficiently these days. A man's ego is involved with powers or energies but a cold, steel machine has no ego. I suppose if a man can levitate, then he is God. They certainly thought so and that is why religion is so confused between the two themes—nobility of heart and head and turning the water into wine. The book is incomplete. It stands in the air. I could only record what I loathed and how it broke me. I had to do that because I really did put that paper up in the post office and it injured an innocent person—the daughter of "Sello". What else could I do but explain my side?

In anxiety that I should suddenly die, I circulated the typescript among all the project people I worked with here. It was simply necessary to show the terrible horror that lead to such actions and a state of mental confusion. People who are turned insane do not maintain a state of control over their insanity. There is a side to insanity that expresses itself as extreme cruelty towards others. But those people ruled. Why else is human society so full of blood?

8. EXTRACT FROM PIECE ENTITLED "GILES: SOME NOTES ON YOUR NOTES AGAIN" (UNDATED) (*KMM44 BHP84*)

I deeply treasure the notes you sent me and I shall keep them in a special place.

Oh yes, I was well aware of the two sides of you even though I saw more of the stiff formal side. I had my private speculations and I used to think: "He is the sort they used to send out in colonial times to rule the empire. The stiff formal side is the administrator and the crazy side helped them cope with wild animals and savages in all the dark jungles of the empire?" How's that for a character analysis?

I agree with you about the creation of a world people may not recognise because I know that in *Maru* and *Power* any resemblance to the real Botswana was purely coincidental. People have a complacent way of saying to me: "Your first book is *just* what Botswana is like, but I don't understand *Maru*. I don't like it." By the time they got to *Power*, they were definitely uneasy! I've had people here walk up to me, stare at me with great unease and then say: "I've just read A QUESTION OF POWER." After that they will say no more—none of the gushing tributes I received for *Rain Clouds*.

Do you remember that passage in Dr Zhivago? Pasternak says the same thing, that the written word is the highest form of human expression—very much as you say, "superior art form. High art." Pasternak has been my bible for years and years and years.

The Serowe book was really a temporary retreat from my own tortures because it is with a sense of dismay that one acknowledges that learning which caused so much suffering, not only to myself but to others too could simply be summed up as "horrible shit". And yet I know that I touched the sources of evil itself and that there was no help. Nothing could break it—it was like some eternal horror that would never meet up with its retribution, while I know that for each thing that I do that is harmful, a retribution of a terrible kind awaits me. So one gives way before one's own needs all the time and patches life up, sometimes tenderly, sometimes violently in an effort not to hurt people too much. Often when I hate deeply and bitterly, I will speak in my softest tone. Often when I love and respect, I will flare up so violently that my victim shudders from end to end.

What would be the point of learning "horrible shit"? It was so systematic and insistent, that learning. Do you mean then that one accepts finally that the world "is cruel and unjust and cruel again"? I have hesitated at a certain crossroad because I think, that unlike you, I don't have a very intellectual approach to life. I may grasp intellectual questions but it is my heart that makes my ideas live. But one might have to complete the last lap of a tortuous existence with no heart. At present it's like I scurry around in anxiety looking for ways and means to keep the slowly dying flame alive—unfortunately love isn't such a an abstract world and so far I have achieved the impossible. One can have a good laugh at people. Anyone can say laughingly and carelessly: "Oh I adore so-and-so. Isn't he wonderful?" Just let me say it and people give a violent start as though at any time I am about to run off with a gentleman or start up a flaming love affair. I am too solid to be an Anna Karenin and I ticked off all her faults in Tolstoy's book. I have a feeling only that man/woman relationships are like some kind of turning point in our age and time . . . .

I hesitate so long at my own crossroad, uncertain of any direction. It is only because I have accomplished too much and more or less, won single handed, in my obscure road of hell, all the crowns and trophies that were going in this age old game of God, the Devil and Eve. I don't like to wear any of them.

I'd hand them on, laughingly, to all those who have no earnings because at present I don't think anyone is going to endure the suffering I've endured. It is really knowledge of battle that teaches you how precarious the victories are. So, unlike you, I am not happy. Sometimes I think this sorrow will always be there and a portion of my life will be permanently warped.

It is all these things that shape my writing. I feel like taking another dive for cover. During the year I wrote the Serowe book, my fingers used to fly over the keyboard and I can hear all the gushing tributes in advance and the relief: "Now that's really Botswana. I like your book." They wouldn't know what "the other world" cost me. They wouldn't know that for three quarter part of the time it is anguish to stay alive and that I am not writing to please them but perhaps waiting and waiting to get beyond my own crossroad and perhaps finding my heart still alive. . . . . .

9. EXTRACT FROM LETTER TO BETTY STEPHENS, OCTOBER 29, 1972 (*KMM 77 BHP 14*)

. . . On Khama, The Great. Yes, I have decided on a biography. Novel writing is such a free world that one tends to develop very strong mental attitudes, often not corresponding to real life. Certainly to be hostile and anti-social is a privilege not always granted to man. To work on the life of a man who took power and used it might make me sound less insane than I am now.

For one thing, at one time the Khama family were the power horses of this country. All influence came from them and they had the reputation of being a very cruel family. Khama, The Great would be tainted with this and that was where I wanted to take off and veer away. It is awful stuff to delve into, tight, vicious mean and futile but the extent of suffering it caused is tremendous. I have so far always manipulated my characters my way—get the hell out of this bloody mess and leave the chips to the bastards but real life is not like that. At one glance Khama, The Great is a replica of all the male heroes of my novels, the same personality type so I am half on sure ground re-creating him. I know ahead what makes him tick.

10. LETTER TO GILES GORDON, JULY 29, 1973
(*KMM44 BPH40*)

P.O. Box 15,
SEROWE, Botswana,
Africa.
29th July, 1973.

Dear Giles,

I was conscious of not having spent so much on postage this month.

Oh yes, I knew that Davis-Poynter were to send me the further £175 on date of publication, but actually James Curry had mentioned some time ago that he would first send me a £200 advance on A QUESTION OF POWER. Later he wrote asking me if I would agree to Heinemann paying Davis-Poynter £100 and then he would send me £100 but I suppose he will send me this £100 after publication or something. In any case I am most grateful to you for getting Davis-Poynter to pay the £175 ahead of publication date. I am not sure whether I am supposed to laugh at such remarks as "perfunctory and businesslike" letters from you. They are not as bad as the letters I am getting from the Davis-Poynter people just now—very strained and formal, brisk and businesslike. They hurried me through so much work, just stopping short of starting each letter: Dear Madam, will you please fill in this form, please correct this—that at the end of correcting the galley proofs of POWER I put in a little note . . . . "May I take a bow to myself as the writer of this book. I don't

think I'll ever produce its equivalent again . . ." I felt pained at
all the rush, rush and formality. It didn't seem like they were
publishing a book at all. They hastened to write back: Oh no, you
aren't the only one who is making a bow. The book has aroused
a storm of praise so far. For the first time I began to relax a little.
I just didn't know what was going on.

Actually I don't mind perfunctory and businesslike letters. A
great change has come over me now that I am moving into old
age. I find myself rather more dignified and appreciative of all
good, courteous human behaviour. I suspect my intellect must
be developing or something, certainly there is a great change in
me. Davis-Poynter had told me about the Booker Prize entry.

I have not done any more work on the SEROWE book but I
had filled in the time reading the biography of TSHEKEDI
KHAMA by MARY BENSON. If James Price is really keen on it,
I can certainly complete the SEROWE, due to my admiration for
Tshekedi Khama and his father, Khama, The Great and partly
for my own involvement in the project work of Serowe.

I noted particularly in the third book, the project parts, that I
seem to be glued to the country. Simply, one cannot do anything
constructive without generating that tremendous sincerity but I
must say that Botswana hasn't been my country for a long time.
I haven't listened to the news for two years, only BBC World Service because there is nothing else that is truthful and sane.
There is nothing else I want to say about the country, only if possible make a bow to Khama, etc, through the SEROWE book but
if James Price does not want it, with my outline and plan, let me
know and I'll just pack up everything and leave the country. I
have been planning this for some time and written letters here
and there and everywhere. And I do have travel documents.

Whoever planned it, down at the government capital of Gaborone, succeeded in letting off a big bomb amongst us. The young
American volunteer, Tom, of my POWER book was deported
from Botswana. Unfortunately, all I said about him in the book
was too true. He was as good as that. People were paralysed with
shock. No reason emerged. All sorts of people were phoned, contacted—there had to be a mistake somewhere—but everyone received a blank, blind reply: "He isn't wanted in the country
anymore." He had a good job—adult literacy classes—
everything looked right and a letter came in the post one morning: "Get out in two weeks time." Just like that. Unfortunately,
there are people and people. The project people and volunteers

know everything there is to know about the country, not bad things, its birds, its wool-weaving and spinning groups, its food, its people maybe its politics. The politics aren't interesting. They are awful shit, and certainly I don't care about it.

Things like, "What do billions of people in the world need? Food." It's a big programme and one can find it anywhere else in the world, plus a new and beautiful relationship with people.

I have long run out of my stay here but the learning has been of such an intense and concentrated nature that I'm not sure I'm normal anymore. Terrible things happen in Africa that give a powerful lever for the Boers and Ian Smith. The people who are victimised by a newly independent African government say from the comparative safety of New York: "I'm glad they threw me out when they did. Look at what came after them. It's much worse."

The ordinary people are very nice here. First I had used my intuition about them. I didn't know Khama. I couldn't link it to anything but now I see that they have his beautiful face.

I wonder where Tom comes in all this. God we don't seem to care where we belong anywhere. It has often seemed enough just to pitch tent and get on with some work. I belong to those kinds of people but it is awfully difficult to just pitch tent and get on with a job. You offend someone and you don't know how. I think there is a force of evil at work here and on this continent. It doesn't want the poor and starving to stop starving and it is against any effort of that kind. You get destroyed struggling against that force.

I could not help noticing that Davis-Poynter are conducting a campaign against the Botswana government on the dust jacket of my book. They said: [of Botswana] that it has "independence of a kind. . . . ." and so refugees there "report to the police once a week. ." It's okay. It is the truth and whatever happens to me, it couldn't be any worse than what I've already been through.

I'm sorry for the long personal digressions again. Some kind of image comes to mind, the sort of people who stand over a cliff of death and laugh their heads off. Funny that Botswana, a God-forsaken bush country can really make a human being like that.

Yours sincerely,
Bessie.

P.S. Don't worry too much about the Khama article, should it be sent back from Blackwoods. It can just rest somewhere. It was good enough work to just stimulate my brain cells on the man. I like such a richly creative personality. Ha, Ha, all his relatives are alcoholics; he was so strict about beer but that sort of thing is just a private joke!

P.P.S. You say no one wants the JACOB story. Could you return it, sea mail? I haven't a spare copy. But with it I could build up a small file of short stories to try on Heinemann at a later stage. There might be many items from the SEROWE book that I cannot use but they could develop into short stories and I could jot them down. As you know the SEROWE book needs no direct analysis on my part but there may be times when I find it a bit tedious and I can sit and dream a bit and jot over a few of my own notes on life, etc. Your typist makes a lot of errors. Read by candle light at night they all show through and are fascinating.

11. EXTRACT FROM LETTER TO MILLY DANIEL, A PUBLISHER, AUGUST 9, 1974 (*KMM63 BHP10*)

. . . . .The work on the Serowe book is not yet complete although I have signed a contract with Davis-Poynter Ltd. I had indeed prepared some additional material for him and was waiting to hear from him before I made any further additions to and alterations on the new book.

There seems to be a misunderstanding. I quote a portion of your letter to Giles: ". . . most of the interviews with younger people living there tend to be with white settlers . . ." I think you are referring to Part Three of the book and I feel I ought to point out that the white people interviewed there and who are working on projects are certainly not "white settlers" but international volunteers who are only here for two to three years and then go back to their countries. All the people I interviewed have already left Botswana and if this would cause confusion, a footnote could be inserted in the book, at the appropriate place *volunteer staff*. The die-hard white settler would never, never, never dream of associating with black people! And how would I ever write about them because I am black. Volunteers are some other dream of finding out about people's humanity and working *together* with them. I am by now feeling highly alarmed. I saw a review of "A Question Of Power", scheduled to appear in the new York Times and the review says in effect that there's something wrong with me because I associate "only with Europeans". Actually, in the ordinary way, with my South African background and real dislike of people who think they are top dog, the wrong sorts of white people would be too scared to even say hullo to me. That I should be thought of as a special defender of the white man! BUT a person would be crazy if people in general were damned forever on the basis of what they looked like. In general, those who now come here, work for a time, are (if you like white people) of a very High order. You tend to forget race in the pursuit of new ideas and work. You are thinking of something else rather than what the person looks like. It is the unusual chain of almost accidental goodness that has made Serowe so rich. There seemed to be no definite plan behind it but Pat van Rensburg opened the door here to a new kind of person. Unfortunately, nothing is defined. People only work and then leave. The volunteers I interviewed had put projects together on no money at all but sheer inventiveness and a will to contribute something to the community . . .

12. Letter to Michael Scammell, December 1, 1974 (*KMM243 BHP3*), partly reproduced in *A Woman Alone* (61).

> Mrs B. Head,
> P.O. Box 15,
> SEROWE, Botswana.
> 1st Dec. 1974.

Michael Scammell,
Writers & Scholars International Ltd,
21 Russell Street,
Covent Garden,
LONDON WC2B SHP

Dear Sir,

I thank you for your paper—survey on censorship—but I prefer not to answer your questionnaire of protest against apartheid. I believe that people cannot protest against evil social systems. The people who create it merely laugh in your face, and keep guns at hand to annihilate you. I believe that the white man in South Africa does not deserve the privilege he is at present enjoying of ruling and being the dominant race of the country because he has not the faintest inkling of how to treat other people, who differ from him in looks, decently.

If you protest and make one gain against apartheid, the South African government, possibly, in terror, has to pass two more repressive laws to liquidate your gain and you end up by increasing the suffering of the people in the country and I am Damn, damn sick of it. Why not simply say that on the whole the white man isn't such a nice form of human life? He isn't nice and I don't like what has been done in that country by those hideous sorts of people who are repelled by the shape of people's noses, hair, complexion—things about which people can do nothing. So what have I got to protest about? I just want the fucking bastards out of the country because they are obscene and horrible and cause endless misery. I am sort of thinking of ways to get them out of there. It takes a bit of time, because it involves a broader question than mere protest—it is a question of evil as a whole, We are likely to remove one horror and replace it with another and those of us who have suffered much do not relish the endless wail of human misery.

My writing is not on anybody's bandwagon. It is on the sidelines where I can more or less think things out with a clear head. We may be at a turning point and need new names for human dignity, new codes of honour all nations can abide by.

I really don't like evil and it is this which bothers me most. The world ought to be a happy place to live in because each life span we live through is so short.

Yours faithfully,
Bessie Head

13. PART OF UNDATED LETTER (*KMM82 BHP6*)

NOTES FOR GARY . . .   B. HEAD

I certainly think that writing, and novel writing in particular is a nationalistic activity, but this expression of national feeling is rather the subdued communication a writer conducts with his society. I have tried to outline this relationship in my third book which has not yet been accepted for publication—in its opening lines . . . "how often was a learner dependent on his society for his soul evolution?" So to a certain extent a writer is so often first referred to by the name of his country and what his readers have discovered about his country, through him. Since my books were published, I have often been referred to as "the Botswana writer," which is not quite true, since South Africa ought to have been my country as I was born there.

The problems outlined in my books are all South African ones but my own country gives people no clothes or a sense of belonging to anything so I have been forced to borrow the national clothes of Botswana to wear as a writer. It is almost impossible to be a writer in South Africa because of the difficulty one encounters when trying to express people's humanity. All the concentration is on people's complexions and a writer cannot write about something so unnatural. In the first place a human being is taught to regard himself as a Coloured or Indian or White or Black. He is one or the other of these things and once he begins to write he is trapped in his complexion and must leave so many people out of his thoughts because he might only know how a Coloured lives but not the day to day living of a White man. It kills all feeling of humanity and caring for everyone, and it is unreal and a nightmare.

If one is Black, as I am, then a writer's problems are mountainous. We grow up with a sense of, in South Africa, that even the birds and trees belong to the white man. They are not things black people have the intelligence to appreciate. And yet, although South Africa made white people rich and comfortable, their ownership of the country is ugly and repellent. They talk about South Africa in tourist language all the time. . . . "this grand and sunny land," they say. No one is living there and the white man who has all the say now is only a tourist and a very horrible one.

When a writer writes about the earth he loves, he is singing a praise song for all his people and he does not want to think of them as black, green and white people, but only people. Then, the earth and the sky and the trees and the birds blend together in his heart like an unending poem. Of all my writing I like best a description of an early morning sunrise in Botswana . . . . .

". . . . . As far as the eye could see it was only a vast expanse of sand and scrub but somehow bewitchingly beautiful. Perhaps he confused it with his own loneliness. Perhaps it was those crazy little birds. Perhaps it was the way the earth had adorned herself for a transient moment in a brief splurge of gold. Or perhaps he simply wanted a country to love and chose the first thing at hand. But whatever it was, he simply and silently decided that all this dryness and bleakness amounted to home and that somehow he had come to the end of a journey. . . ."

That is what I mean by borrowing the clothes of Botswana because I have no country and no one.

14. EXTRACT FROM LETTER TO BEATA, MARCH 9, 1975 (*KMM25 BHP19*)

Thank you for your letter of 25th Feb. Oh, yes indeed, I'd love the book on re-incarnation. I accept it as fact; it provides a continuity of experience, but also to me it replaces hereditary in summing up a human personality. It also accounts for love of various kinds—that people tend to travel together and work together and share chores, and they do this over and over again. There is an area of life that is completely confused—people make a terrible commotion over their feelings for each other, doing apparently irrational things when they meet someone they are particularly responsive to—as though some hidden back history sets off a kind of explosion. It fascinates me because I always sort out my human relationships along these lines and tell people quite freely we've met before somewhere.

Oh, I do a lot without habitual activity, frustrations and joys. I just live with myself. It's not so bad. Botswana, my version of it, makes people from outside fall terribly in love with the place. My two most recent books are very much local people books and I had them read by some friends from South Africa. It was my great delight to see how they imitated what they had read in the books—the silence of the place which has a special quality and the way they knew that they could immediately move with and talk to the people—half the introductions had been made already. So I don't know if I am the right person to ask about Botswana, most certainly I am recording a special part of it and never leave Serowe. I stay here for years and years. Here in Serowe, you can start anything you like and dream whatever you like and once you have read my fourth book—*Serowe: The Village Of The Rain-Wind*—you will see why. The village can take any new idea, dream or invention—everyone comes here and it is one of the most developed villages in Botswana. Once you've read that book you can decide about Botswana. The inventions and dreams spread to all parts but this is its true Mecca. The provisional date of publication of the Serowe book is October, by Davis-Poynter again. None of the dreams here get Africanised because all sorts of people work together—maybe not perfectly but things get going on an international scale. I have sat in one place and seen the whole world here. A lot of the projects do not belong to the government. They belong to the people who build them up. It's when you get on the government line, where there may be money that you can't do much.

15. LETTER TO STEPHEN GRAY, THE WRITER AND CRITIC, MAY 2, 1976 (*KMM14 BHP4*)

P.O. Box 15,
SEROWE, Botswana.
2nd May, 1976.

Dear Stephen,

I have just received Sol Plaatje's MHUDI c/o your publishers, Hugh Keartland.

!!! I'm afraid I've forgotten I'm a lady and here I am turning cartwheels and flipping over on my back in sheer joy! I am almost out of my mind with joy!

Firstly, I was sitting in Mbulelo's house that Sunday, waiting for the train back to Serowe, when I mentioned to him that my research on Khama, The Great was going badly as I have had a difficult time with the Botswana National Archives re the loan of research material. I told him I had mainly worked on the land question. He straight-away got up and loaned me his copy of MHUDI. He seemed shocked at his generosity because he said in a strangled voice that it was very expensive. I then earnestly promised to return his precious book to him by registered post. WHEN I READ THIS BEAUTIFUL BOOK, I was absolutely in despair. I needed to copy the whole book out by hand so as to keep it with me. The whole book is beautiful. It is more than a classic; there is just no book on earth like it. All the stature and glamour of the writer are in it.

Well, you can imagine how I feel now on having my own MHUDI. NEVER has a gift been SO WELCOME. For a year I have struggled with research on Khama. A lot is missing and has to be filled in by assumption. Much was available to me through the writings of Mackenzie on the desperate struggle the Baralong Chiefs waged to save the land from the Boers but you find a gap in records. You only know that Khama would allow no Boer to settle in his land—he blocked their migration northwards with the aid of the British. But you have to assume he knew more than the records tell. A whole piece of my work fell into place with MHUDI. I had a terrible time with Mackenzie's

Austral Africa Vol 1&2, which mainly deal with Baralong tribes near Kuruman..

Thank you so much and thank you also for your own book 1 SA pon a time. I swear I wouldn't have understood that language had you not explained it to me. I have been doing mostly pressured historical reading for a year but I'll get down to your book as soon as I am able.

Yours sincerely,
Bessie.

16. Extract from letter to Alberti, the American chargé d'affaires in Gaborone, September 1, 1978
(*KMM20 BHP18*)

. . . . . . Don Jones had already passed through Serowe with some of your good news and your new marriage and I sent back little messages myself to the effect that I had shared some of your past suffering and joy and the little memo I had wanted to make to it—the dedication of my *Serowe* book was causing me considerable anguish. The book fell into the trap of inflation where publishers only now want to make money out of a writer. In the past I never made money for them. I was only a writer who drew good reviews "for being concerned about mankind". Something horrible has happened to that kind of writer under inflation. They have had to count back on whether we are an investment or not. I seem to have only one last life-line left—Heinemann Educational books in London. They hung on to the *Serowe* book and would not reject it for months and months and in spite of entreaties and pleas from my side, they still refuse to reject it. They are about the only publisher I have left and about the only publisher that can afford to hold a writer like me who is not on the best-selling list. The point I am trying to make in this long ramble is that when your wife visited me that Saturday, so long ago, with Lee Nichols, she looked at me with wonder and worship. Hundreds of people pass through my life, but no one looks at me with wonder and worship. People come to me and talk about themselves because they think my writing is on their wave length. Your wife said nothing. From the moment we met, she never once took her glance off my face and then all through the interview with Lee Nichols, she tried to squeeze herself into a corner so that she could be as quiet as a mouse and not disturb anything. I might be explaining something you knew very well.

But that is how your family became a part of my life. Don Jones said everyone holds you in such high honour that I can only imagine that your new life is as beautiful as your former life.

I am pleased that you have enjoyed "The Collector Of Treasures", and that it struck such a responsive chord in you. I am very well aware indeed that black women in America have the same problems as black women in Africa—where they find themselves faced with men who have abdicated from all responsibility and I have read those women writers in America who have articulated the problem. Americans as such, and black people there who are Americans, would tend to me to express problems in infinitely more complicated ways. I was frightened by much that was communicated to me like women's drift towards lesbianism and indiscriminate love-making so that some of the work I did seemed to have a fairy-tale quality to it. Much of my research here is contained in the title story, "The Collector Of Treasures". When I sorted it out I said to myself: "You cannot solve a problem unless you create an attractive ideal." The man, Paul Thebolo serves, to me, as that attractive ideal, to outline the new direction. I am inclined to take short cuts like that but life can be much more horrifying.

17. LETTER TO TONY HALL, AN AGRICULTURALIST WHO HAD WORKED WITH THE FARMERS' BRIGADE IN SEROWE, DECEMBER 30, 1978 (*KMM47 BHP40*).

> P.O. Box 15,
> Serowe,
> Botswana.
> 30th Dec. 1978.

Dear Tony,

Thank you for the Christmas presents. Mine to your family will be delayed again as I hope to send you a copy of my history of Serowe. Heinemann have indicated that they'd like to accept it but they are slow to contract for it. Howard thanks you for his gift. He reads quite a lot and has often amazed me at the books he has brought home; I've eagerly sat down and read them myself—they range from crime to Freud to various versions of Marxism.

First for my news. I haven't got anything off the ground yet but I hope to go down to Gaborone on the 16th Jan to see the U.N.

people and give everything a push. I felt so safe and cared for when I stopped over in London on my last trip that when we leave here I'll extend the stopover and let you know.

I have a long week-end here so I have time to reply to your very interesting paper. I carefully marked out portions of it where I wished to expand on your own thoughts. I have many beautiful things that I often re-read and I want to place them next to your own thoughts. I am convinced that man's intuitive sense is at one. When you take in world literature and man's spiritual experience as a whole you find that there is mutual agreement and not hostility but oh the anguish this has caused me—the rich big view. I've had a sense of people wanting to kill me all the time for the big rich view. No one got "A Question Of Power" right, except strangely, the wife of Pat van Rensburg, Liz. She said to me: "What I love about the book is that it proposes learning wisdom from ordinary people." "A Question Of Power" is the great bow to the ordinary man as opposed to the great bow to the powerful, single dominating God. No one spotted this except she and I did not love the woman. I was totally out of sympathy with her, but she sharply caught on to what I was getting at. The book so tortured people, they were frightened that they were losing their God in the sky and they hate me for having jolted them out of this love affair. I cannot solve the mystery of Jesus Christ, the demand to place implicit faith in a single dominating personality: No one comes unto the father, except by me. Take salvation from me alone. It's here on a plate. This has fascinated mankind. Oh they've loved it so much, but not the whole world. But it's been big enough to include the whole world. I shy away from the single powerful, dominating figure. All should be Christ. As you write: If you truly follow Christ you will only be content when all are Christ.

You can see my method in "A Question Of Power". I was struggling with total darkness and only glimpses of light. I had no control over the experiences I recorded and I said towards the book's end that I knew nothing but if I knew I would tell the simple truth. The experience frightened me enough to make me record it but I admit to the book being badly scrambled. I did not know the truth but a fearful hell was in front of me. My attitude at that time was let me get the hell out of hell. But I will work piece-meal like that. If I only see so much, I'll say so with humility. And people can trust me perfectly. I am ashamed of nothing because I don't want to be the Being in the Sky. I want to be me and me is oh so jolly most times. That was why I used the D.H.

Lawrence quote at the beginning of my book. "only Man can fall from God, only Man . ." It follows then that Man is God. That is all I was saying.

You may feel in your bones as you say that there may be a second coming. You know people really hate the being coming down on clouds of glory and they'd shoot at it in caseit disturbs the stock market. Perhaps I prefer that sudden insight that there are so many Christs. But it is a little more than this with me. I bow to all mankind has achieved so far. I bow to Marxism and stand close to it in the sense that it is important to feed and clothe and house mankind. No religious leader could break open that hard vicious door of the privileged few who lived on and exploited the many. But they do not acknowledge man's holiness. They will kill and kill and kill and I hate their arrogance. Perhaps I imagine a world where people see they are God and the greeting changes and people say to each other "Good-morning God." You couldn't possibly kill God if it was you, could you? You couldn't possibly exploit or do any evil to God and God and God. That's more or less your "triumph of love". I do not like the hysteria of Christianity but the broad and natural, working and building on all that's been done by mankind, just a natural patterning of events.

My foster mother was not Indian. She was coloured like me. Each evening she prayed loudly to God, but then so did all black people. Once they caught on to the idea of God, plus Jesus Christ, they clung desperately to it but everything else was taken away from them and they were misused and exploited. I have lain back in anguish at one's sheer helplessness in the face of that situation. But it was South Africa's apartheid laws that forced me to a library donated to the community by an Asian man. He of course stuffed it with Hindu philosophy. Lord it's a rich world. I read nothing else for two years. India was religion itself, the whole land and the life of the spirit was mapped out to the last possible detail. Men sat down and concentrated on the unreal world which was very real to them and then carefully mapped out their observations. The height of Hinduism is austere discipline and loftiness in meditation on the spirit. It has that element of miracle performing which is so attractive to people but it was frowned on generally by the austere thinkers. I have some of those books. That world is accessible and most of the religious terms can be translated into English. The only untranslatable term is the word Shiva. It was the great symbol of God as man and there are a thousand Shivas, all lost in the clouds of meditation. So many living men were Shiva. The religious disciplines were carefully mapped out according to men's capacities. Men are not alike in temperament. Some men are all love so the discipline they have to follow is Bakhti Yoga, the discipline of love. Some men are all intellect so the discipline they have to follow is Jana Yoga, the discipline of knowledge. Some men are all courage so the discipline they have to follow is Raja Yoga the discipline of the warrior (the Bagvad Gita is the discipline of the warrior for example). Lord, it's a strange beautiful free flowing world full of unusual insights that many people outside that world would find unacceptable. Apparently mankind's destiny flows in major cycles roughly covering spans of two thousand years. The destructive cycle is the Kali Yuga (Yuga is that span of time—the rise to dominance of the female principle in the era of the Kali Yuga.) They maintain that the Kali Yuga, the rise of the female principle has always brought death and destruction to the world. It leads into the golden age of mankind but this has never been achieved because women have always brought about the downfall of the world or men. I laughed a bit when they let loose Mrs Ghandi on India and she brought about that mess. The world, they say is now in the Kali Yuga again, with the rise to dominance of the female principle. Does this not make sense. Look at the wild loud shout of the woman's liberation movement. They are after something but they don't know what and it takes awful turns and messes in America, wild indiscriminate sex and lesbianism. But that's what they mapped out. To correspond with this cycle of the Kali Yuga they spotted a new and fearful female principle. Mother Kali, they call her and her description goes as follows:

. . . . She wears a garland of human heads and a girdle of human arms. She has four arms. The lower left hand holds a severed human head and the upper grips a blood-stained sabre. One right hand offers boons to Her Children; the other allays their fears. She combines the terror of destruction with the reassurance of motherly tenderness. She is the Cosmic power, the totality of the Universe, the glorious harmony of the pairs of opposites. She deals out death as she creates and preserves. She has three eyes, the third being the symbol of divine wisdom; they strike dismay into the wicked, yet pour out affection for Her devotees. Mother Kali is the creator. Nay, she is deeper. She is the Universal mother, the All Powerful. She takes away the last trace of ego and merges it in the consciousness of the Absolute. She stands on the bosom of her husband, Shiva, the Absolute, who lies prostrate at her feet. She appears to be reeling under the spell of wine. She is the highest symbol of all the forces of nature, the synthesis of their opposites, The Ultimate Divine in the form of woman . . .

That's the vision the Hindu saints saw of the woman who leads the destructive era of the Kali Yuga. She leads it into the golden age of mankind. Mankind has never reached this. Its destiny has always been broken at the Kali Yuga, but this they maintain is the turning point into the golden age, or in your own words, "the triumph of love".

I love the above grisly description of course as I am very familiar with Hindu philosophy and lived with Asian people in Durban for two years. I sat with them on the floor while they offered sacrifices before terrible looking gods and Goddesses like the above then ate the sacrificial food which was extremely tasty and delicious. So this is a natural part of my life.

Let me quote you something more tender from the British writer D. H. Lawrence:

> We live to stand alone and listen to the Holy Ghost. The Holy Ghost is inside us and who is many Gods. Many Gods come and go, some say one thing and some say another, and we have to obey the God of the innermost hour. It is the multiplicity of gods within us make up the Holy Ghost. The next era is the era of the Holy Ghost . . .

That's more in your line, more tender than the rugged, terrific, astounding visions of India. But they are all okay. Mankind does not really disagree at the level of intuition.

I hope this gets you going somewhere. I loved the wide generosity of your paper.

Much love to all.
Bessie.

18. LETTER TO ROMALETA FRANCIS, A STUDENT, JULY 11, 1980 (*KMM342 BHP5*)

Bessie Head,
Post Restante,
Gaborone,
Botswana,
Southern Africa.
11th July, 1980.

Dear Ms. Romaleta Francis,

Thank you for your letter of 23ʳᵈ June and for your paper on my novel A QUESTION OF POWER.

I hardly recognised my novel in your symbolic interpretation of it, but you are excused. A QUESTION OF POWER is a novel readers take fierce possession of. The canvas on which the tale is drawn is BIG, the tale drawn on that canvas, small, sketchy and uncertain. There are wide spaces between each uncertain idea and sketch in which the narrator, Elizabeth, constantly says: I am not sure. I do not understand. But this, roughly, is the way things happened, I think I shall interpret the experience this way. What do you think? This very attitude of uncertainty is an open invitation to the reader to move in and re-write and reinterpret the novel in his/her own way. So A QUESTION OF POWER is a book that is all things to all men and women.

To a psychiatrist it is a description of a wretched form of schizophrenia which is very distressing, but it throws light on the world of insanity about which not so much is known.

To a woman's liberationist the book is pure woman's lib. illuminating some dark and hidden intent on the part of the male of the species to eliminate the female of the species.

To an idealist who would remove poverty and suffering from the world, the book is the ultimate in wonder, the great answer to human suffering.

To the idealist who dreams about the riddle of life and puzzles over it, the wide open spaces of the book are an endless delight, a temptation to re-write, re-dream and reinterpret the story.

So, A QUESTION OF POWER was as strenuous to live and write as it is to read and study and being such it has a place of its own. It is not a bestseller. The majority heartily dislike it and most people left off reading it after page 50 and said many unpleasant things to me such as writers don't go writing books of *that* sort; they write *nice* books and it was a pity I ruined my reputation because most of my books are *nice*.

I admit that A QUESTION OF POWER is autobiographical. The vastness of the canvas was influenced by my belief in Hinduism and a belief in re-birth and re-incarnation. When I began to have unusual experiences I believed then that my past lives were upheaving and that I was faced with eternal and well-known foes. The personalities of Sello and Dan are touched by eternal interpretations of good and evil. A belief in rebirth influences one to a view that each individual, no matter what their origin and background, is really more than what they are. Each individual is the total embodiment of human history and a vast accumulation of knowledge and experience (Freud's view, as well, that this vast accumulation of knowledge and experience is stored in the sub-conscious and that the human individual is a greater mystery than one would suppose and not all flat and two dimensional). This view of Freud and of Hinduism opposes Christianity which proposes the short life span and the brink of the abyss. If you have been good you will go to heaven and eternal life. If you have been bad you will die when you die; you will be obliterated. Hinduism proposes the eternal and gentle continuity of human life, the eternal renewal in birth, the new life that rests on a billion spans of lives. These views influence me profoundly. Always when I meet each individual living being I say: "Ah, here is the total embodiment of human history." More often feeling an individual's wealth of achievement I say: "Ah, here's God." I am inclined to share the title of God among mankind and this makes people extremely uncomfortable. But it is the base of my life and a feeling of reverence for people and the reason why the canvas of A QUESTION OF POWER was so vast.

South Africa is really a part of southern Africa. Southern Africa, which includes countries like the former Rhodesia, Angola and Mozambique, was made one whole economic trading unit during colonial times. The people held in severe bondage were people in Angola, Mozambique, Rhodesia, South Africa and Namibia. Often in South Africa people's protest, and there was always a build-up to a point of protest and demonstration, was minimal. A few police bullets could break protest in a day. I have noted that since the liberation of Angola and Mozambique, which were most unexpected, people's protest in South Africa has become more militant. No longer could a demonstration be broken by a few bullets. The Soweto uprising, which involved all black people throughout South Africa, went on for months and months and cost an enormous amount of lives. This uprising corresponded to the liberation of Angola and Mozambique. The most recent uprising began soon after the most unexpected granting of independence to Zimbabwe (Rhodesia) and the rise to power of a popular black leader. This protest goes on and on with a great loss of lives. It is as though the impossible is happening. Really monstrous and formidable power structures, just disappear overnight. This seems to madden black people in South Africa. They just rush before police and army bullets, completely without fear, maddened by the thought that the horrors just give way. I feel that this is going to build up to a gigantic momentum and they are one day going to rise up and tear the white man to shreds in South Africa. There is less and less fear. There is only hope and courage now.

Yours sincerely,

Bessie Head

19. LETTER TO LEE NICHOLS, VOICE OF AMERICA BROADCASTER IN WASHINGTON, SEPTEMBER 23, 1980 (*KMM122 BHP16*)

Bessie Head,

P.O. Box 1930,

Gaborone,

Botswana,

Southern Africa.

23rd Sept. 1980.

Dear Mr. Nichols,

Thank you for your letter of Sept. 4th which I received through the Embassy here in Gaborone. I am sending this letter through USICA in Gaborone.

I took a cable to you to the USICA office requesting if there was time that two more books be added to the list you already have:

1. *The Collector of Treasures* (short stories, Heinemann African Writers Series, London, 1977).

2. *Serowe: The Village Of The Rain-Wind* (non-fiction, Heinemann African Writers Series, London 1981) This book is at the moment with the printers and I await the galleys for correction. It will be out in 1981 for sure.

My news? I left Serowe some months ago, driven from my small nook there by financial desperation. I could no longer live on my book royalties as the cost of living soars every day. United Nations Development Programme (World Food Programme section) had long asked me to work for them on the basis of rural development work I had done in Serowe. Well this whole year passed by with protracted negotiations about the job and still they have not confirmed it. They asked me if I could work in the

Gaborone office for two years but the red tape they go in for is endless. In the meanwhile my expenses in Gaborone, to complete work on a historical novel were paid for by CUSO (Canadian Universities Service Overseas) and World Lutheran federation. So that is what I have been doing.

I know it's still summer your side so you cannot yet write me one of those marvellous letters filled with snow.

Yours sincerely,
Bessie Head

20. LETTER TO TAHIRAH, A STUDENT, SEPTEMBER 17, 1982 (*KMM346 BHP6*)

Bessie Head,
P.O. Box 15,
Botswana.
17th Sept. 1982.

Dear Tahirah,

All right, persistent lady, I'll take your questions from 1 to 8.

1. From the ages one to thirteen I was cared for by a foster parent and then transferred to a missionary orphanage in Durban—St Monica's Home, Hilary. Attached to the mission I attended Umbilo Road High School and then took my teacher training while still attached to Umbilo Road High with Springfield Training College. On that base I continued educating myself.

2. In South Africa I was merely a part of the black community. I taught for two years in Durban and sought lodgings with an Asian family. Thus, I learned that Asian people were more discriminated against than me, a coloured. Coloureds had never been a threat to the white race but the woman who offered me lodging, had to apply for a special permit to visit friends in Johannesburg. Asian people were restricted to Natal. God, the horror of that land!

3. Botswana is a tribal, tribal land if you care to touch that side of it. Strange, I have seen white people only look at white people and talk to their own as though their own were unique to them. Here I have seen black people do the same. Their own is unique to them. I can count black people who have walked into my home. Two women and one man.

One woman I worked with on a garden project and she is the Kenosi of *A Question of Power*. The other woman was a principal of a secondary school whose life story is on page 83 of *Serowe: Village of the Rain Wind*. The man is my neighbour, Martin Morolong who did a translation on page xviii of *Serowe: Village of the Rain Wind*. He has done many more translations from Setswana to English for me than that, knocked in nails I can't reach and given me money loans. I have lived here for 18 years and those are the only three black people known to me. I seek no one. Life is pleasant enough. One always greets and is greeted. I am not lonely. I have a big international world. The whole world has bought my books and the whole world walks to my door. I receive visitors from all parts of the world, journalists etc. But some complicated things happened to me here which I will elaborate on in answer to question 6.

4. I had refugee status here for 15 years. After thirteen years I was exhausted by having to report to the police every Monday. I applied for citizenship. They quickly refused. Two years later they offered it with no further request from me. That was 1979. I accepted the offer. It is terrifying to travel on the U.N. refugee travel document. You can be imprisoned. I struggled for years and years to leave Botswana but could find no where else to go.

5. A professor, a black American, has said of me: "It is difficult to know which audience she is addressing." I am a highly individualistic person and the two books that express this extreme individualism are *Maru* and *A Question of Power*. People complain and complain that the two books are inaccessible. But in Holland the first books published reflected an African world that was accessible—*When Rain Clouds Gather* and *The Collector of Treasures*. What they mean by the English is African is that this was a former British Protectorate so English and Setswana are both official languages. English, wherever it travels, has the remarkable quality to take on local colour and so a kind of Setswana English is spoken here, clear, sharp, and vivid. I have a good ear for English as it is spoken so what you read in most of my books is a kind of Setswana English. I fear I lived a too solitary life here and find the local language extremely difficult to grasp though I have used dictionaries and many other books to try and learn it.

6. Some complicated things happened to me here. All right,

cancel Elizabeth and let me explain. As soon as I arrived in the country, I felt a deep sense of disturbance. Someone, as I explain in *Question*, entered the hut I was living in and identified himself as a real living man in the village. He's dead now. I would beg that you never use his real name, but he was Seretse Khama, the first president of Botswana. I am not sure the character of Sello is entirely he. I was appalled by the nervous breakdown and the things I said then. Most lines in Part One do not belong to him. They belong to me. I was struggling to sort out a frightening experience. Lines like this belong to me. I thought "That man is the root cause of human suffering." Then I made him say it: "I thought too much of myself. I am the root cause of human suffering." In August 1968 that man did some fatal things. He announced something to the people. On a Saturday morning some pictures were widely distributed. It was of a man, a woman and a child. A little boy approached me and offered me a picture. I refused to accept it, which I regret now, as I have no proof to back what I am saying. But I walked into the house of a friend and asked: "What are those pictures about?" She said: "They are religious pictures," and she looked very frightened. Soon after these people began to attack me. If they caught my eye, they spat on the ground. Three boys aged about 16 approached my son as he was playing in the yard and stoned him. One of the boys shouted: "I don't care. I won't do anything for you." They thought the man wanted to marry me and they went wild. He had superior status. I was an inferior. A young man shouted at me quite out of the blue: "You think you are something but you are just a bloody bastard bushman." I did not think any of these things. The man was only a personality in my mind as you correctly observe. The man *never once, never once* approached me in real life. He took elaborate precautions to create an impassable barrier between him and me, so I don't know him as a real man. I only know rumours. He had cheap sex and slept around with many women. I was some kind of desperation in his life, so deep that it was terrifying. I don't know what he said to the people but he knew me and he never made *one* mistake. He never associated his name publicly with an inferior woman. I have the courage to stand alone against the whole world and I walked steadily through the storm of publicity he raised. I saw black people here as being no different from the Boer. They are blind in their racialism and cruelty and they are no different from the white man. BUT, they did not spit at me for too long or hurt my little boy who was six years old and had caused them no harm. I did not change my routine. I was living then on a refugee allowance of $3.00 a month and a diet of tea. I did not live behind barred doors with security guards like the man did, but without defence, so that they had spat at me and stoned my child. They did not reason that I had not issued those pictures. I did not know what the man wanted from me. This particular society is VERY dangerous. It is male dominated. A man has no faults. They move straight towards a woman and would kill her. The heights of its horror I have experienced because of that man, its racialism and its cruelty to women. But in essence I would not have broken down had I only to face Botswana society. At one stage they realised it was not in their interest to spit at me, they recognised that courage and ignored me because they were not sure of what was going on. I would not have broken down except for the torture of that nightmare world.

7. You ask: You ask, what future world is offered to Elizabeth by Sello. Nothing. The book still belongs to me. I may elaborate on it some day. But it is the sort of book that grows with one's life. I acknowledge that I was not alone, that I was learning, but that is my book and it will grow with my life.

8. You ask: You repeatedly mention homosexuals? What significance? About Part two students have repeatedly asked me to explain the significance of rubbish? What is the significance of the panties? There's no significance in all the rubbish of Part two except that the man Dan did not want the man Sello to approach Elizabeth in real life, hence all the wild violence, abuse and sudden alternations between tenderness and insanity: "My darling, I've been here for sometime. I've watched over everything." Alternated with: "You are a dog, you are filth, you are a coloured dog." Alternated with: "My darling, if I lose you I'll have nothing left." Alternated with: "When I go I go on for one hour. You can't do that. You haven't got a vagina." That really broke me. I am not a woman who arouses men physically. I can make quick contact with a man but the range of my physical experience is very limited. My husband was sexually impotent and that really scared me and put me off any desire to

experiment sexually. I was scared most men would be like that and I could not endure such humiliation. Later, I looked back with humour on that shout: "You haven't got a vagina." It was the shout of a man who could not approach me either and he was saying, the grapes must be sour anyway, after Aesop's fable of the wolf and the grapes. But the shocking cruelty of Part two induced the breakdown.

yours sincerely, Bessie Head

21. Letter to Susan Gardner, June 18, 1983 (*KMM288 BHP11*)

Bessie Head,
P.O. Box 15,
Serowe,
Botswana.
18th June 1983.

Ms. Susan Gardner,
Department of Comparative & African Lit.
University of the Witwatersrand.
1 Jan Smuts Avenue,
Johannesburg 2001.
South Africa.

Dear Ms. Gardner,

Thank you for your letters of 30th May and 7th June.

Thank you for all the feedback material. Many people have taken from me and given nothing in return. Thank you for your great courtesy in handing my re-typed page 2 of the interview to Prof. Mphahlele which stated that I did not work with him at Drum publications because he had just left the office when I arrived. That was all I cared about. I am no social pusher and name dropper.

Thank you, Ravan Press has sent me all the monies they owe me.

The mistake in receiving you and the students was entirely mine. I work in a world where there are no rules. For what I offer there is sometimes a bottle of wine, more often there is nothing. My relationship with the university world has been most unpleasant. Very seldom do I take trips abroad. The University people despise me, the self-made writer. They look at me with a sick grin and say they only pay $12 an hour for a class. I go down well with an audience and students because I love people and have a wide range of interests. When they realise that my work is good, they still look at me with a sick grin and shift the fee to $50.

Some things choke me. I quote Pat's thesis: "I would like to thank Professor R. Nethersole for generously allocating money from Comparative Literature funds for helping to subsidise the trip to Botswana." It was anticipated that I would work a whole day with you and the students for nothing. Never, never again will I do this. Never, never again will I receive students and lecturers from South Africa.

I quote your post card of 17.5.83: "Wits would in any event pay for me (and anyone you wanted to see) to drive up." Why should I be so anxious to see the well-heeled? I am desperately poor.

Any further correspondence from you will be returned unopened. Should you make a mistake of trying in any way to contact me or approach me I will write a letter of complaint to the University administration.

Yours sincerely,
Bessie Head

22. Letter to Christine Green, literary agent, May 31, 1984 (*KMM27 BHP119*)

Bessie Head,
P.O. Box 15,
Serowe,
Botswana.
31st May 1984.

Ms. Christine Green,
John Johnson Authors" Agents Ltd,
Clerkenwell House,
45/47 Clerkenwell Green,
London EC1R OHT.

Dear Christine,

Thank you for your letter of 23rd May and enquiries about the proposed project of my autobiography. I have enclosed three pages of rough notes about my development as a writer. I would plan the autobiography as follows:

I would like the book entitled as *LIVING ON A HORIZON*—a title definitive of one who lives outside all possible social contexts, free, independent, unshaped by any particular environment, but shaped by internal growth and living experience.

I have a good idea of how I work. I work well and quickly with material drawn from living experience, *Maru* was lived for one year and then rapidly typed out in three months. *A Question Of Power* was lived for three years and rapidly typed out in six months. Research work has been much more difficult for me and taken a much longer time. The autobiography would have the category of research for I would have to set up a workshop and draw on notes, papers and letters written over the years. I would like one year clear for this book.

About finance. I understood that a contract and a commission are two different things; that money obtained through a commission would not have to be paid back. Is this so? When you said a sizeable sum of money would be offered I immediately thought of £5,000. Could you get as much money for me as possible? I need to pay my son's airfare back from Canada, which is about $2,500 and I need to renovate my house—the roof is leaking badly.

About photographs. I have three of my youth, one taken when I was six years old. I need these three treated in a special way. Could they be reproduced and the originals sent back to me? I have a lot of photos of my life in Botswana and these I can part with.

Resume of the planning of the book: I would divide the book into two parts—my life in South Africa (27 years) and my life in Botswana (20 years). I have parted with information about the circumstances of my birth but always kept the details as vague as they were given to me. I was thrust into life with no living relatives in sight. My mother was a white woman. Her major tragedy was that her family were very upper class, of Scottish origin and very wealthy, I suspect, involved in mining developments in Johannesburg. The family bred race horses. They were the top strata of South African society. My mother had been married and returned to the family home after a broken marriage. She then muddled and destroyed her life completely. She sought some warmth and love from a black man who tended the family race horses; and so she acquired me. In white South Africa terms the ultimate horror had been committed, that a white woman had had sex with a black man. When the family found out they succeeded in classifying my mother as insane, sped her down away from the family home in Johannesburg to a small town, Pietermaritzburg and locked her up in the Pietermaritzburg Mental hospital where she gave birth to me. I was then removed from her, but she made stipulations. She asked that I should be given her exact same name—Bessie Amelia Emery, and that attention and care be paid to my education and that some of her money be set aside for my education. She was never let out of the mental hospital and committed suicide when I was six years old. They tell me no details were available about my father. I fear they killed him instantly. I have kept the details spare like that but the opposite is the truth about my mother. She caused so much disturbance that there was a thick file on her. One copy was sent to St Monica's Home, Hilary, Durban, where I was partly reared. When I caused any disturbance the file would be brought out and read to me on the understanding that I should not make a noise because my mother had been insane. I might be insane like her too. So I acquired this spare information. I do not believe the Pietermaritzburg Child Welfare Society would release my mother's file to me, because of her status. Other countries honour their citizens and help them find their relatives but not white South Africa. I am as anxious to avoid any knowledge of my mother's white relatives as they were anxious to destroy my mother and disown me. I do not want to know them. Can the early beginnings remain as spare as that? I can offer no more information on my mother except what was told to me when I was a child.

I was partly reared by a foster mother and partly by British missionaries. Although I only have a high school education, the base of my learning fulfilled all my mother's wishes. I was richly educated in South Africa and on a solid base continued to educate myself. This would form the first part of the book.

It is my Botswana experience that would form the bulk of the book. It is incredibly rich in learning, both inwardly and socially. I express a surprise about this because everything happened to me unawares, grew upon me slowly and in a natural way. In the end it could be said that so far all my books have been set in Serowe, that I had not anticipated that books would grow out of a writer's life and that a special and harmonious relationship would unfold between me and my environment. All this experience has been outlined in my books and the biography would be like a filler to questions students of my work have addressed to me over the years because a special relationship developed between me and students of my work. I only needed to write a book

and the most original students in the world would write to me and acquire a first class pass for the M.A. and P.H.D thesis!
     I hope this answers all your questions,
                    Yours sincerely,
                    Bessie Head

23. LETTER TO ELIZABETH FAIRBAIRN, LITERARY AGENT, OCTOBER 21, 1985 (*KMM27 BHP174*)

                                        Bessie Head,
                                        P.O. Box 15,
                                        Serowe,
                                        Botswana.
                                        21st Oct. 1985.

Ms. Elizabeth Fairbairn,
John Johnson Authors' Agent Ltd,
Clerkenwell House,
45/47 Clerkenwell Green,
London EC1R OHT.

Dear Ms. Fairbairn,

Thank you for the contracts for my autobiography and your letters of 7th and 14th October, which I have received at the same time. I return both contracts to you unsigned, by express post. I approve all the clauses in the contract, except clause 3(d), whereby payment will be made to me in three parts. I had understood that the £7,500 would be paid to me in a lump sum and not in three parts. It had not been discussed. I need the £7,500 immediately. Could you make a special appeal to William Heinemann on my behalf? The roof of my house leaks so badly that when it rains, the rain pours into the house. It was built in 1969. Plastic pipe was used for the plumbing. Last year the pipe burst with age and heat. I had to dis-connect it. I draw water with great difficulty to my house. I have a weak back and cannot carry heavy weights. I have been in hospital twice for severe back pain. The full payment for the autobiography will ease these problems and ease the constant struggle to survive and so expedite the work on the autobiography.
     I have written to the Dutch man about his request for an interview. I have a bit of problem about the interview in my home. I was abused by some lecturers of the University of the Wit-

watersrand. I had one of my private papers stolen and one of my friends tampered with in an unpleasant way. Should I send you a full report about this? I do the interview when I travel and am a guest but I am terrified to receive people in my home. I know people make an effort to concentrate on my work so I always offer to reply to enquiries by post.

Heinemann/ AWS. do not have the rights to *Maru*. They only have a sub-lease for their edition from Victor Gollancz Ltd, 50% of which I share with that publisher. I contract independently after that. John Johnson have arranged a number of contracts with me for *Maru*. There is the question of the advance for me. Heinemann AWS have world rights to *A Question Of Power*, *The Collector Of Treasures* and *Serowe: Village of the Rain Wind*. I have here with me the Zimbabwe Publishing House edition of *Maru*. I await your investigations and report to me.

> Yours sincerely,
> Bessie Head.

24. LETTER TO ELIZABETH FAIRBAIRN, JANUARY 16, 1986 (*KMM27 BHP203*)

> Bessie Head,
> P.O. Box 15,
> Serowe,
> Botswana.
> 16th Jan. 1986.

Ms. Elizabeth Fairbairn,
John Johnson (Authors' Agent) Ltd,
Clerkenwell House,
45/47 Clerkenwell Green,
London EC1R OHT

Dear Ms. Fairbairn,

Thank you for your letter of 9th January and the request by Cherry Farrow to do a documentary film on *Serowe: Village of the Rain Wind*. Would you present her with a few problems?

1. I assume she will film the village. I would not allow it for people to be tampered with or filmed or interviewed, without a stipulated fee. I did not take anything from people when I worked with them. I offered them a little payment

for the valuable information they gave me. The agreement was P6.00 or £3.00 or a gift copy of the book. When the book was published I pressed this upon James Currey who was working with me at that time. He kindly sent me 100 gift copies for my contributors. All my contributors wanted the book, not the money.

2. Part three, the Swaneng Project collapsed completely. It existed for eleven years. There's nothing left of it. The training complex has been leased to business people. The project did what the government could not do. It took in 800 trainees and was supported by aid from Holland, Sweden, Denmark, Norway etc. The government could only afford to train 20 students in agriculture. This was later raised to 120 but 3,000 students apply each year for agricultural training. So the Swaneng project was spectacular; the book was written when it was in full swing and the students were on the site. In 1979 the donor aid countries raised a query and sent over their researchers. The brigades were not becoming self-supporting as they had promised to be. They found this hugely-weighted training programme and little productive work. The donor countries withdrew their aid. That was the end of the Serowe brigades.

The book exists because the brigades were a part of the history of the village—a hundred year history of self-help. I cannot help worrying about the lady's project. What I have recorded is an era that has died and passed on. Individual business enterprise has taken over. The village is still as pretty as I describe it in the opening passages of the book but the lady would have to have a very sound reason for taking on this project. Would you present these problems to her?

Yours sincerely,
Bessie Head

25. EXTRACT FROM LETTER TO ELIZABETH FAIRBAIRN, JANUARY 30, 1986 (*KMM27 BHP264*)

. . . . I hope my comments will put the lady Cherry Farrow off the idea of filming Serowe. I have a dread of anyone coming here. They take from people and give nothing and then sell their product for thousands and thousands. No one comes near me now for the interview. I head them off straight at the gate. I permit no stranger an entry. I am content with the quiet audience of students who do their theses on my books.

I have a letter from Adam Lively of William Heinemann. They request the autobiography by September this year. I am able to meet the deadline. I proudly boast a new fridge but it allows me to stay home five days at a time with food stored in the freezer box. They wish that the three-in-one volume be published together with the autobiography in March 1987 and they wish that I come to England at that time. I have written to them to give them the go ahead to plan for my publicity trip. May I ask if they are drawing up a contract with you for the three-in-one volume?

26. THE FOLLOWING TWO PIECES WERE INCLUDED IN A LETTER TO JANE CLEGG, A CRITIC, JULY 16, 1978 (*KMM457 BHP*)

Influences In One's Writing Life

Some Notes on D.H. Lawrence—by Bessie Head

Lawrence was very much a part of my youth—I was first introduced to him at high school and for some time after that acquired as much of his work as I could. Somehow I am thankful that he was such a dominant part of my reading life when younger because one has less power then to discriminate and reject. One merely suffers through experience. Lawrence is so great as a writer and his work covers such an extensive area of human experience that he lends himself to all sorts of purposes—kindly scholarly appraisal and all those labels, the true father of modern literature, the originator of the "idea" novel in english and so on. All I was aware of at one time was that Lawrence was deeply disturbing to read. I think he affects one like that when one is still dependent, wanting to learn codes of conduct and really searching for some answers to life's puzzles. Lawrence attracts and holds one because, essentially, he is the Great Teacher, patient, detailed and absolutely truthful about the message he is transmitting. There were also frontiers he was travelling on, not new to human experience, but new was his interpretation of what may properly be called the hidden darkness, the hells of the world within individuals.

I appreciated his contemptuous remark in a letter to Constance Garnett, the translator of Dostoyevsky: " . . . I don't like him (Dostoyevsky). He hides at the feet of Jesus." And indeed I would have to re-read *The Brothers Karamazov* again because I cannot recall the pretty tendernesses of the holy father whose philosophy made up the bulk of the novel. I am inclined to pretty tendernesses myself. It is not distinctive. It is like the air one cannot do without. My memory of Lawrence is that hard, mean, yappy voice, that deep undertone of malice and hate that threaded its way through almost everything he wrote. It was this which was so deeply disturbing to me; it was a totally foreign view to expound but strangely a reality to millions of people who have suffered on this earth. There was nothing he wrote about people that was not disturbing. He only totally subdued the malice and hate in those essays, on those days he spent utterly alone with the earth and when, towards evening, a small wild flower fell asleep in the palm of his hand. (Who but he and Van Gogh could make the earth vibrate and glow like that?) That hard yappy voice is also subdued in *Lady Chatterley* with an isolation that includes only the earth and a woman. It was the only novel of Lawrence that I read with relief and without anxiety. But what I am trying to say is that an acquaintance with Lawrence is an acquaintance with real reality, that he had his finger on something deeply awry in human nature, something that could not hide at the feet of Jesus, something that he toweringly had control of—a world full of evil. If I say Lawrence and evil, that's not the total story. But Lawrence and evil move together like a continually unfolding dialogue. Somewhere at the back of my mind, that early acquaintance with Lawrence seems to be the only reason for my survival and sanity today. I wasn't intended to survive the view of evil I recorded in *A Question Of Power*. But it was as though he had mapped out that unfamiliar terrain where only the horrific occurs and life is so weirdly askew that it can do nothing but remain askew. There's no salvation there whatsoever, no devil to overcome, no hope, no nothing, only a sustained horror.

Lawrence said: "Art for my sake". I agree but the canvas Lawrence worked on was vast indeed. I take the view that we don't live once but that we've lived billions of times on this earth, so that each living individual could be said to be the total embodiment of human history. Lawrence was like that, way behind the English miner's son, the totality of all that he had ever been, right to primeval times (a word he was so fond of) as though by that word primeval, he was indicating how total was the assessment he was making. No one could interpret himself to himself the way Lawrence did, no one had access to insights into evil and its workings as he did. His method seemed to be two-fold, quietly laying out a hoary man, a horror and side by side slowly building up a new man, with new values, depending on what riches life was offering him as he lived.

I would like to tackle *Sons and Lovers* to illuminate the above. It's one of those books that are all awry and yet no book promises more from the opening chapters. The lay-out of the small mining town is panoramic and utterly absorbing. One settles down to read one of the most fascinating books ever written and then bang! mid-way the novel is dead. The heroes on whom Lawrence lavishes love and attention, Mrs Morel and the boy, Paul Morel, are on the wrong side of the fence. One does not have any love at all for the horrific woman and Lawrence presents her in all her horror, sparing no detail. There's that glorious man, Morel, a part of the early panorama and a part of the general kindnesses and humanity of the surrounding people. They are all poor but Morel arranges the rent payments in such a way that his wife never has a moment's worry about it, such as the other wives have. Family life, we find out, is so central to his existence, that when he finally becomes aware that something is wrong with the woman he married, he assaults her, he gets stone drunk, but he cannot leave her. Morel is so rich as a man that he flings around tendernesses like a billionaire. There's a part where he walks in. His wife is pregnant. His voice went tender: "I brought thee something and something for the little ones . . ." To every tenderness she replies: "Ugh, don't bother me with your natter . . ." He flings around absent-minded tendernesses on the children: "Hullo, my pretty . . ."

That boy Paul Morel has all the horrors of his mother. He says of the ordinary mining-men: "I don't like them. They are common." His mother accepts many kindnesses from the local women; they help her with her pregnancies but they are common too. Mid-way in the novel the boy Paul Morel, has totally ousted his father and he and his mother carry on their strange love affair. It doesn't matter what happens, only he and his mother exist: "Their eyes met . . ." I got sick of it. The book was like ash in my mouth. I peeped at the end and there she was the horror, opening the door to Paul's girl friends with hostile stares, shouting "he's not here," and slamming the door again. The experience between mother and son is intense yes, spiritual yes, but spiritual evil.

Lawrence writes: ". . . as her sons grew up she selects them as lovers—first the eldest, then the second . . . when they come to manhood, they can't love because their mother is the strongest power in their lives . . . William gives his sex to a fribble, and the mother holds his soul . . . the younger son decides to leave his soul in his mother's hands and goes for passion . . ."

There was a lot of that in Lawrence, dark dungeons where one demon holds down the soul of the other demon. They laughingly do nothing beyond their horrors that sometimes it's a relief they were at least surrounded by normal people. The father, Morel, is so male, so normal, so human. They keep him out of the secret, funny game. They despise him but they do not despise themselves for the perverts they are. One is just left with this disturbing tale and that it was all written the wrong way.

I have here an essay on Lawrence: *Pilgrim of the Apocalypse* by Horace Gregory and among other things, he casually brings together the two novels, *Sons and Lovers* and *Lady Chatterley*. He asks: "Just what did Lawrence want with the Indians and his search for the ultimate male type?" Horace Gregory maintains that the ultimate male for Lawrence had been in his own father. He compares Mellors and Morel. Everytime Mellors speaks of love, he breaks into the tender Nottinghamshire dialect spoken by Morel in *Sons and Lovers. Lady Chatterley* is such a peaceful, reflective novel that one almost feels the new man laying himself out. I have never read a biography of Lawrence but the little that has come through about his life and his marriage do not seem at all pleasant. He was a violent enough reading experience simply because Lawrence was religious in action. He was making something for himself while alive. He was acknowledging all his horrors but only replacing them with the truly supreme—not the mystical and absent, but only what life offered him.

There is that symbol he used, the phoenix rising from its *own* ashes. The key word is *own*, to find redemption in one's own power. Lawrence seemed so clear to me after my own view of evil. Initially, I thought I would retrack him for the enlightenment he offered. Then I found that I could not make the effort. It is not my natural terrain. I acknowledge evil for its own sake, that it is there and laughingly, full of rubbish, that is of no use to mankind. I felt that Lawrence gathered all that rubbish together, and he was full of rubbish and burnt it on a huge ash heap. This making of a new man was only stated in intuitive terms.

There is absolutely no difference between the inner dungeons described by Lawrence and the more real dungeons described by Pasternak in *Zhivago*. But Pasternak, the man, is not the source of human suffering. I greatly fear that words like—"in me are people without names/ children, stay-at-homes, trees/ I am conquered by them all/ and that is my only victory"—are not the words of a man who has the power to change the world or rule the world, but he ensures day to day survival.

Some notes on Camara Laye & exile, etc.

Statements on politics and exile were made by Dennis Brutus, Lewis Nkosi, Pierre Bambote and Camara Laye. Brutus and Nkosi have written down their views about being South African writers in exile. I just did not pay heed to what Brutus was saying as he was so loathsome to me. But Lewis Nkosi talked to me privately about being helplessly addicted to whisky. He said its source was a sense of lostness and loneliness in his life in London. But there is a wonderful charm in Lewis. He is a scholar. He did not seem to be talking about death because he became very alert when we discussed the writings of Ayi Kwei Armah and others and he has a book of criticism of African literature which will be published next year. So it looks like he was only worried and ashamed about alcohol. Once we were invited for coffee in the afternoon. Our host presented us with the coffee and everyone kept politely silent. Lewis in anguish asked for whisky. The host obliged. Soon everyone partook of that whisky bottle and he glowed with relief. "My disease is catchy," he said. I am not sure Lewis" problem is lostness and loneliness in London and a longing for South Africa. I worked with him on Drum Publications in Johannesburg and he was a misfit there too. Then, he was struggling away from the black world. He never talked to us, the black staff on the paper but seemed then to hunger only to communicate with white people with whom he associated. He never liked the black world and I was somewhat amazed when he talked to me. So, I could not sort him out, except that there is an undying charm in the man.

Pierre Bambote's exile from the Central African Republic seems to be only temporary. He fled the Bokassa regime and talked about what has become evident in world news—that Bokassa killed school children with his own hands.

The most gruesome story of exile was told by Camara Laye. Fifteen years ago he was among the cadres who formed the first government of Guinea with Sekou Toure. It soon became evident that Toure was killing off his comrades one by one. Camara Laye had been posted as Guinea's ambassador to Ghana. He was filled with anxiety and abandoned his post and fled to Sierra Leone. Then he made an error. He sent his wife back to Ghana to wind up his family affairs. She was arrested at the airport and imprisoned for eight years. He fled with his seven children to France. The years of anxiety and the strain of rearing seven children broke his health. He lives on tablets from day to day. The threads of his writing were broken and he can only write fairy stories for children. He said: I am the only living member of the cadres who formed the first government with Sekou Toure. "I am alive because I fled."

Camara Laye might represent that feeling of suddenly shrivelling up in a creative sense but it is not so easy to say so. A book or books are an accumulation of living observation. Sometimes one gives one's all in a few books. Sometimes a dam waits to burst and then the great masterpiece or masterpieces come pouring out. I can never tell with myself because I live on a very violent cycle. I tend to crash right down to rock bottom where nothing exists and suddenly take a violent and unexpected upward swing. The two pivots are absolutely necessary for me, not peaceful even-keel day to day work. I have to pause and drop. Sometimes I have to wait and wait until I can control my material.

27. AN ARTICLE, UNDATED (*KMM187 BHP19*)

News about Berlin (for my friends)

Bessie Head.

They told me June was the month for roses in Berlin. They blazed away in deep red and pale pink hues on every available patch of earth. Never have I seen a city of such fantastic beauty, planted out with flowers and trees. We lived in the very posh, expensive area of Charlottenberg but worked each evening in the Kunstlerhaus Bethanien, in the slums of Krozberg. A German writer Erica Runge was obsessed that I see the stark horror of Krozberg where blocks of old buildings were massed together and where no air and sunlight penetrated and where no flowers and trees grew. Krozberg was crowded with Turkish immigrants and thousands of little children playing on the streets. Charlottenberg was an endless stream of women with slender figures with not a child in sight. Erica Runge walked me through endless courtyards in Krozberg, showing me the bullet holes of the last war and the crumbling buildings where people still lived. Two things amazed me. What could be called the slum area of West Berlin was spotlessly clean and without smells like Charlottenberg. Secondly, slogan after slogan was painted on the crumbling walls. There were endless slogans about the Vietnam war and the atom bomb—the latest passion being "Support Swapo for an independent Namibia!"

The writers on the programme:

My main initial worry was that I would dislike the writers on the programme. They were all the well-known and established writers of Africa and I feared that they would be completely self-centred and absorbed in their own fame. Of our whole group I really disliked Dennis Brutus and the two French-speaking writers, Mongo Beti and Ahmadou Kourouma. Mongo Beti and Kourouma were strange men indeed. Our programme proceeded with such difficulty and chaos that at one point when nothing made sense any more we began to realise that we were being presented to the German public by our organiser, Dagmar Heusler, as mindless savages from darkest Africa, we began to pull together to nail her to the ground. The two French-speaking writers at that point threw themselves into her embrace.

Dennis Brutus was a tragedy all of his own making. I think he had attended too many literary conferences of this kind. We were constantly under pressure to talk and explain ourselves. There was not a moment's free time when a microphone did not appear before our mouths. For my part I grimly held onto the village from which I had come. I did not like the news media men and women. They are hard-eyed, vicious and greedy. I pitted the whole village of Serowe against them and the slow unfoldment of rural development and I would not budge from this. To my surprise the interviews would run into four or five hours. God knows how many interviews I have on my life in Serowe and God knows where they went! But suddenly in Rome, on my way back, the tremendous battering of the past days overwhelmed me. For a moment I thought I had gone insane. My head was a confused roar. I stood still in the airport, rocking to and fro, on the point of collapse. There was a point at which Dennis Brutus had gone completely insane and did not know it. His face was always set in grim hard lines. His eyes were hard and greedy like the news media men. His eyes restlessly swept the room to see who noticed or was taking note of the great Brutus. Horror of horror, he never stopped talking. He talked all the time in a slow, unending drawl. His voice was horrible to hear because he clipped words back into his mouth and you could not really hear what he was saying. The charm of human dialogue was long lost to him. He had long stopped absorbing any learning from life but was only offering life himself, Brutus, dead and deadly dull in an unending stream. He expressed opinions on everything in sight in a final flat dead voice. No one could have a counter opinion. You could not even ask him the time or any simple ordinary human question. He would only look right through you. He only laughed at his own jokes. The only redeeming feature was that he noticed something was wrong with Dagmar Heusler. But Dennis Brutus was a lesson and a warning. Should writers attend conferences of this kind? What happens to the creative man within? What happens to all those moments of quiet, dreaming tenderness. Some dreams are so tender that they can never be communicated in words.

There was something sly and skulking about Nuruddin Farah but he never came near enough to bother me much. I only observed at a distance that he was not so nice and that my great love, Taban Lo Liyong, hated him.

For the rest, all the writers were men of great dignity, at peace with themselves. Particularly outstanding as a man was Lenrie Peters, a surgeon and writer from Gambia. He and Taban Lo Liyong, I loved most. Taban loved to clown and clown and take off his shoes and walk around barefoot. Taban was an open, generous and straight-forward man. Chinua Achebe was always peaceful and even-keel and on the whole there was a great feeling of harmony amongst us, with no one pushing for anything and everyone in pleasant agreement with the other. This was to help us greatly because for the first few days complete chaos was presented to us. A programme was written down on paper but the programme was not supposed to work. When we asked our programme organiser, Dagmar Heusler about times to assemble or any direct, practical questions as to the work at hand—that was what she could not stand. She did not want it like that. She wanted us paralysed, broken and speechless. Most of the writers began to suffer from a deep depression.

Dagmar Heusler, the programme organiser: Before we arrived in Berlin, Ms. Dagmar Heusler was the lady who wrote us very nice letters. Several writers, including myself, had the same thought in mind—to take her a gift because we had liked her letters so much. Mongo Beti went further. He wrote and asked her to marry him.

The first evening we met my liking for Ms. Heusler was over and I immediately began to worry about how I was going to survive her. She invited me to dinner and spent a long time explaining to me that there were three capitalist devils in Berlin, a certain Eckhardt, the over-all boss of the festival, a certain Klicker, her boss on the literature programme and Dr. Haerdter, the manager of the Kunstlerhaus where we were to work. We never met Klicker and Eckhardt. We saw Dr. Haerdter every evening at the Kunstlerhaus but had no communication with him beyond a greeting. He was a silent man, who only smiled and shook hands. We were to notice as the days went by that when we asked Ms. Heusler a direct question about work or time she would reply that either Klicker, Eckhardt or Haerdter, hated her. That evening she also told me that the German government (west, that is) did not approve of our presence in Berlin because we were Marxists. We were there because she had strenuously fought our cause. She next began to attack my person. She said in a very disappointed voice that from my letters she had assumed that I was an emancipated woman. The extreme disappointment in her voice implied that I was not. She also observed that English was the most inferior language in the world. The most superior language was Italian. It had a thousand words for saying "get up", whereas in English you could only say "get up" and nothing more. She also asked me if I liked action or peace. I said I liked peace.

Before we arrived in Berlin Ms. Heusler informed us that air fares, board and accommodation would be provided. She now informed me that I could only eat breakfast at the hotel. We would have to purchase lunch and supper out of an allowance of DM40 per day. She would let me have some money at 1 o'clock the following day. I never saw Ms. Heusler for 3 days. On the first day she sent a young lady to ask me if I was hungry. She would lend the young lady DM50 to take me to a meal and pay back the young lady the following day. I was so embarrassed that I told the young lady I was not hungry. The second day no one approached me. I stayed alone in my hotel room and was taken for a meal by the German writer, Erika Runge. On the third day at 5pm, Ms. Heusler phoned and asked me to come downstairs. She asked me in a gay and amused voice how I liked Berlin. I did not like *my* situation. I had left home with fifty dollars and it was not going to last long in Berlin. The cheapest meal was DM11. Everything else cost DM31 in Charlottenberg. I looked her straight in the face and asked her if I was supposed to purchase lunch and supper out of my own money. She looked startled and uncertain and then said airily: "Oh, thank you for reminding me. DM1000 is due to you—DM500 for food, DM500 for your public reading. Would you like it all at once?" I wanted nothing more to do with her so I said yes. She gave me DM500.

Eventually it turned out I had received the highest sum of money of all the writers. For six days Achebe, Taban, Lenrie Peters, Mongo Beti and Kourouma received no food allowance. They had to purchase food out of their own money. Other writers were given either DM100 or DM200. On the Sunday she called a meeting. It was a subtle appeal to us to ask her for no more money. It was a mad rambling story. First Eckhardt the big boss had lost his job because he had abused the money. (Eckhardt remained the boss of everything till we left). Secondly, the German government had removed DM80000 from the allowance allocated to us because we were Marxists.

Another drama was going on in the hotel. Ms. Heusler booked us in and was paying the major bill. She ordered the hotel not to transfer any incoming calls to our rooms. But we would find discrete notes each day in our hotel boxes. I myself received a wild message: Mr Reital phoned. Phone him back! Urgent! I knew no Mr Reital nor was there a number to phone.

The public readings were long drawn-out agony. Some writers had lengthy English texts. The lengthy English text was read. The German translation was read. This for two hours. From 7.30pm. to 11.30pm. This for two writers per evening. The first evening Ulli Beier, the father of African literature moderated. He knew most of the Nigerian and Ghanaian authors personally and had published their first poems and stories. He had made notes on us all to introduce us to the German audience. The second evening Ulli was driven off and his place taken by Ms. Heusler. Her low deep modulated voice flowed like a river over the stunning amplifier system. The excuse was that his notes were too long. They were not. It was the German translations of English and French texts that were too long. She modulated on the writers without reference to notes, implying that Ulli had to read his notes but she could sail over us. She knew our works so well.

Lenrie Peters preceded me. No writer has been allowed to

greet the German audience. He suddenly turned and flashed a smile and greeted people and established a chatty relationship with the audience. He said that he was sorry that Ulli Beier had been removed from the programme as Ulli had published his first poem.

On Wednesday everything came to a head. I came down to the reception lounge and the writers were counting the insults. We had to go to a workshop and organise it ourselves. Ms. Heusler, the organiser, turned up two hours later. We were handed workshop topics in German and had to ask for an English translation of the topics before we could proceed. The workshop proceedings were being taped but if so only Ms. Heusler knew this and had access to the tapes. Deep secrecy surrounded the tapes and there were a thousand people who wanted the material because the topics and discussions were valuable, often deeply moving. Six of the writers had been forced by political circumstances into exile and had not lived in Africa for years and years and could no longer write about Africa. Camara Laye said he now wrote fairy tales. He is the author of "The African Child". Next, Chinua, Lenrie Peters, George Hallet and Gavin Jantjes were leaving the following day. They had not been paid a food allowance nor for their public readings. Next, a lecturer from Frankfurt had brought his students to see us. He asked Ms. Heusler if we could talk to his students. At first she said no, then she said: "You can take Taban Lo Liyong because he needs the money". All the writers were looking indignantly at each other. No one wanted to go to the third workshop. Gavin Jantjes, frantic about his money phoned Ms. Heusler with that message. She replied that we could only get our money if our return air tickets were photocopied. He began to try to frantically grab our air tickets while everyone shouted no, no, no. This is a further humiliation. Somehow we moved off in the bus to the workshop. No one wanted to start the workshop. Ms. Heusler was not available. The discussion about humiliation and indignity continued and delightfully was being taped into Ms. Heusler's secret tapes. Eventually Lenrie Peters tried to bring order. We had a very few select German guests in our midst. It was suggested that we continue for the benefit of our guests and settle scores with Ms. Heusler later. Then someone suddenly turned to me and said: What do you say, Bessie? I grabbed the microphone and shouted: "We are fools to continue. We are nothing but Ms. Heusler's black dogs". The two French-speaking writers began to bang the table loudly. They said: "We object to this woman's language!

That is no way to speak in a conference hall!" (Mongo Beti and Kourouma). Shaking with anger I stood up and walked out. A German journalist ran after me. He said: "If you say you are Ms. Heusler's black dogs, then we are Ms. Heusler's white dogs. She treats us the same way." Just then Ms. Heusler came speeding towards us. The journalist said: "Turn now and tell her what you told us". I was beside myself with rage. I began shouting at the top of my voice, an incoherent jumble of things—that she dare not insult Taban Lo Liyong, that she was right at death's door. I was about to kill her. She looked back coolly and innocently: "I don't know what you are talking about," she said.

German people began running in all directions. They were phoning, Eckhardt, Klicker and Haerdter. No one talked to us before this showdown. Then Berlin people had a lot to say about Ms. Heusler. She had got the job as our literary organiser by selling her vagina to a man who had a lot of power. They asked Klicker to fire her on the spot. He kept silent, frightened of the man who had the power. But Ms. Heusler was irrelevant from that moment onwards. I certainly never saw her again. What I saw was the whole of Berlin and love in abundance. No matter which way I turned I saw the glowing face of a Berliner. People had seemed cold and removed. The people are also violently emotional. I don't know how many people embraced me and kissed me wildly on both cheeks.

I brought Ulli Beier back on the programme. Like Lenrie Peters I turned to the audience, smiled and greeted and chatted for a bit. After that day I know a thousand things about Berlin and Germany and statistics of unemployment because people never stopped talking to me freely and joyfully.

At six o'clock on the evening of that Wednesday all the writers were paid their full allowance. Dr. Haerdter said that the German government had not taken away the money. It had been in the office all the time, Ms. Heusler did not want to part with it. I am sorry so much attention goes to Ms. Heusler. She was real and very dangerous. To this day we do not know if it was only she or another and she who worked hard to present us to the German public as mindless savages. If they wished to do so, why did they choose the most articulate writers in Africa? Why was there such a muddle? Or was it only she, a pathetic mentally ill woman? A part of the experience was terrifying. But there are solid, honest, good and wonderful people in Berlin.

28. AN ARTICLE, UNDATED (*KMM457*)

Khama, The Great

Very little must have changed for the old man who shuffled his way into our project garden, early that morning. Intent on performing an ancient tribal duty, he was quite oblivious of the fact that our local industries project, "Boiteko" was straining to be an imitation of the Chinese commune and Ujamaa villages of Tanzania. In a corner of our workshop stands a blackboard on which a dedicated Marxist had copied out some of the thoughts of Mao Tse-tung on how to encourage a spirit of co-operation among people working on a collective enterprise. That morning the old man unconsciously demonstrated that African custom is ahead of the strenuous and exhausting programme Mao outlined for China—co-operation among the people is already there.

After a curt nod in my direction (I am an outsider and foreigner), the old man turned to my garden work partner, Bosele, and talked to her briefly. As he kept silent, her only comment was: "Ow," said in a sympathetic voice. The old man turned and walked away. She remained thoughtful and serious, so I asked:

"What did the old man say?"

"He has come to tell me about the death of Abotseng's child during the night," she said.

"Is Abotseng your relative?" I asked.

She looked up at me, then rested back from the crouched position of transplanting onions. It was time again to explain "the law" to one who did not know. Time and time again she had explained "the law" across the vegetable beds. It was a law so sacred, personal, immediate that it was written in the heart. It dictated how man should care for man.

"Abotseng is not my relative," she said. "But we live in the same village. When there is a death we must all help. The old man always goes to each person in the morning to tell about a death. I might bring a bucket of water to wash the body. Other women might go into the bush to collect wood for the fire. The men must agree to dig the grave. People who cannot offer help must present a proper excuse or they will be hated. It is our custom."

Did Mao Tse-tung need to add anything on that? And yet, for the economics of poverty, his literature and outlines for development threaded its way through all the work projects we undertook, as though our work was part African, part something new. But our work environment had to be taken into account too. Bamangwato area is unlike any other area in the country. It is always part African, part something else. Bamangwato people claim a long line, eight they say, of turbulent and erratic geniuses among their leadership of chiefs and the smouldering flame of it can be tracked down to Khama, The Great.

Of course I'd heard of him as soon as I arrived in Botswana. Little children can recite in a sing-song all the details about a cow: "we use every part of it," they sing and they have an enchanting dance about cows—their horns turn up, their horns turn down and they move their hands this way and that. Little children in school also parrot off in sing-song all the achievements of Khama, The Great: "He abolished bogadi," they sing. "He abolished the drinking of beer. He abolished witchcraft. He abolished polygamy. He abolished . . . . . ."

My knowledge of Khama, The Great might have grown no further than that if it hadn't been that at the time I was reading Edgar Snow's RED STAR OVER CHINA, acquaintances in England had written to ask me to uncover some detail about their great granddad, John Mackenzie, who had been a missionary in Botswana, years and years ago. I'd been going through a state, like a sort of working nightmare over Snow's book—the terrible descriptions of inhuman cruelty and poverty . . . . . .

"Have you ever seen a man—a good honest man who has worked hard, a "law-abiding citizen", doing no serious harm to anyone—when he has had no food for more than a month? It is a most agonising sight. His dying flesh hangs from him in wrinkled folds; you can clearly see every bone in his body; his eyes stare out unseeing, and even if he is a youth of twenty he moves like an ancient crone, dragging himself from spot to spot . . ." This is the sort of writing one turns to again and again struggling to penetrate the deep anguish of so many human beings who have died through the greed of others.

In my efforts to track down the missionary, John Mackenzie, the literature of that time, the invasion into Southern Africa by the whites, particularly the Boers, began to read as terrible as Snow's descriptions of pre-revolutionary China—the evil was the same, *land greed*, then gold greed. John Mackenzie, the missionary, exists in his relationship to Khama, The Great. As you begin to read and read a picture slowly emerges of a towering personality, the Lincoln of Southern Africa. Lincoln is the only majestic title I can give to a man like Khama. And the greatness of the missionaries like Mackenzie was that they saw the greed of the white man, were repelled by it and contributed to the drafting of the great land tenure laws Khama and two chiefs handed to Queen Victoria when they sought to make Botswana a British Protectorate.

"that the land is not saleable, and that this law is good" because "the South Africa Company wants to take our land and sell it so that they may see gain; The South Africa Company wants to impoverish us so that hunger may drive us to become the white man's servants and dig in his mines and gather his wealth."

I know a bow is made to the two chiefs, Bathoen and Sebele, who accompanied Khama to England but the lofty beauty of those words ". . . . That the land is not saleable, and that this law is good . . ." exclusively belong, in my mind, to the personality of Khama. Chiefs Bathoen and Sebele controlled other tribal areas but the strength and stability of Botswana comes entirely from the thorough revolution Khama made, all at once, from top to bottom of the Bamangwato area. Times have to change and a rare genius is a man who makes them change all at once.

They say colonial rule lasted for one hundred years in Africa, but in Botswana for only eighty. There was a gap of about twenty years before the Boers and other white traders, land-seekers, gold seekers reached his borders but not a gap for reports to reach him about a pattern that had unfolded of the white man's behaviour in South Africa. They were a people of different values and concepts of wealth who encountered a culture where, for one thing the land was not the African man's wealth; it was just there to be used as needed. If there were a concept of wealth it was in cattle. In this age and time when words like "the inferior natives" can be re-examined, it is clear to see whose behaviour at that time was most inferior, and still is. The Boers started out on a career of theft from a people who had not direct sense of possession. They continue it to this day, only now they call their stealing by nice legal names like the Group Areas Act. Is there any difference between what is happening in South Africa now and what happened to Livingstone's house in Kolobeng, Botswana?

. . . . . "Livingstone travelled back (to Botswana) only to discover that during his absence the Boers had again raided Kolobeng, shot many of Sechele's people and driven them away. His house had been ruined, all his furniture carried away and all his diaries of his early travels and adventures destroyed . . . ."

A black man of the personality of Khama, can then, like Lincoln formulate certain broad principles, untorn himself by the turmoil of his times as so many black men were. It wasn't only against the white man's greed that his land laws formed a block of protection for his people; he turned towards tribal society and undid its self-undoing weaknesses, the sorts of weaknesses where one bad cause could forever corrupt his world and where God had not yet fulfilled himself, in many ways. The endless abolishments he made helped open the tight, closed door of custom to new things.

Two portraits of the man, Khama, are available, the one drawn up by the white missionaries, the other that can be pieced together from conversations with villagers. The former so lifts him above and out of context of his society that one has an unpleasant sensation of reading about the one black man who really *made it* into the white man's world. He is left hanging there somewhere in the air, a phenomenon of achievement it is hard to equal. Great attention is drawn to the conflict between his father, Segoma, described as a "heathen" and the so called "Christian" element in Khama. Segoma is presented in such degrading terms that in the end he appears like a devil capable of all evils. His son, Khama, rises at his expense.

Re-linked, re-written, the story of Khama and his father would read something like this: All I had later was given me by my father. My father made me the great man I am, even though he did it by default.

The clue to the conflict comes out of the diary of David Livingstone. Livingstone, while intent on his missionary work was such a beautiful and sensitive recorder of human personality that a vivid word portrait is left of Segoma, the father of Khama. Towards evening one day, Livingstone and Segoma sat in a hut together in discussion on things philosophical. A mood of deep brooding fell upon Segoma then he turned towards Livingstone and said: " My heart is proud and angry ... " Before Livingstone could reply, Segoma abruptly stood up and left the hut.

In contrast to this, from out of the fading Victorian photographs of Khama, stares a serene, composed face, with humorous eyes.

Under ordinary circumstances then the conflict between father and son would have been explained as the mutual antipathy of two personalities who are like poison to each other; for from Livingstone's portrait in words we get the impression of Segoma, the man, as turbulent, emotional, moody and full of himself, with all his life processes out of control. The face of Khama, the humorous eyes, is the face of a man in full control of himself and others. It is also the face of a natural law-maker. How is it in Africa we are told then that personality conflicts are due to one man being a "heathen" and the other a "Christian"?

In the village of Serowe I met the youngest grandson of Khama, the Great, also named Segoma. I told him that I had become deeply interested in the life of his grandfather but laughingly added that he sounded like the white man's pet.

"On the contrary", he said. "Khama conducted all his affairs with foreigners through his secretary, Rathosa. He preferred to talk Setswana. He is one of the most popular leaders we have ever had but for a reason especially appreciated by my people. He had what the old people call the gifts a man is born with. For instance, I have a university education. It does not impress the old people. They have asked me to display my own gifts, not something acquired outside myself."

After reading all I had found available on Khama, the Great, I was left with the peculiar feeling that one other ancient African custom had all along been one jump ahead of mankind. Only today do we have the world wide pre-occupation with co-operation and communal ownership, as opposed to individual profit and gain. But as far as African land laws were concerned, it had always been there that the land was the common property of all men. The little children should take note and add an amendment to their village chants about Khama, the Great. Yes indeed he had abolished one hundred and one tribal customs but he did not abolish the ancient tribal land laws. It was this very law that had been the undoing of all the tribes of Southern Africa. A whole lot of good forces, moved into place at that time between him, Queen Victoria and the British Government and these he used as a powerful block, for his country, against the land grabbing Boers. It must have been the personality of the man, his gift to make noble and coherent to a rather horrible people, an innate nobility in some aspect of African life.

When are a man's times not tense with challenge? One senses in the trend of liberated or independent Africa that the image of terrible greed has merely shifted from a white face, to a black face. Those of us who work on small village communal projects look forward, perhaps, to another African Lincoln-like figure such as Khama, the Great, who will make a general summary of Africa's nobility which will act as a powerful block against Africa's greed.

—The End.

29. THE FOLLOWING IS THE TYPESCRIPT OF AN INTERVIEW
BETWEEN HEAD AND ELLEN BICK MEIER. MEIER PUBLISHED AN
ARTICLE ON HEAD IN *INFORMATION* UNDER A TITLE WHICH
TRANSLATED MEANS "THE WORLD WITHOUT MEN." THE
VERSION HERE BEARS A DIFFERENT TITLE (*KMM446 BHP6*)

A Writer with Earth under her Nails.

Interview with Bessie Head.

How did you become a writer?

For a while I was a journalist, and inside every journalist hides a novelist. This was a crucial point. I have, however, always been engaged in writing.

Who has influenced your writing?

When I was around twenty I happened to read a biography on Brecht, "The Choice of Evils". It was especially his style and method that influenced me. When he built up his didactic plays they were based on research which also included statistical facts. This fascinated me and stayed in the back of my head: to be able to use literature in this way and most of my writings, novels and short stories—are based on facts from reality, like development of rural projects. I have never hesitated to use facts and figures—gathered through research—for a novel.

In "A Question of Power" for example the narrator is involved in a development project in the rural areas. The basic facts of the starting up of the project is part of the book together with many everyday events and all the difficulties and results of working together and sharing things.

You have been part of a collective with women from rural areas yourself.

As I have told you in "A Question of Power" which is an autobiographical novel, I was in charge of the growing of vegetables. The problem was that the project did not yield enough profit for the women to live on. We had a nursery, a vegetable garden and a small-scale industry producing gooseberry-jam. I was working on a voluntary basis. I started some renewals that became useful during draughts. In Serowe there were several projects: A weavery, a laundry with soap production, a pottery and a textile unit. The whole list is there, in a "A Question of Power". The women came to learn a skill. But they also came for another reason. You see, they had experienced the break-down of the traditional family-structure. They were alone with a lot of children born outside marriage. The society was out of balance: there were more women than men. These women joined the development projects in the country, and I was entirely preoccupied with growing vegetables and storing all their life-stories inside me—about their poverty and their struggles. This place was where I gathered most of the facts that became part of "The Collector of Treasures". The women joined the projects to be able to find solutions to their problems.

What do you consider your main literary topics?

My books are about choices and the constant attempt of avoiding the sources of power. These are the choices which have been essential to me as a writer, and sometimes I put the question to myself if these are the choices that Africa is faced with.

In "A Question of Power" the power problem is carried through to its inner core, and this does not appeal to people. The book is a precise account of what happened to me during a breakdown after one year of insomnia.

The assumption of the book is that the two male principal characters are gods in human disguise. We give the gods nicknames—they are the "almighty", the "protector of all". Imagine if you meet one of these human gods. If you give complete confidence to another person, you cannot be sure that this person is the opposite of what is said about him. Because, if a person is almighty who can prevent him from being a rude libertine or one who prosecutes his fellow-men with that incredible power. I believe that Jesus was a good man, but where in history do you find leaders, people in positions of power who have been nothing but a source of suffering for their fellow-men. People believe in the existence of a good creator who can protect them. This is not true. My book disturbs people because they need something supernatural to rule over them. But they never put a question to whether this idea is not the source of suffering to mankind. People ought to question and analyse what it is that rules them—if it is love, compassion, use value, friendliness or if it is the incredible god or gods who are brutal and cruel. I wrote the book to regain my self-respect which was battered after the breakdown. But also to study how people can survive the kind of horror I have gone through—it was a kind of defence, a reason to keep on living.

What are you working at now?

I have just finished: Serowe: Village of the Rain Wind.

The title covers some of my private experiences. I lived in Serowe during the drought when you could smell the rain in the wind, but you never got a drop. During the drought we have a teasing small rain playing around the small blue mountains around the village. You can see the rain falling in the distance, sheets of rain. The wind passes through the rainy part and you can smell it, but you never get a single drop of it yourself. This can drive people mad. The book starts with a description of the climate—the drought that I have experienced. It is not a novel but a portrait of the village based on interviews with 94 Serowe dwellers of all ages. It is based on their words. My next project is a new kind of book—a historic fiction. This is a difficult way for me to work. I want to describe the foundation of the Bechuanaland Protectorate (now Botswana). It is a noble story. My thesis is that the big surrender of land to the colonial powers in a way stopped here. The resistance is personified by the old chief, Khama the Third. He would not be my hero, had he not been able to share his power. The old chiefs possessed great power, because they also possessed supernatural power—the power to make rain, the power of life and death. They were considered next to the almighty—next to God. Perhaps this also explains some of the problems of independent Africa and the fact that the only charge of leadership has been through coups and murders.

Why are there in your opinion so few African women writers?

In the Serowe district I have experienced that the women were unbelievably suppressed in a completely men-dominated society. Also the women are illiterate. You cannot overcome centuries of oppression in one day and become conscious.

Ellen Bick Meier.
Information August 1980

References

Works by Bessie Head

Head, Bessie. 1975. Preface to "Witchcraft." *Ms Magazine*. November.

————. 1981. *Serowe: Village of the Rain Wind*. London: Heinemann.

————. 1984. *A Bewitched Crossroad*. Craighall: Donker.

————. 1985. "Why Do I Write?" Reproduced from *Mmegi wa Dikgang* 7. KMM286, BHP5, Bessie Head Papers, Khama III Memorial Museum, Serowe, Botswana.

————. 1986. *A Question of Power*. London: Heinemann. (First published in 1974.)

————. 1987. *When Rain Clouds Gather*. London: Heinemann. (First published in 1969.)

————. 1987. *Maru*. London: Heinemann. (First published in 1971.)

————. 1990. *Tales of Tenderness and Power*. London: Heinemann.

————. 1990. *A Woman Alone: Autobiographical Writings*. Edited by Craig Mackenzie. Oxford: Heinemann.

————. 1992. *The Collector of Treasures*. London: Heinemann. (First published in 1977.)

————. 1993. *The Cardinals*. Cape Town: David Philip.

Secondary Material

Adler, Michelle, Susan Gardner, Tobeka Mda, and Patricia Sandler. 1989. "Interview with Bessie Head." In *Between the Lines*, edited by Craig Mackenzie and Cherry Clayton, 7–29. Grahamstown: NELM.

Allen, C. 1965. *Modern Discoveries in Medical Psychology*. London: Pan Books.

Beeton, D. R. 1980. "Preserving a Cultural Heritage: A South African Past Present and Future." *Communiqué* 5.2:1–10.

Belsey, Catherine. 1992. "True Love: The Metaphysics of Romance." *Women: A Cultural Review*. 3.2:181–92.

Benjamin, Jessica. 1990. *The Bonds of Love*. London: Virago Press.

Benjamin, Walter. 1970. *Illuminations*. Edited by Hannah Arendt. London: Jonathan Cape.

Berger, John. 1976. "Stories Walk Like Men." *New Society* 37:409–10.

Berger, Roger A. 1990. "The Politics of Madness in Bessie Head's *A Question of Power.*" In *The Tragic Life,* edited by Cecil Abrahams, 31–43. Lawrenceville, NJ: Africa World Press.

Bergonzi, Bernard. 1970. *The Situation of the Novel.* London: Macmillan and Co.

Blake, William. 1982. "The Divine Image." In *William Blake, Selected Poems,* edited by P. H. Butter, 17. London and Melbourne: Dent.

Blythe, Ronald. 1981. Foreword. In *Serowe: Village of the Rain Wind* by Bessie Head. London: Heinemann, AWS.

Brown, Lloyd W. 1979. "Creating New Worlds in Southern Africa: Bessie Head and the Question of Power." *Umoja* 3.1:43–53.

———. 1981. *Women Writers in Black Africa.* Westport, CO: Greenwood.

Buber, Martin. 1949. *Paths in Utopia.* London: Routledge and Kegan Paul.

Butler, Marilyn. 1985. "Against Tradition: The Case for a Particularized Historical Method." In *Historical Studies and Literary Criticism,* edited by Jerome J. McGann, 25–47. Madison: University of Wisconsin Press.

Campbell, Elaine. 1985. "Bessie Head's Model for Agricultural Reform." *Journal of African Studies* 12.2:82–85.

Chase, Joanna. 1982. "Bessie Head's *A Question of Power.* Romance or rhetoric?" *ACLALS Bulletin* 6.1:67–75.

Chetin, Sara. 1989. "Myth, Exile, and the Female Condition: Bessie Head's *The Collector of Treasures.*" *Journal of Commonwealth Literature* 24.1:114–37.

Chinweizu, Onwuchekwa Jemie, and Ihechukwu Madubuike. 1983. *Towards the Decolonization of African literature.* Washington, DC: Howard University Press.

Cixous, Hélène. 1976. "The Laugh of the Medusa." *Signs* 1:875–93.

———, and Catherine Clément. 1986. *The Newly Born Woman.* Minneapolis: University of Minnesota Press.

Clayton, Cherry. 1988. "A World Elsewhere: Bessie Head as Historian." *English in Africa* 15.1:55–69.

Coward, Rosalind. 1990. "Female Desire: Women's Sexuality Today." In *Feminist Literary Theory,* edited by Mary Eagleton, 145–48. Oxford: Basil Blackwell.

Davison, Carol Margaret. 1990. "A Method in the Madness: Bessie Head's *A Question of Power.* In *The Tragic Life*, edited by Cecil Abrahams, 19–29. Lawrenceville, NJ: Africa World Press.

Daymond, M. J. 1988. "Bessie Head, *Maru* and a Problem in her Visionary Fable." In *Short Fiction in the New Literatures in English*, edited by J. Bardolph, 247–52. Commonwealth Literature and Language Studies. Nice: Faculté des Lettres et Sciences Humaines.

———. 1993. Introduction. In *The Cardinals* by Bessie Head, vii–xviii. Cape Town: David Philip.

de Beauvoir, Simone. 1988. *The Second Sex.* London: Picador.

Dourley, J. P. 1990. "Jung's Impact on Religious Studies." In *C. G. Jung and the Humanities: Towards a Hermeneutics of Culture*, edited by Karin Barnaby and Pellegrino D'Acierno, 36–44. London: Routledge.

Dovey, Teresa. 1989. "*A Question of Power*: Susan Gardner's Biography versus Bessie Head's Autobiography." *English in Africa* 16.1:29–38.

Driver, Dorothy. 1990. "The Child's Mother Grabs the Sharp End of the Knife: Women as Mothers, Women as Writers." In *Rendering Things Visible*, edited by Martin Trump, 225–55. Johannesburg: Ravan Press.

Eagleton, Terry. 1992. *Marxism and Literary Criticism*. London: Routledge.

Eilersen, Gillian Stead. 1995. *Bessie Head—Thunder Behind her Ears*. Claremont, South Africa: David Philip.

Ellmann, Maud. 1994. *Psychoanalytic Literary Criticism*. London & New York: Longman.

Evasdaughter, Elizabeth N. 1989. "Bessie Head's *A Question of Power* Read as a Mariner's Guide to Paranoia." *Research in African Literature* 20.1:72–83.

Feder, Lillian. 1980. *Madness in Literature*. Princeton: Princeton University Press.

Felman, Soshana A. 1978. *Literature and Psychoanalysis*. Baltimore: Johns Hopkins University Press.

Felski, Rita. 1989. *Beyond Feminist Aesthetics: Feminist Literature and Social Change*. Cambridge: Harvard University Press.

Finnegan, Ruth. 1970. *Oral Literature in Africa*. London: Oxford University Press.

Fordham, Frieda. 1991. *An Introduction to Jung's Psychology*. Harmondsworth: Penguin Books.

Forgacs, David. 1992 . "Marxist Literary Theories." In *Modern Literary Theory*, edited by Ann Jefferson and David Robey, 166–203. London: Batsford.

Fradkin, Betty. 1978. "Conversations with Bessie." *World Literatures Written in English* 17.2:427–34.

Frank, Katherine. 1984. "Feminist Criticism and the African Novel." *African Literature Today* 14:34–48.

Freud, Sigmund. 1939. *Moses and Monotheism*. London: Hogarth Press.

Frye, Northrop. 1975. "Blake's Treatment of the Archetype." In *English Romantic Poets: Modern Essays in Criticism*, edited by M. H. Abrams, 55–71. London: Oxford University Press.

———. 1990. *Anatomy of Criticism*. Harmondsworth: Penguin Books.

Gagiano, Annie. 1996. "Finding Foundations for Change in Bessie Head's *The Cardinals*." *The Journal of Commonwealth Literature* 31.2:47–60.

Gardner, Susan, and P. E. Scott, 1986. *Bessie Head: A Bibliography*. Grahamstown: National English Literary Museum.

Gilbert, Sandra M. 1986. "Introduction: A Tarantella of Theory." In *The Newly Born Woman* by Hélène Cixous and Catherine Clément, ix–xviii. Minneapolis: University of Minnesota Press.

———, and Susan Gubar. 1979. *The Madwoman in the Attic: The Woman Writer and the Nineteenth-Century Literary Imagination*. New Haven: Yale University Press.

Goody, J. R., and Ian Watt. 1963. "The Consequences of Literacy." In *Literacy in Traditional Society*, edited by Jack R. Goody, 27–68. Cambridge: Cambridge University Press.

Gordimer, Nadine. 1978. *The Conservationist*. Harmondsworth: Penguin.

Gordon, Giles. 1981. Letter to Bessie Head, February 2. KMM44 BHP, Bessie Head Papers, Khama III Memorial Museum, Serowe, Botswana.

Gover, Daniel. 1990. "The Fairy Tale and the Nightmare." In *The Tragic Life*, edited by Cecil Abrahams, 113–21. Lawrenceville, NJ: Africa World Press.

Grant, Jane. 1981. "Encounters with Remarkable Men." *Review South*, August: 55.

Guthkelch, A. C. 1914. Introduction to *The Utopia of Sir Thomas More*, xi–xxv. London: G. Bell and Sons.

Hall, James A. 1977. *Clinical Uses of Dreams*. New York: Grune and Stratton.

Hampson, Daphne. 1990 *Theology and Feminism*. Oxford: Blackwell.

Harrow, Kenneth W. 1995. *Thresholds of Change in African literature: The Emergence of a Tradition*. London: James Currey.

Hartman, Geoffrey H. 1975. "Nature and the Humanization of the Self in Wordsworth." In *English Romantic Poets: Modern Essays in Criticism*, edited by M. H. Abrams, 123–32. London: Oxford University Press.

Heywood, Christopher. 1976. *Aspects of South African literature*. London: Heinemann Educational Books.

———. 1991. *"The Story of an African Farm:* Society, Positivism, and Myth." In *The Flawed Diamond*, edited by Itala Vivan, 26–39. Sydney: Dangaroo Press.

Holst Petersen, Kirsten. 1991. "South Africa." In *The Commonwealth Novel Since 1960*, edited by Bruce King, 125–41. London: Macmillan.

Holzinger, Tom. 1974. Letter to Bessie Head, August 10. KMM48 BHP8, Bessie Head Papers, Khama III Memorial Museum, Serowe, Botswana.

Ibrahim, Huma. 1996. *Bessie Head: Subversive Identities in Exile*. Charlottesville: University Press of Virginia.

James, Adeola. 1990. *In Their Own Voices*. London: James Currey.

JanMohamed, Abdul. 1983. *Manichean Aesthetics: The Politics of Literature in Colonial Africa*. Amherst: University of Massachusetts Press.

Jeffreys, Sheila. 1990. *Anticlimax—A Feminist Perspective of the Sexual Revolution*. London: The Women's Press.

Jelinek, Estelle C. 1980. *Women's Autobiography*. Bloomington: Indiana University Press.

Jenkins, Keith. 1995. *On "What is History?"* London and New York: Routledge.

Johnson, Joyce. 1990. "A Novelist at the Crossroad: Bessie Head's *A Bewitched Crossroad. Kunapipi* 12.3:126–32.

Joyce, James. 1964. *A Portrait of the Artist as a Young Man*. London: Penguin.

Jung, C. G. 1934. *Modern Man in Search of a Soul*. London: Kegan Paul, Trench, Trubner & Co.

———. 1967. *Collected Works*. Princeton: Bollingen Foundation, Princeton University Press.

Keen, Sam. 1969. *Apology for Wonder*. London and New York: Harper and Row.

Kitchen, Paddy. 1981. "Peace in Serowe." *The Listener*, 2 July: 23–24.

Kugler, Paul. 1990. "The Unconscious in a Postmodern Depth Psychology." In *C. G. Jung and the Humanities: Towards a Hermeneutics of Culture*, edited by Karin Barnaby and Pellegrino D'Arcieno, 307–18. London: Routledge.

Kunene, Mazisi. 1976. "South African Oral Traditions." In *Aspects of South African Literature*, edited by Christopher Heywood, 24–41. London: Heinemann Educational Books.

Langen, R. 1989. "Progresses of the Soul: Affliction in Three Novels of Colour." Paper given at the ACLALS Silver Jubilee Conference, University of Kent, 24–31 Aug: 1–15.

Lessing, Doris. 1989. *The Grass is Singing*. London: Paladin Books.

Light, Alison. 1990. "'Returning to Manderley'—Romance Fiction, Female Sexuality and Class." In *Feminist Literary Theory*, edited by Mary Eagleton, 140–45. Oxford: Basil Blackwell.

Lukács, Georg. 1969. *The Meaning of Contemporary Realism*. London: Merlin Press.

———. 1970. *Writer and Critic*. London: Merlin Press.

———. 1971. *The Theory of the Novel*. Cambridge, MA: The MIT Press.

Mabuza, Lindiwe. 1988. "To a Comrade. In Power to the people: A glory to creativity." In *Criticism and Ideology*, edited by Kirsten Holst Petersen and Anne Rutherford, 186–92. Uppsala, Sweden, The Scandinavian Institute of African Studies.

Mackenzie, Craig. 1988. "Short Fiction in the Making: The Case of Bessie Head." In *Short Fiction in the New Literatures in English*, edited by J. Bardolph, 237–45. Commonwealth Literature and Language Studies. Nice: Faculté des Lettres et Sciences Humaines.

———. 1989a. *Bessie Head, An Introduction*. Grahamstown: National English Literary Museum.

———. 1989b. "Bessie Head's *The Collector of Treasures*: Modern story-telling in a traditional Botswanan village." *World Literature Written in English* 27.2:139–48.

Marquard, Jean. 1978. "Bessie Head: Exile and Community in Southern Africa." *London Magazine* 18.9/10:48–61.

———. 1979. "The Farm: A Concept in the Writing of Olive Schreiner, Pauline Smith, Doris Lessing, Nadine Gordimer and Bessie Head." *Dalhousie Review* 59.2:293–307.

May, Charles E. 1984. "The Nature of Knowledge in Short Fiction." *Studies in Short Fiction* 21:327–38.

McLuskie, Kathleen, and Lynn Innes. 1988. "Women and African Literature." *Wasafiri* 8:3–7.

Milosz, Czeslaw. 1990. "On Hope." In *Literature in the Modern World*, edited by Dennis Walder, 357–62. Oxford: Oxford University Press.

Modisane, Bloke. 1963. *Blame Me on History*. London: Thames & Hudson.

Mofolo, Thomas. 1961. *Chaka*. London: Heinemann.

Moi, Toril. 1990. "Sexual/Textual Politics: Feminist Literary Theory." In *Feminist Literary Theory*, edited by Mary Eagleton, 231–33. Oxford: Blackwell.

Mphahlele, Ezekiel. 1959. *Down Second Avenue*. London: Faber & Faber.

———. 1962. *The African Image*. London: Faber & Faber.

Mukherjee, Arun P. 1990. "Whose Post-Colonialism and Whose Postmodernism?" *World Literature Written in English*. 30.2:1–9.

Mzamane, Mbulelo V. 1984. "The Uses of Traditional Oral Forms in Black South African Literature." In *Literature and Society in South Africa*, edited by Landeg White and Tim Couzens, 147–60. New York: Longman.

Nasta, Susheila. 1991. Introduction. In *Motherlands: Black Women's Writing from Africa, the Caribbean and South Asia*, edited by Susheila Nasta, xiii–xxx. London: The Women's Press Ltd.

Neumann, Erich. 1973. *The Origins and History of Consciousness*. Princeton: Bollingen Series.

Nichols, Lee. 1981. "Bessie Head." In *Conversations with African Writers: Interviews with Twenty-Six African Authors*, edited by Lee Nichols, 48–57. Washington DC: VOA.

O'Connor, Frank. 1963. *The Lonely Voice: A Study of the Short Story*. London: Macmillan.

Ogunbesan, Kolawole. 1979. "The Cape Gooseberry Also Grows in Botswana: Alienation and Commitment in the Writings of Bessie Head." *Presence Africaine* 109:92–106.

Olney, James. 1973. *An Approach to African Literature*. Princeton: Princeton University Press.

Ong, Walter J. 1982. *Orality and Literacy*. London: Methuen.

Parthasarathy, R. 1989. "The Exile as Writer: On Being an Indian Writer in English." *The Journal of Commonwealth Literature*. 24.1:1–4.

Peek, Andrew. 1985. "Bessie Head and the African Novel." *SPAN: Journal of the South Pacific Association for Commonwealth Literature and Language Studies* 21:121–36.

Ravenscroft, Arthur. 1976. "The Novels of Bessie Head." In *Aspects of South African Literature*, edited by Christopher Heywood, 174–86. New York: Africana.

"Report A" from agent on *Serowe: Village of the Rain Wind*. Undated. KMM456, BHP19, Bessie Head Papers, Khama III Memorial Museum, Serowe, Botswana.

Rich, Paul. 1984a. "Romance and the Development of the South African Novel." In *Literature and Society in South Africa*, edited by Landeg White and Tim Couzens, 120–37. New York: Longman.

———. 1984b. "The Civilization Idea: An essay on Nadine Gordimer's *July's People* and J.M. Coetzee's *Waiting for the Barbarians*." *Research in African Literature* 15.3:365–93.

Roland, Alan. 1978. *Psychoanalysis, Creativity and Literature*. New York: Columbia University Press.

Ronge, Barry. 1985. *A Bewitched Crossroad*. Fair Lady, 20 March, 27

Rooney, Caroline. 1991. "Dangerous Knowledge and the Poetics of Survival: A Reading of *Our Sister Killjoy* and *A Question of Power*." In *Motherlands: Black Women's Writing from Africa, the Caribbean and South Asia*, edited by Susheila Nasta, 99–126. London: The Women's Press Ltd.

Rorty, Richard. 1989. *Contingency, Irony, and Solidarity*. Cambridge: Cambridge University Press.

Rose, Jaqueline. 1994. "On the Universality of Madness: Bessie Head's *A Question of Power*." *Critical Inquiry* 20:401–18.

Sarvan, Charles. 1990. "Bessie Head: Two Letters." *Wasafiri* 12:11–15.

Schreiner, Olive. 1983. *The Story of an African Farm*. London: Hutchinson & Co.

Sepamla, Sipho. 1988. "To What Extent is the South African Writer's Problem

Still Bleak and Immense?" In *Criticism and Ideology*, edited by Kirsten Holst Petersen and Anne Rutherford, 186–92. Uppsala, Sweden: Scandinavian Institute of African Studies.

Sillery, Anthony. 1954. *Sechele: The Story of an African Chief*. Oxford: Ronald.

———. 1965. *Founding a Protectorate: History of Bechuanaland 1815–1895*. London: Mouton & Co.

Singer, June. 1990. "On William Blake: Reason versus Imagination." In *C. G. Jung and the Humanities: Towards a Hermeneutics of Culture*, edited by Karin Barnaby and Pellegrino D'Acierno, 162–73. London: Routledge.

Snitow, Ann Barr. 1990. "Mass Market Romance: Pornography for Women is Different." In *Feminist Literary Theory*, edited by Mary Eagleton, 134–40. Oxford: Blackwell.

Tucker, Margaret E. 1988. "A 'Nice-Time Girl' Strikes Back: An Essay on Bessie Head's *A Question of Power*." *Research in African Literatures* (19.2:170–81

Tucker, Martin. 1991. *Literary Exile in the Twentieth Century: An Analysis and Biographical Dictionary*. New York: Greenwood.

Van der Post, Laurens. 1985. "The 'Turbott Wolfe' Affair." In *Turbott Wolfe*, by William Plomer, 9–55. Oxford: Oxford University Press.

Van Rensburg, Patrick. 1978. *The Serowe Brigades*. London: MacMillan Education.

Vigne, Randolph. 1991. *A Gesture of Belonging: Letters from Bessie Head, 1965–1979*. London: SA Writers.

Watts, Jane. 1989. *Black Writers from South Africa*. London: MacMillan.

Weedon, Chris. 1993. *Feminist Practice & Poststructuralist Theory*. Oxford: Blackwell.

White, Hayden. 1987. *The Content of the Form*. Baltimore: John Hopkins University Press.

White, Victor. 1964. *God and the Unconscious*. London and Glasgow: Fontana Books.

Wilhelm, Cherry. 1983. "Bessie Head: The Face of Africa." *English in Africa* 10.1–13.

Wilkinson, Jane. 1991. "Nature and Art in Olive Schreiner's *The Story of an African Farm*. In *The Flawed Diamond*, edited by Itala Vivan, 107–20. Sydney: Dangaroo Press.

Wimsatt, W. K. 1975. "The Structure of Romantic Nature Imagery." In *English Romantic Poets: Modern Essays in Criticism*, edited by M. H. Abrams, 25–36. London: Oxford University Press.

Index

240